EXTREME
OWNERSHIP

Dawn breaks over South-Central Ramadi. Task Unit Bruiser, Charlie Platoon sniper overwatch deep into enemy territory with AH-64 Apache gunship overhead. Enemy fighters shot thousands of rounds at the helicopter as they overflew the city.

(Photo courtesy of the authors)

EXTREME
OWNERSHIP

HOW U.S. NAVY SEALS LEAD AND WIN

JOCKO WILLINK

AND

LEIF BABIN

ST. MARTIN'S PRESS 〽 NEW YORK

EXTREME OWNERSHIP. Copyright © 2015, 2017 by Jocko Willink and Leif Babin. All rights reserved. Printed in the United States of America. For information, address St. Martin's Press, 175 Fifth Avenue, New York, N.Y. 10010.

www.stmartins.com

Designed by Omar Chapa
Maps by Emily Langmade

The Library of Congress has cataloged the first hardcover edition as follows:

Willink, Jocko.
   Extreme ownership : how U.S. Navy SEALs lead and win / by Jocko Willink and Leif Babin. — First edition.
      pg. cm.
  ISBN 978-1-250-06705-0 (hardcover)
  ISBN 978-1-4668-7496-1 (ebook)
  1. Iraq War, 2003–2011—Campaigns—Iraq—Anbar (Province).
2. Leadership—United States.   3. United States. Navy. SEALs. Task Unit Bruiser.   4. United States. Navy. SEALs. Officers—Biography.   5. Iraq War, 2003–2011—Personal narratives, American.   I. Babin, Leif.   II. Title. III. Title: How U.S. Navy SEALs lead and win.
  DS79.764.A63W55 2015
  303.3'4—dc23

                          2015025571

ISBN 978-1-250-18386-6 (hardcover)

Our books may be purchased in bulk for promotional, educational, or business use. Please contact your local bookseller or the Macmillan Corporate and Premium Sales Department at 1-800-221-7945, extension 5442, or by email at MacmillanSpecialMarkets@macmillan.com.

Second Edition: November 2017

*Dedicated to Marc Lee, Mike Monsoor, and Ryan Job
—three courageous warriors, SEAL teammates, and friends—
who valiantly wielded their big machine guns on the mean streets of
Ramadi and laid down their lives so that others might live.*

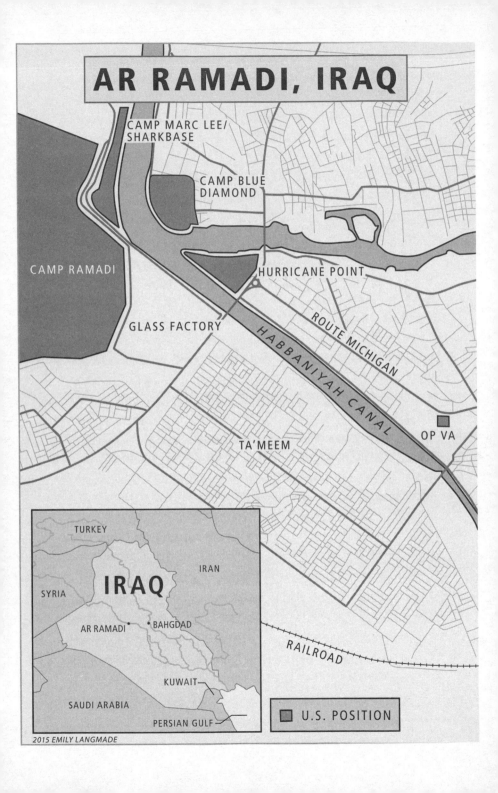

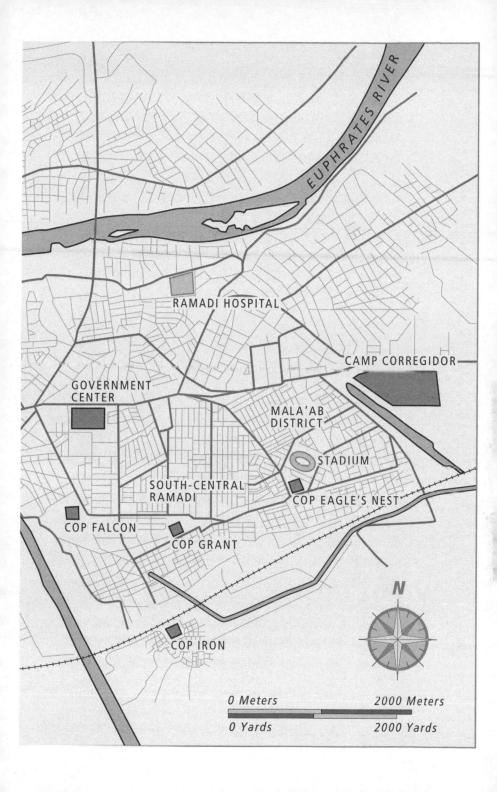

CONTENTS

FOREWORD

Of the many exceptional leaders we served alongside throughout our military careers, the consistent attribute that made them great was that they took absolute ownership—Extreme Ownership—not just of those things for which they were responsible, but for everything that impacted their mission. These leaders cast no blame. They made no excuses. Instead of complaining about challenges or setbacks, they developed solutions and solved problems. They leveraged assets, relationships, and resources to get the job done. Their own egos took a back seat to the mission and their troops. These leaders truly *led*.

In the years since we left active duty, we have worked with multitudes of business professionals, from senior executives to frontline managers, across a vast range of industries, including finance, construction, manufacturing, technology, energy, retail, pharmaceutical, health care, and also, military, police, fire departments, and emergency first responders. The most successful men and women we've seen in the civilian world practice this same breed of Extreme Ownership. Likewise, the most successful high-performance teams we've worked with demonstrate this mind-set throughout their organizations.

Since the publication of *Extreme Ownership,* we've heard from readers across the United States and around the world whose lives have been strongly impacted for good. They've told us how implementing its principles changed their lives and made them better: a more productive employee, a more supportive spouse, or a more engaged parent. Once people stop making excuses, stop blaming others, and take ownership of everything in their lives, they are compelled to take action to solve their problems. They are better leaders, better followers, more dependable and actively contributing team members, and more skilled in aggressively driving toward mission accomplishment. But they're also humble—able to keep their egos from damaging relationships and adversely impacting the mission and the team.

We've heard countless stories about how applying these combat leadership principles have helped readers accomplish what others, or even they themselves, had previously thought impossible. *Extreme Ownership* has helped people all over the world launch a successful company or nonprofit, receive a major promotion, land a better job with greater responsibility and more opportunity for growth, hit numbers far beyond expectations, achieve special recognition as an exceptional team member, or accomplish their goals, whatever they may be.

Every day we hear new stories—different people, different businesses, different industries. The details change. The characters are diverse. There are always slight differences in the way things unfold. But their outcomes are ultimately the same. "I can't believe how well that works" is a common response.

The principles are simple, but not easy. Taking ownership for mistakes and failures is hard. But doing so is key to learning, to developing solutions, and, ultimately, to victory. Those who successfully implement these principles run circles around the rest of the world.

Since the release of *Extreme Ownership*, the fundamental principles of combat leadership that we learned on the battlefield of Iraq have been exposed to, understood, and implemented by hundreds of thousands of readers around the world. We've worked with thousands more individuals through our leadership consulting business, Echelon Front, and reached a vast audience on social media. We've also been fortunate to receive feedback from many of them on a daily basis. Their responses have been incredible.

We've heard from readers who called the book: "life-changing," "the best leadership book I've ever read," and "exactly what I needed to hear." They explain how they have learned even more on the second, third, or fourth read through the book. There can be no higher compliment to us as authors than to observe the scores of *Extreme Ownership* copies we have signed with multiple color tabs marking well-underlined, highlighted, and dog-eared pages with scribbled notes in the margins that serve as testament to the book's frequent use as a ready reference guide for engaged leaders navigating the challenges of business and life. Such testimonials and observations inspire us to work even harder ourselves.

But what's been even more gratifying is to hear about are the *RESULTS.*

We get reports from military leaders on the front lines putting the principles to work against our nation's enemies; these leaders are "leading up the chain of command" to receive the green light for approval to launch on critical battlefield missions or utilize crucial resources. Chief executive officers of massive, global companies detail how they have initiated Extreme Ownership in their organizations and observed their personnel throughout the chain of command step up and lead. We hear from first responders who utilize the lessons from *Extreme Ownership* in their official training programs to lead their troops in stressful and dangerous situations. All of their stories have reinforced what we learned in the SEAL Teams: leadership is the most important thing on the battlefield and the principles of good leadership do not change regardless of the mission, the environment, or the personalities of those involved. Leading is leading.

We worked with the division of a construction company that faced the grim possibility of shutdown due to systemic safety problems. But once its employees implemented Extreme Ownership, the division not only solidified their right to operate, but it also earned a top position in safety at the company. We've helped companies streamline their manufacturing process, make deadlines on the delivery of product, and complete vast projects on time and under budget. We've guided young, capable, eager leaders struggling in antagonistic relationships with their bosses to implement the mind-set of no excuses and no one else to blame. By taking ownership, checking their egos, and accepting the blame for a difficult relationship, they repaired relationships and regained the trust of their leaders. As a result, they achieved recognition above their peers and throughout their industry for exceptional performance. We've heard from leaders in the medical profession who tell us how explaining the "why" to their team and communicating orders in a "simple, clear, and concise" manner greatly enhanced their team's performance and saved lives in the operating room.

We've watched fire department battalion training chiefs utilize *Extreme Ownership* as a handbook, teaching their firefighters to implement "Cover and Move" to better function as a team, enabling them to more effectively serve their communities while better protecting their firefighters in harm's way. We've seen police officers promoted into leadership positions of greater authority and responsibility attribute their success directly to the principles of *Extreme Ownership*.

A number of school teachers, educators, and coaches have

told us how the concepts of this book have made them better, delivering greater impact and improving the lives of their students and athletes. Pastors and mission groups have relayed to us how *Extreme Ownership* made their teams more effective, delivering greater impact to the lives of people in need.

We've even heard from spouses who tell us how *Extreme Ownership* saved their marriage. Once they stopped pointing fingers and casting blame on their wife or husband, they were able to look inwardly at what they could take ownership of to produce a better outcome. As a result, their relationships were repaired and strengthened.

To see such far-reaching, extraordinary impact is deeply meaningful to us. We wrote this book to truly help others—leaders and aspiring leaders—to be better: to lead more successful and fulfilling lives, become more engaged and effective people, to have a greater impact for good on everyone around them.

Helping others live better lives is also a way for us to honor the legacy and heritage of those we served with in combat who gave their last full measure. We owe them everything.

We believe in these principles because we have witnessed their extraordinary results, not only on the battlefield, but also in business and in life. We look forward to watching the message continue to spread far and wide and to seeing the mind-set of Extreme Ownership continue to enable every leader, every follower, and every person to become even more effective and to fulfill their ultimate purpose: *lead* and *win*.

GET AFTER IT.

—Jocko Willink and Leif Babin
July 2017

PREFACE

"So, there I was. . . ."

Plenty of glorified war stories start like that. In the SEAL Teams, we make fun of those who tell embellished tales about themselves. A typical war story told in jest about something a SEAL did usually begins like this: "So, no shit, there I was, knee-deep in grenade pins. . . ."

This book isn't meant to be an individual's glorified war story. As SEALs, we operate as a team of high-caliber, multitalented individuals who have been through perhaps the toughest military training and most rigorous screening process anywhere. But in the SEAL program, it is all about *the Team*. The sum is far greater than the parts. We refer to our professional warfare community simply as "the Teams." We call ourselves "team guys." This book describes SEAL combat operations and training through our eyes—from our individual perspectives—and applies our experience to leadership and management practices in the business world.

Yet, our SEAL operations were not about us as individuals;

our stories are of the SEAL platoon and task unit we were lucky enough to lead. Chris Kyle, the SEAL sniper and author of the best seller *American Sniper,* which inspired the movie, was one member of that platoon and task unit—Charlie Platoon's lead sniper and point man in Task Unit Bruiser. He played a part in the combat examples in this book, as did a host of other teammates who, though deserving of recognition, remain out of the spotlight. Far from being ours alone, the war stories in this book are of the brothers and leaders we served with and fought alongside—the Team. The combat scenarios describe how we confronted obstacles as a team and overcame those challenges together. After all, there can be no leadership where there is no team.

Between the Vietnam War and the Global War on Terrorism, the U.S. military experienced a thirty-year span of virtually no sustained combat operations. With the exception of a few flashes of conflict (Grenada, Panama, Kuwait, Somalia), only a handful of U.S. military leaders had any real, substantial combat experience. In the SEAL Teams, these were the "dry years." As those who served in heavy combat situations in the jungles of Vietnam retired, their combat leadership lessons faded.

All that changed on September 11, 2001, when the horrific terrorist attacks on the U.S. homeland launched America once again into sustained conflict. More than a decade of continuous war and tough combat operations in Iraq and Afghanistan gave birth to a new generation of leaders in the ranks of America's fighting forces. These leaders were forged not in classrooms through hypothetical training and theory, but through practical, hands-on experience on the front lines of war—the front echelon.* Leadership theories were tested in combat; hypotheses put through trials of

---

* Based on our leadership lessons learned from the front echelon on the battlefield, we named our company Echelon Front, LLC.

fire. Across the ranks of the U.S. military services, forgotten war-time lessons were rewritten—in blood. Some leadership principles developed in training proved ineffective in actual combat. Thus, effective leadership skills were honed while those that proved impractical were discarded, spawning a new generation of combat leaders from across the broad ranks of all U.S. military services—Army, Marine Corps, Navy, Air Force—and those of our allies. The U.S. Navy SEAL Teams were at the forefront of this leadership transformation, emerging from the triumphs and tragedies of war with a crystallized understanding of what it takes to succeed in the most challenging environments that combat presents.

Among this new generation of combat leaders there are many war stories. After years of successful operations, including the heroic raid that killed Osama bin Laden, U.S. Navy SEALs have piqued the public's interest and received more attention than most of us ever wanted. This spotlight has shed light on aspects of our organization that should remain secret. In this book, we are careful not to remove that shroud any further. We do not discuss classified programs or violate nondisclosure agreements surrounding our operational experiences.

Many SEAL memoirs have been written—some by experienced and well-respected operators who wanted to pass on the heroic deeds and accomplishments of our tribe; a few, unfortunately, by SEALs who hadn't contributed much to the community. Like so many of our SEAL teammates, we had a negative view when SEAL books were published.

Why then would we choose to write a book? As battlefield leaders, we learned extremely valuable lessons through success and failure. We made mistakes and learned from them, discovering what works and what doesn't. We trained SEAL leaders and watched them implement the principles we ourselves had learned with the same success on difficult battlefields. Then, as we worked with businesses in the civilian sector, we again saw the leadership principles we followed in combat lead to victory for the companies and executives we trained. Many people, both in the SEAL Teams and in the businesses we worked with, asked us to document our lessons learned in a concrete way that leaders could reference.

We wrote this book to capture those leadership principles for future generations, so that they may not be forgotten, so that as new wars begin and end, such crucial lessons will not have to be relearned—rewritten in more blood. We wrote this so that the leadership lessons can continue to impact teams beyond the battlefield in all leadership situations—any company, team, or organization in which a group of people strives to achieve a goal and accomplish a mission. We wrote this book for leaders everywhere to utilize the principles we learned to lead and win.

Who are we to write such a book? It may seem that anyone who believes they can write a book on leadership must think themselves the epitome of what every leader should aspire to be. But we are far from perfect. We continue to learn and grow as leaders every day, just as any leaders who are truly honest with themselves must. We were simply fortunate enough to experience an array of leadership challenges that taught us valuable lessons. This book is our best effort to pass those lessons on, not from a pedestal or a position of superiority, but from a humble place, where the scars of our failings still show.

We are Jocko Willink and Leif Babin, SEAL officers who served together in Ar Ramadi, Iraq, during Operation Iraqi Freedom. There, we became intimately familiar with the humbling trials of war. We were lucky enough to build, train, and lead high-performance, winning teams that proved exceptionally effective. We saw firsthand the perils of complacency, having served on a battlefield where at any time the possibility of our position being overrun by a large force of well-armed enemy fighters was quite real. We know what it means to fail—to lose, to be surprised, outmaneuvered, or simply beaten. Those lessons were the hardest, but perhaps the most important. We learned that leadership requires belief in the mission and unyielding perseverance to achieve victory, particularly when doubters question whether victory is even possible. As SEAL leaders, we developed, tested, confirmed, and captured an array of leadership lessons as well as management and organizational best practices. We then built and ran SEAL leadership training and helped write the doctrine for the next generation of SEAL leaders.

Our SEAL task unit served through the bulk of what has become known as the "Battle of Ramadi." But this book is not intended as a historical account of those combat operations. In a concise volume such as this, we cannot possibly tell the stories of service and sacrifice by the U.S. military men and women who served, fought, bled, and died there. We—the authors and the SEALs we served with in Ramadi—were tremendously humbled by the courage, dedication, professionalism, selflessness, and sacrifice displayed by the units we served with under both the U.S. Army 2nd Brigade, 28th Infantry Brigade Combat Team, and the U.S. Army 1st Brigade, 1st Armored Division—the Ready First Brigade Combat Team. These included a distinguished list of courageous and storied units, both U.S. Army and Marine Corps. It would require an entire book (or series of books) to detail their heroism and unfaltering dedication to the mission and our country. God bless them all.

Inside that Band of Brothers carrying out the broader fight for Ramadi was our SEAL task unit: Naval Special Warfare Task Unit Bruiser. Again, the combat experiences relayed in the following chapters are not meant for historic reference. Although we have used quotes to impart the message of conversations we had, they are certainly not perfect, and are subject to the passage of time, the constraints of this format, and the shortfalls of memory. Our SEAL combat experiences depicted in this book have been carefully edited or altered to conceal specific tactics, techniques, and procedures, and to guard classified information about when and where specific operations took place and who participated in them. The manuscript was submitted and approved through the Pentagon's Security Review process in accordance with U.S. Department of Defense requirements. We have done our utmost to protect the identities of our brothers in the SEAL Teams with whom we served and for those still serving in harm's way. They are silent professionals and seek no recognition. We take this solemn responsibility to protect them with the utmost seriousness.

We took the same precaution with the rest of the warriors in the Ready First Brigade Combat Team. We have used, almost entirely, rank alone to identify these brave Soldiers and Marines.* This is by no means meant to detract from their service, but only to ensure their privacy and security.

Likewise, we have done our utmost to protect the clients of our leadership and management consulting company, Echelon Front, LLC. We have refrained from using company names, changed the names of individuals, masked industry-specific information, and in some cases altered the positions of executives and industries to protect the identities of people and companies. Their confidentiality is sacrosanct. While the stories of our lessons learned in the business world are based directly on our real experiences, in some cases we combined situations, condensed timelines, and modified story lines to more clearly emphasize the principles we are trying to illustrate.

The idea for this book was born from the realization that the principles critical to SEAL success on the battlefield—how SEALs train and prepare their leaders, how they mold and develop high-performance teams, and how they lead in combat—are directly

---

* In accordance with U.S. Department of Defense policy, the term "Soldier" will be capitalized for "U.S. Soldier" throughout this book, as will "Marine" for "U.S. Marine."

applicable to success in any group, organization, corporation, business, and, to a broader degree, life. This book provides the reader with our formula for success: the mind-set and guiding principles that enable SEAL leaders and combat units to achieve extraordinary results. It demonstrates how to apply these directly in business and life to likewise achieve victory.

EXTREME
OWNERSHIP

Task Unit Bruiser SEALs unleash lethal machine gun fire and 40mm grenades on insurgents during a clearance operation in southeast Ramadi.

(Photo courtesy of the authors)

INTRODUCTION

Ramadi, Iraq: The Combat Leader's Dilemma

Leif Babin

Only the low rumble of diesel engines could be heard as the convoy of Humvees* eased to a stop along the canal road. Iraqi farm fields and groves of date palms spread for some distance into the darkness in all directions. The night was quiet. Only the occasional barking of a distant dog and a lonely flickering light gave any indication of the Iraqi village beyond. If intelligence reports were accurate, that village harbored a high-level terrorist leader and perhaps his entourage of well-armed fighters. No lights were visible from the convoy, and darkness blanketed the road, blacking out most of the surroundings to the naked eye. But through the green glow of our night-vision goggles a flurry of activity could be seen: a platoon of Navy SEALs kitted up with helmets, body armor, weapons, and gear, along with an element of Iraqi soldiers, dismounted from the vehicles and quickly aligned in patrol formation.

---

* High Mobility Multipurpose Wheeled Vehicle, or HMMWV, spoken as "Humvee."

An explosive ordnance disposal (EOD) bomb technician pushed forward and checked out a dirt bridge that crossed the canal ahead. Insurgents often planted deadly explosives at such choke points. Some were powerful enough to wipe out an entire vehicle and all its occupants in a sudden inferno of flying jagged metal and searing heat. For now, the way ahead appeared clear, and the assault force of SEALs and Iraqi soldiers stealthily pushed across the bridge on foot toward a group of buildings where the terrorist reportedly took refuge. A particularly evil insurgent responsible for the deaths of American Soldiers, Iraqi security forces, and innocent civilians, this notorious al Qaeda in Iraq emir had successfully evaded capture for months. Now was a critical opportunity to capture or kill him before his next attack.

The SEAL assault force patrolled up a narrow street between the high walls of residential compounds and moved to the door of the target building.

BOOM!

The deep concussion from the explosive breaching charge shattered the quiet night. It was a hell of a wake-up call for the occupants inside the house as the door blew in, and aggressive, well-armed men with weapons ready for a fight entered the house. The Humvees pushed forward across the bridge, down the narrow street wide enough only for a single vehicle, and came to a stop in security positions around the target building. Each vehicle's turret contained a SEAL manning a heavy machine gun, ready to provide fire support if things went sideways.

I was the ground force commander, the senior SEAL in charge of this operation. I had just stepped out of the command vehicle and onto the street near the target building, when suddenly someone yelled: "We've got a squirter!" It was our EOD operator nearby who had seen the "squirter," meaning someone fleeing the target building. Perhaps it was the terrorist himself or someone with information on his whereabouts. We couldn't allow him to escape.

The EOD operator and I were the only ones in position to pursue him, so we sprinted after the man. We chased him down a narrow alleyway, around a group of buildings, and down another dark alleyway that paralleled the street where our Humvees were parked. Finally, we caught up to him, a middle-aged Iraqi man in a traditional Arabic robe, or *dishdasha*. As we were trained, he was quickly forced to the ground and his hands controlled. Those hands didn't possess a weapon, but he might have a grenade in his pocket or, worse, be wearing an explosive suicide belt under his clothing. Anyone associated with such a high-level terrorist might have such deadly devices, and we couldn't assume otherwise. Just to be sure, he had to be searched quickly.

In that instant, I became keenly aware that we were all alone in the world, totally separated from our unit. The rest of our SEAL assault force didn't know where we were. There hadn't been time to notify them. I wasn't even sure exactly where we were located relevant to their position. All around us were darkened windows and rooftops of uncleared buildings, where enemy fighters might be lurking, preparing to attack and unleash hell on us at any second. We had to get back and link up with our troops ASAP.

But even before we could cuff the man's hands and begin a pat-down search for weapons, I heard movement. As I looked down the alleyway through my night-vision goggles, suddenly seven or eight men rounded the corner not forty yards from us. They were heavily armed and rapidly moving toward us. For a split second, my mind questioned what my eyes were seeing. But there it was: the unmistakable outlines of AK-47 rifles, an RPG-7*

---

* RPG-7, Russian designed shoulder-fired rocket, widely distributed and highly popular among America's enemies for its deadly effectiveness. Contrary to popular belief, "RPG" does not stand for "Rocket Propelled Grenade" but is an acronym for the Russian "Ruchnoy Protivotankovy Granatamyot," which roughly translates: "handheld antitank grenade launcher."

shoulder-fired rocket, and at least one belt-fed machine gun. They weren't there to shake our hands. These were armed enemy fighters maneuvering to attack.

Now, the two of us—the EOD operator and I—were in a hell of a tight spot. The subdued Iraqi man and possible terrorist we were holding had not yet been searched, a situation that carried huge risks. We needed to fall back and link up with the rest of our force. Now, with a larger enemy force maneuvering on us with heavier firepower, the two of us were outnumbered and outgunned. Finally, I desperately needed to resume my role as ground force commander, dispense with handling prisoners, and get back to my job of command and control for the assault force, our vehicles, and coordination with our distant supporting assets. All this had to be accomplished immediately.

I had deployed to Iraq before, but never had I been in a situation like this. Though combat is often depicted in movies and video games, this was not a movie and it certainly was no game. These were heavily armed and dangerous men determined to kill American and Iraqi troops. Were any of us to fall into their hands, we could expect to be tortured in unspeakable ways and then decapitated on video for all the world to see. They wanted nothing more than to kill us and were willing to die by the dozen to do so.

Blood pumping, adrenaline surging, I knew every nanosecond counted. This situation could overwhelm the most competent leader and seasoned combat veteran. But the words of my immediate boss—our task unit commander, Lieutenant Commander Jocko Willink—echoed in my head, words I'd regularly heard during a full year of intensive training and preparation: "Relax. Look around. Make a call." Our SEAL platoon and task unit had trained extensively through dozens of desperate, chaotic, and overwhelming situations to prepare for just such a moment as this. I understood how to implement the Laws of Combat that Jocko had taught us: Cover and Move, Simple, Prioritize and Execute, and Decentralized Command. The Laws of Combat were the key to not just surviving a dire situation such as this, but actually thriving, enabling us to totally dominate the enemy and *win*. They guided my next move.

Prioritize: Of all the pressing tasks at hand, if I didn't first handle the armed enemy fighters bearing down on us within the next few seconds nothing else would matter. We would be dead. Worse, the enemy fighters would continue their attack and might kill more of our SEAL assault force. This was my highest priority.

Execute: Without hesitation, I engaged the enemy fighters moving toward us with my Colt M4 rifle, hammering the first insurgent in line carrying the RPG with three to four rounds to the chest, dead center. As he dropped, I rapidly shifted fire to the next bad guy, then to the next. The muzzle flashes and report of the rifle announced to all within earshot that a firefight was on. The group of enemy fighters hadn't bargained for this. They panicked, and those who could still run beat a hasty retreat back the way they had come. Some crawled and others dragged the wounded and dying around the street corner and out of sight as I continued to engage them. I knew I had hit at least three or four of them. Though the rounds had been accurate and impacted the enemy fighters' centers of mass, the 5.56mm round was just too small to have much knock-down power. Now the bad guys were around the corner, some no doubt dead or gravely wounded and soon to be. But surely those who were unscathed would regroup and attack again, likely rounding up even more fighters to join their efforts.

We needed to move. There was no time for a complex plan. Nor did I have the luxury of providing specific direction to my shooting buddy, the EOD operator next to me. But we had to execute immediately. Having dealt with the highest priority task—armed enemy fighters maneuvering to attack—and with that threat at least temporarily checked, our next priority was to fall back and link up with our SEAL assault force. To do this, the EOD operator and I utilized Cover and Move—teamwork. I provided cover fire while he bounded back to a position where he could cover me. Then I moved to a new position to cover for him. Thus, we leapfrogged our way back toward the rest of our team with the prisoner in tow. As soon as we reached the cover of a concrete wall in a perpendicular alleyway, I kept my weapon at the ready to cover while the EOD operator conducted a quick search of the prisoner. Finding no weapons, we then continued back and linked up with our team and, once there, handed off the prisoner to the designated prisoner-handling team with the assault force. Then I resumed my role as ground force commander, directing my mobility commander in charge of the vehicles to move a Humvee with its .50-caliber heavy machine gun to a position where we could repel any further attacks from the direction the enemy fighters had come. Next I had our SEAL radioman communicate with our Tactical Operations Center (TOC) located miles away to keep them informed and get the TOC spinning to coordinate air support to assist us.

For the next half hour, the insurgent fighters attempted to maneuver on us and dumped hundreds of rounds in our direction. But we remained one step ahead of them and repeatedly beat back their attacks. The man we had chased down turned out not to be our target. He was briefly detained for questioning, turned over to a detention facility, but then released. We didn't find our target that night. The al Qaeda in Iraq emir had apparently departed sometime prior to our arrival. But we killed at least a handful of his fighters and we collected valuable intelligence on his operations and organization. Though the operation failed to achieve its primary objective, we did demonstrate to the terrorist and his cronies that there were no areas where they could safely hide. This likely forced him (in the short term, at least) to focus efforts on his own preservation rather than plotting his next attack. In that, we had helped protect American lives, in addition to Iraqi security forces and innocent civilians, which was at least a consolation prize.

→ For me, the biggest gain was in leadership lessons learned. Some were simple, as in the acknowledgment that before any combat operation, I needed to do a much more careful map study to memorize the basic layout and the area around the target for those times when I couldn't immediately access my map. Some lessons were procedural, like establishing clear guidance for all our operators about just how far we should chase squirters without first coordinating with the rest of the team. Other lessons were strategic: with proper understanding and application of the Laws of Combat, we had not only survived a difficult and dangerous situation but dominated. As an entire generation of SEAL combat leaders and I would learn, these Laws of Combat could be applied with equal effectiveness in an intense firefight or in far less dynamic or high-pressure situations. They guided me through months of sustained urban combat in Ramadi, throughout my career as a SEAL officer, and beyond.

Those same principles are the key to any team's success on the battlefield or in the business world—any situation where a group of people must work together to execute a task and accomplish a mission. When applied to any team, group, or organization, the proper understanding and execution of these Laws of Combat would mean one thing: victory.

LEADERSHIP: THE SINGLE MOST IMPORTANT FACTOR
Leif Babin and Jocko Willink

This book is about leadership. It was written for leaders of teams large and small, for men and women, for any person who aspires to better themselves. Though it contains exciting accounts of SEAL combat operations, this book is not a war memoir. It is instead a collection of lessons learned from our experiences to help other leaders achieve victory. If it serves as a useful guide to leaders who aspire to build, train, and lead high-performance winning teams, then it has accomplished its purpose.

Among the legions of leadership books in publication, we found most focus on individual practices and personal character traits. We also observed that many corporate leadership training programs and management consulting firms do the same. But without a team—a group of individuals working to accomplish a mission—there can be no leadership. The only meaningful measure for a leader is whether the team succeeds or fails. For all the definitions, descriptions, and characterizations of leaders, there are only two that matter: effective and ineffective. Effective leaders lead successful teams that accomplish their mission and win. Ineffective leaders do not. The principles and concepts described in this book, when properly understood and implemented, enable any leader to become effective and dominate his or her battlefield.

Every leader and every team at some point or time will fail and must confront that failure. That too is a big part of this book. We are by no means infallible leaders; no one is, no matter how experienced. Nor do we have all the answers; no leader does. We've made huge mistakes. Often our mistakes provided the greatest lessons, humbled us, and enabled us to grow and become better. For leaders, the humility to admit and own mistakes and develop a plan to overcome them is essential to success. The best leaders are not driven by ego or personal agendas. They are simply focused on the mission and how best to accomplish it.

As leaders, we have experienced both triumph and tragedy. The bulk of our combat experiences and the stories told in this book come from what will always be the highlight of our military careers: SEAL Team Three, Task Unit Bruiser, and our historic combat deployment to Ar Ramadi, Iraq, in 2006 through what became known as the "Battle of Ramadi." Jocko led Bruiser as task unit commander. Leif and his SEALs of Charlie Platoon, including lead sniper and point man Chris Kyle, the "American Sniper," and their brother SEALs in Delta Platoon fought in what remains some of the heaviest, sustained urban combat operations in the history of the SEAL Teams. Bruiser SEALs played an integral role in the U.S. Army 1st Armored Division, Ready First Brigade's "Seize, Clear, Hold, and Build" strategy that systemically liberated the war-torn, insurgent-held city of Ramadi and radically lowered the level of violence. These operations established security in the most dangerous and volatile area in Iraq at the time and set the conditions for the "Anbar Awakening," a movement that eventually turned the tide for the United States in Iraq.

In the spring of 2006 when Task Unit Bruiser first arrived in Ramadi, the war-torn capital city of Al Anbar Province was the deadly epicenter of the Iraqi insurgency. Ramadi, a city of four hundred thousand, was a total war zone marred by rubble-pile buildings and bomb craters—the scars of continuous violence. At that time, U.S. forces controlled only about one-third of the city. A brutal insurgency of well-armed and determined enemy fighters controlled the rest. Every day, brave U.S. Soldiers and Marines were bloodied. The Camp Ramadi medical facility saw a near constant flow of severely wounded or dead. Valiant U.S. military surgical teams desperately fought to save lives. A U.S. intelligence report leaked to the press grimly labeled Ramadi and Anbar Province "all but lost." Virtually no one thought it possible that U.S. forces could turn the situation around there and win.

Through the summer and fall of 2006, Jocko orchestrated Task Unit Bruiser's contribution to the Ready First Brigade's efforts as his SEAL platoons fought side by side with U.S. Army Soldiers and Marines to clear out enemy-held areas of the city. Leif led Charlie Platoon's SEALs in scores of violent gun battles and highly effective sniper overwatch missions. Delta Platoon fought countless fierce battles as well. Together, Task Unit Bruiser SEALs—snipers, riflemen, and machine gunners—killed hundreds of enemy fighters and disrupted enemy attacks on U.S. Soldiers, Marines, and Iraqi security forces.

Bruiser SEALs frequently spearheaded the Ready First operations as the first U.S. troops on the ground in the most dangerous, enemy-held neighborhoods. We secured buildings, took the high ground, and then provided cover as Soldiers and Marines moved into contested areas and Army combat engineers furiously worked to build and fortify outposts in enemy territory. Bruiser SEALs and the Ready First Soldiers and Marines built a bond that will forever be remembered by those who served there. Through much blood, sweat, and toil, the Ready First Combat Team and Task Unit Bruiser accomplished the mission. The violent insurgency was routed from the city, tribal sheikhs in Ramadi joined with U.S. forces, and the Anbar Awakening was born. Ultimately, in the months following TU Bruiser's departure, Ramadi was stabilized and the level of violence plummeted to levels previously unimaginable.

Tragically, Task Unit Bruiser paid a tremendous cost for the success of these operations: eight SEALs were wounded and three of the best SEAL warriors imaginable gave their lives. Marc Lee and Mike Monsoor were killed in action; Ryan Job was blinded by an enemy sniper's bullet and later died while in the hospital recovering from surgery to repair his combat wounds. These losses were devastating to us. And yet they were only three of nearly one hundred U.S. troops killed in action that were part of the Ready First Brigade Combat Team, each one a tragic, immeasurable loss.

Despite the doubters and naysayers, Ramadi was won, the city stabilized, and the populace secured. By early 2007, enemy attacks plunged from an average of thirty to fifty each day throughout much of 2006, to an average of one per week, then one per month.

Ramadi remained a model of stability and one of the safest areas of Iraq, outside the historically stable Kurdish-controlled north, for years afterward.

These operations were victorious but also extremely humbling; the takeaways—both good and bad—vast. The Battle of Ramadi provided a litany of lessons learned, which we were able to capture and pass on. The greatest of these was the recognition that leadership is the most important factor on the battlefield, the single greatest reason behind the success of any team. By leadership, we do not mean just the senior commanders at the top, but the crucial leaders at every level of the team—the senior enlisted leaders, the fire team leaders in charge of four people, the squad leaders in charge of eight, and the junior petty officers that stepped up, took charge, and led. They each played an integral role in the success of our team. We were fortunate for the opportunity to lead such an amazing group of SEALs who triumphed in that difficult fight.

Upon returning home from combat, we stepped into critical roles as leadership instructors. For many years, Navy SEAL leadership training consisted almost entirely of OJT (on the job training) and mentoring. How a junior leader was brought up depended entirely on the strength, experience, and patient guidance of a mentor. Some mentors were exceptional; others, lacking. While mentorship from the right leaders is critical, this method left some substantial gaps in leadership knowledge and understanding. We helped to change that and developed leadership training curriculum to build a strong foundation for all SEAL leaders.

As the officer in charge of all training for the West Coast SEAL Teams, Jocko directed some of the most realistic and challenging combat training in the world. He placed new emphasis on training leaders in critical decision making and effective communication in high-pressure situations to better prepare them for combat. Leif ran the SEAL Junior Officer Training Course, the basic leadership training program for every officer who graduated from the SEAL training pipeline. There, he reshaped and enhanced training to more effectively establish the critical leadership foundations necessary for new SEAL officers to succeed in combat. In these roles, we helped guide a new generation of SEAL leaders who continue to perform with unparalleled success on the battlefield, validating the leadership principles we taught them.

Some may wonder how Navy SEAL combat leadership principles translate outside the military realm to leading any team in any capacity. But combat is reflective of life, only amplified and intensified. Decisions have immediate consequences, and everything—absolutely everything—is at stake. The right decision, even when all seems lost, can snatch victory from the jaws of defeat. The wrong decision, even when a victorious outcome seems all but certain, can result in deadly, catastrophic failure. In that regard, a combat leader can acquire a lifetime of leadership lessons learned in only a few deployments.

We hope to dispel the myth that military leadership is easy because subordinates robotically and blindly follow orders. On the contrary, U.S. military personnel are smart, creative, freethinking individuals—human beings. They must literally risk life and limb to accomplish the mission. For this reason, they must believe in the cause for which they are fighting. They must believe in the plan they are asked to execute, and most important, they must believe in and trust the leader they are asked to follow. This is especially true in the SEAL Teams, where innovation and input from everyone (including the most junior personnel) are encouraged.

Combat leadership requires getting a diverse team of people in various groups to execute highly complex missions in order to achieve strategic goals—something that directly correlates with any company or organization. The same principles that make SEAL combat leaders and SEAL units so effective on the battlefield can be applied to the business world with the same success.

Since leaving the SEAL Teams, we have worked with companies across a wide array of industries, from the financial, energy, technology, and construction sectors to the insurance, auto, retail, manufacturing, pharmaceutical, and service sectors. Having trained and worked with a large number of leaders and company leadership teams, we have witnessed the extraordinary impact in increased efficiency, productivity, and profitability that results when these principles are properly understood and implemented.

The leadership and teamwork concepts contained in this book are not abstract theories, but practical and applicable. We encourage leaders to do the things they know they probably should be doing but aren't. By not doing those things, they are failing as leaders and failing their teams. While rooted in common sense and based on the reality of practical experience, these principles require skill to implement. Such concepts are *simple, but not easy,** and they apply to virtually any situation—to any group, team, organization, or individual seeking to improve performance, capability, efficiency, and teamwork. They are sometimes counterintuitive and require focused effort and training to implement in practice. But this book provides the necessary guidance so that anyone can apply the principles and, with dedication and discipline over time, master them and become effective leaders.

ORGANIZATION AND STRUCTURE

The lessons we learned as SEAL leaders through our combined years of experience are numerous. For this book, we have focused our efforts on the most critical aspects: the fundamental building

---

* "Simple, not easy" is a phrase used often by former UFC fighter and World Champion Brazilian jiu-jitsu black belt Dean Lister, a three-time Submission Grappling World Champion.

blocks of leadership. The book derives its title from the underlying principle—the mind-set—that provides the foundation for all the rest: Extreme Ownership. Leaders must own everything in their world. There is no one else to blame.

This book is organized into three parts: Part I: "Winning the War Within"; Part II: "The Laws of Combat"; and Part III: "Sustaining Victory." "Winning the War Within" develops the fundamental building blocks and mind-set necessary to lead and win. "The Laws of Combat" covers the four critical concepts (described earlier) that enable a team to perform at the highest level and dominate. Finally, "Sustaining Victory" discusses the more nuanced and difficult balance that leaders must navigate in order to maintain the edge and keep the team perpetually operating at the highest level.

Each chapter focuses on a different leadership concept, each unique though closely related and often mutually supporting. Within each chapter there are three subsections. The first identifies a leadership lesson learned through our U.S. Navy SEAL combat or training experience. The second subsection explains that leadership principle. The third demonstrates the principle's application to the business world, based on our work with a multitude of companies in a broad range of industries.

We believe in these leadership concepts because we have seen them work time and again, both in combat and in business. Their proper application and understanding ensure effective leaders and high-performing teams that produce extraordinary results. These principles empower those teams to dominate their battlefields by enabling leaders to fulfill their purpose: *lead* and *win*.

PART I

WINNING THE WAR WITHIN

U.S. Army M1A2 Abrams Main Battle Tank from Task Force Bandit as seen through a SEAL sniper loophole. Task Force Bandit (1st Battalion, 37th Armored Regiment of the 1st Brigade, 1st Armored Division) was an outstanding unit with whom Bruiser SEALs worked closely. They were aggressive, professional, and courageous. Loopholes, created by either explosives or manual tools, allowed SEAL snipers to observe and engage enemy fighters while remaining somewhat protected from enemy fire.

(Photo courtesy of the authors)

CHAPTER 1
Extreme Ownership

Jocko Willink

THE MALA'AB DISTRICT, RAMADI, IRAQ: FOG OF WAR

The early morning light was dimmed by a literal fog of war that filled the air: soot from tires the insurgents had set alight in the streets, clouds of dust kicked up from the road by U.S. tanks and Humvees, and powdered concrete from the walls of buildings pulverized by machine gun fire. As our armored Humvee rounded the corner and headed down the street toward the gunfire, I saw a U.S. M1A2 Abrams tank in the middle of the road up ahead, its turret rotated with the huge main gun trained on a building at almost point-blank range. Through the particle-filled air, I could see a smoky-red mist, clearly from a red smoke grenade used by American forces in the area as a general signal for "Help!"

My mind was racing. This was our first major operation in Ramadi and it was total chaos. Beyond the literal fog of war impeding our vision, the figurative "fog of war," often attributed to Prussian military strategist Carl von Clausewitz,* had descended upon us, and it was thick with confusion, inaccurate information, broken communications, and mayhem. For this operation, we had four separate elements of SEALs in various sectors of this violent, war-torn city: two SEAL sniper teams with U.S. Army scout snipers and a contingent of Iraqi soldiers, and another element of SEALs embedded with Iraqi soldiers and their U.S. Army combat advisors assigned to clear an entire sector building by building. Finally, my SEAL senior enlisted advisor (a noncommissioned officer) and I rode along with one of the Army company commanders. In total, about three hundred U.S. and Iraqi troops—friendly forces—were operating in this dangerous and hotly contested neighborhood of eastern Ramadi known as the Mala'ab District. The entire place was crawling with *muj* (pronounced "mooj"), as American forces called them. The enemy insurgent fighters called themselves *mujahideen*, Arabic for "those engaged in jihad," which we shortened for expediency. They subscribed to a ruthless, militant version of Islam and they were cunning, barbaric, and lethal. For years, the Mala'ab had remained firmly in their hands. Now, U.S. forces aimed to change that.

The operation had kicked off before sunrise, and with the sun now creeping up over the horizon, everyone was shooting. The myriad of radio networks (or nets) used by the U.S. ground and air units exploded with chatter and incoming reports. Details of U.S. and Iraqi troops wounded or killed came in from different sectors. Following them were reports of enemy fighters killed. U.S. elements tried to decipher what was happening with other U.S. and Iraqi units in adjacent sectors. U.S. Marine Corps ANGLICO (Air-Naval Gunfire Liaison Company) teams coordinated with American attack aircraft overhead in an effort to drop bombs on enemy positions.

---

* "War is the realm of uncertainty," *On War* by Carl von Clausewitz (1780–1831), Prussian general and military theorist. Clausewitz never actually used the term "Fog of War."

Only a few hours into the operation, both of my SEAL sniper elements had been attacked and were now embroiled in serious gunfights. As the element of Iraqi soldiers, U.S. Army Soldiers, and our SEALs cleared buildings across the sector, they met heavy resistance. Dozens of insurgent fighters mounted blistering attacks with PKC* Russian belt-fed machine guns, deadly RPG-7 shoulder-fired rockets, and AK-47 automatic rifle fire. As we monitored the radio, we heard the U.S. advisors with one of the Iraqi Army elements in advance of the rest report they were engaged in a fierce firefight and requested the QRF (Quick Reaction Force) for help. This particular QRF consisted of four U.S. Army armored Humvees, each mounted with an M2 .50-caliber heavy machine gun, and a dozen or so U.S. Soldiers that could dismount and render assistance. Minutes later, over the radio net, one of my SEAL sniper teams called for the "heavy QRF," a section (meaning two) of U.S. M1A2 Abrams Main Battle Tanks that could bring the thunder with their 120mm main guns and machine guns. That meant my SEALs were in a world of hurt and in need of serious help. I asked the U.S. Army company commander we were with to follow the tanks in, and he complied.

Our Humvee rolled to a stop just behind one of the Abrams tanks, its huge main gun pointed directly at a building and ready to engage. Pushing open the heavy armored door of my vehicle, I stepped out onto the street. I had a gut feeling that something was wrong.

Running over to a Marine ANGLICO gunnery sergeant, I asked him, "What's going on?"

"Hot damn!" he shouted with excitement. "There's some *muj*

---

* PK for Pulemet Kalashnikova, a Russian-designed belt-fed medium machine gun that fires a deadly 7.62x54R (7.62mm x 54mm rimmed) cartridge, generally in hundred-round (or more) belts. The PKM/PKS are common variants. The U.S. military in Iraq frequently used the designation "PKC," with the Cyrillic spelling for "PKS."

in that building right there putting up a serious fight!" He pointed to the building across the street, his weapon trained in that direction. It was clear he thought these *muj* were hard-core. "They killed one of our Iraqi soldiers when we entered the building and wounded a few more. We've been hammering them, and I'm working to get some bombs dropped on 'em now." He was in the midst of coordinating an airstrike with U.S. aircraft overhead to wipe out the enemy fighters holed up inside the building.

I looked around. The building he pointed to was riddled with bullet holes. The QRF Humvees had put over 150 rounds from a .50-caliber heavy machine gun into it and many more smaller caliber rounds from their rifles and light machines. Now the Abrams tank had its huge main gun trained on the building, preparing to reduce it to rubble and kill everyone inside. And if that still didn't do the job, bombs from the sky would be next.

But something didn't add up. We were extremely close to where one of our SEAL sniper teams was supposed to be. That sniper team had abandoned the location they had originally planned to use and were in the process of relocating to a new building when all the shooting started. In the mayhem, they hadn't reported their exact location, but I knew it would be close to the point where I was standing, close to the building the Marine gunny had just pointed to. What really didn't add up was that these Iraqi soldiers and their U.S. advisors shouldn't have arrived here for another couple of hours. No other friendly forces were to have entered this sector until we had properly "deconflicted"—determined the exact position of our SEAL sniper team and passed that information to the other friendly units in the operation. But for some reason there were dozens of Iraqi troops and their U.S. Army and Marine combat advisors in the area. It made no sense to me.

"Hold what you got, Gunny. I'm going to check it out," I said, motioning toward the building on which he had been working to coordinate the airstrike. He looked at me as if I were completely crazy. His Marines and a full platoon of Iraqi soldiers had been engaged in a vicious firefight with the enemy fighters inside that house and couldn't dislodge them. Whoever they were, they had put up one hell of a fight. In the gunny's mind, for us to even approach that place was pretty much suicidal. I nodded at my senior enlisted SEAL, who nodded back, and we moved across the street toward the enemy-infested house. Like most of the houses in Iraq, there was an eight-foot concrete wall around it. We approached the door to the compound, which was slightly open. With my M4 rifle at the ready, I kicked the door the rest of the way open only to find I was staring at one of my SEAL platoon chiefs. He stared back at me in wide-eyed surprise.

"What happened?" I asked him.

"Some *muj* entered the compound. We shot one of them and they attacked—hard-core. They brought it." I remembered what the gunny had just told me: one of their Iraqi soldiers had been shot when he entered the compound.

At that moment, it all became clear. In the chaos and confusion, somehow a rogue element of Iraqi soldiers had strayed outside the boundaries to which they had been confined and attempted to enter the building occupied by our SEAL sniper team. In the early morning darkness, our SEAL sniper element had seen the silhouette of a man armed with an AK-47 creep into their compound. While there were not supposed to be any friendlies in the vicinity, there were many enemy fighters known to be in the area. With that in mind, our SEALs had engaged the man with the AK-47, thinking they were under attack. Then all hell broke loose.

When gunfire erupted from the house, the Iraqi soldiers outside the compound returned fire and pulled back behind the cover of the concrete walls across the street and in the surrounding buildings. They called in reinforcements, and U.S. Marines and

Army troops responded with a vicious barrage of gunfire into the house they assumed was occupied by enemy fighters. Meanwhile, inside the house our SEALs were pinned down and unable to clearly identify that it was *friendlies* shooting at them. All they could do was return fire as best they could and keep up the fight to prevent being overrun by what they thought were enemy fighters. The U.S. Marine ANGLICO team had come very close to directing airstrikes on the house our SEALs were holed up in. When the .50-caliber machine gun opened up on their position, our SEAL sniper element inside the building, thinking they were under heavy enemy attack, called in the heavy QRF Abrams tanks for support. That's when I had arrived on the scene.

Inside the compound, the SEAL chief stared back at me, somewhat confused. He no doubt wondered how I had just walked through the hellacious enemy attack to reach his building.

"It was a blue-on-blue," I said to him. Blue-on-blue—friendly fire, fratricide—the worst thing that could happen. To be killed or wounded by the enemy in battle was bad enough. But to be accidently killed or wounded by friendly fire because someone had screwed up was the most horrible fate. It was also a reality. I had heard the story of X-Ray Platoon from SEAL Team One in Vietnam. The squads split up on a night patrol in the jungle, lost their bearings, and when they bumped into each other again in the darkness, they mistook each other for enemy and opened up with gunfire. A ferocious firefight ensued, leaving one of their own dead and several wounded. That was the last X-Ray Platoon in the SEAL Teams. Henceforth, the name was banished. It was a curse—and a lesson. Friendly fire was completely unacceptable in the SEAL Teams. And now it had just happened to us—to my SEAL task unit.

"What?" the SEAL chief asked with utter disbelief.

"It was a blue-on-blue," I said again, calmly and as a matter of fact. There was no time to debate or discuss. There were real bad guys out there, and even as we spoke, sporadic gunfire could be heard all around as other elements engaged insurgents in the vicinity. "Now what do ya got?" I asked, needing to know his status and that of his men.

"One SEAL fragged in the face—not too bad. But everyone is rattled. Let's get them out of here," replied the chief.

An armored personnel carrier (APC)* had arrived with the heavy QRF and was sitting out front. "There's an APC out front. Get your boys loaded up," I told him.

"Roger," said the chief.

The SEAL chief, one of the best tactical leaders I'd ever known, quickly got the rest of his SEALs and other troopers down to the front door. They looked more rattled than any human beings I had ever seen. Having been on the receiving end of devastating .50-caliber machine gun rounds punching through the walls around them, they had stared death in the face and did not think they would survive. But they quickly got it together, boarded the APC, and left for the nearby U.S. forward operating base—except the SEAL chief. Tough as nails and ready for more, he stayed with me, unfazed by what had happened and ready for whatever came next.

I made my way back over to the Marine ANGLICO gunny. "The building is clear," I told him.

"Roger that, Sir," he replied, looking surprised as he quickly reported it on the radio.

"Where's the captain?" I asked, wanting to find the U.S. Army company commander.

"Upstairs, here," he replied motioning toward the building we were in front of.

---

* M113 armored personnel carrier, a tank-tracked vehicle first used by U.S. forces in Vietnam, employed in Iraq for troop transport and casualty evacuation. With a crew of two or three, it can carry up to ten personnel.

I walked upstairs and found the company commander hunkered down on the roof of a building. "Everyone OK?" he asked.

"It was a blue-on-blue," I replied bluntly.

"What?" he asked, stunned.

"It was a blue-on-blue," I repeated. "One Iraqi soldier KIA,* a few more wounded. One of my guys wounded, fragged in the face. Everyone else is OK, by a miracle."

"Roger," he replied, stunned and disappointed at what had transpired. No doubt, as an outstanding leader himself, he felt somewhat responsible. But having operated in this chaotic urban battlefield for months alongside Iraqi soldiers, he knew how easily such a thing could happen.

But we still had work to do and had to drive on. The operation continued. We conducted two more back-to-back missions, cleared a large portion of the Mala'ab District, and killed dozens of insurgents. The rest of the mission was a success.

But that didn't matter. I felt sick. One of my men was wounded. An Iraqi soldier was dead and others were wounded. We did it to ourselves, and it happened under my command.

When we completed the last mission of the day, I went to the battalion tactical operations center where I had my field computer set up to receive e-mail from higher headquarters. I dreaded opening and answering the inevitable e-mail inquiries about what had transpired. I wished I had died out on the battlefield. I felt that I deserved it.

My e-mail in-box was full. Word had rapidly spread that we had had a blue-on-blue. I opened an e-mail from my commanding officer (CO) that went straight to the point. It read: "SHUT DOWN. CONDUCT NO MORE OPERATIONS. INVESTIGATING OFFICER, COMMAND MASTER CHIEF, AND I ARE EN ROUTE." In typical fashion for a Navy mishap, the CO had appointed an investigating

---

* killed in action

officer to determine the facts of what happened and who was responsible.

Another e-mail from one of my old bosses stationed in another city in Iraq, but privy to what was happening in Ramadi, read simply, "Heard you had a blue-on-blue. What the hell?"

All the good things I had done and the solid reputation I had worked hard to establish in my career as a SEAL were now meaningless. Despite the many successful combat operations I had led, I was now the commander of a unit that had committed the SEAL mortal sin.

A day passed as I waited for the arrival of the investigating officer, our CO, and command master chief (CMC), the senior enlisted SEAL at the command. In the meantime, they directed me to prepare a brief detailing what had happened. I knew what this meant. They were looking for someone to blame, and most likely someone to "relieve"—the military euphemism for someone to fire.

Frustrated, angry, and disappointed that this had happened, I began gathering information. As we debriefed, it was obvious there were some serious mistakes made by many individuals both during the planning phase and on the battlefield during execution. Plans were altered but notifications weren't sent. The communication plan was ambiguous, and confusion about the specific timing of radio procedures contributed to critical failures. The Iraqi Army had adjusted their plan but had not told us. Timelines were pushed without clarification. Locations of friendly forces had not been reported. The list went on and on.

Within Task Unit Bruiser—my own SEAL troop—similar mistakes had been made. The specific location of the sniper team in question had not been passed on to other units. Positive identification of the assumed enemy combatant, who turned out to be an Iraqi soldier, had been insufficient. A thorough SITREP (situation report) had not been passed to me after the initial engagement took place.

The list of mistakes was substantial. As directed, I put together a brief, a Microsoft PowerPoint presentation with time-lines and depictions of the movements of friendly units on a map of the area. Then I assembled the list of everything that everyone had done wrong.

It was a thorough explanation of what had happened. It out-lined the critical failures that had turned the mission into a night-mare and cost the life of one Iraqi soldier, wounded several more, and, but for a true miracle, could have cost several of our SEALs their lives.

But something was missing. There was some problem, some piece that I hadn't identified, and it made me feel like the truth wasn't coming out. Who was to blame?

I reviewed my brief again and again trying to figure out the missing piece, the single point of failure that had led to the inci-dent. But there were so many factors, and I couldn't figure it out.

Finally, the CO, the CMC, and the investigating officer arrived at our base. They were going to drop their gear, grab some food at the chow hall, and then we would bring everyone together to debrief the event.

I looked through my notes again, trying to place the blame.

Then it hit me.

Despite all the failures of individuals, units, and leaders, and despite the myriad mistakes that had been made, there was only one person to blame for everything that had gone wrong on the operation: me. I hadn't been with our sniper team when they engaged the Iraqi soldier. I hadn't been controlling the rogue ele-ment of Iraqis that entered the compound. But that didn't matter. As the SEAL task unit commander, the senior leader on the ground in charge of the mission, I was responsible for everything in Task Unit Bruiser. I had to take complete ownership of what went wrong. That is what a leader does—even if it means getting fired.

If anyone was to be blamed and fired for what happened, let it be me.

A few minutes later, I walked into the platoon space where everyone was gathered to debrief. The silence was deafening. The CO sat in the front row. The CMC stood ominously in the back. The SEAL that had been wounded—fragged in the face by a .50-caliber round—was there, his face bandaged up.

I stood before the group. "Whose fault was this?" I asked to the roomful of teammates.

After a few moments of silence, the SEAL who had mistakenly engaged the Iraqi solider spoke up: "It was my fault. I should have positively identified my target."

"No," I responded, "It wasn't your fault. Whose fault was it?" I asked the group again.

"It was my fault," said the radioman from the sniper element. "I should have passed our position sooner."

"Wrong," I responded. "It wasn't your fault. Whose fault was it?" I asked again.

"It was my fault," said another SEAL, who was a combat advisor with the Iraqi Army clearance team. "I should have controlled the Iraqis and made sure they stayed in their sector."

"Negative," I said. "You are not to blame." More of my SEALs were ready to explain what they had done wrong and how it had contributed to the failure. But I had heard enough.

"You know whose fault this is? You know who gets all the blame for this?" The entire group sat there in silence, including the CO, the CMC, and the investigating officer. No doubt they were wondering whom I would hold responsible. Finally, I took a deep breath and said, "There is only one person to blame for this: me. I am the commander. I am responsible for the entire operation. As the senior man, I am responsible for every action that takes place on the battlefield. There is no one to blame but me. And I will tell you this right now: I will make sure that nothing like this ever happens to us again."

It was a heavy burden to bear. But it was absolutely true. I was the leader. I was in charge and I was responsible. Thus, I had to take ownership of everything that went wrong. Despite the tremendous blow to my reputation and to my ego, it was the right thing to do—the only thing to do. I apologized to the wounded SEAL, explaining that it was my fault he was wounded and that we were all lucky he wasn't dead. We then proceeded to go through the entire operation, piece by piece, identifying everything that happened and what we could do going forward to prevent it from happening again.

Looking back, it is clear that, despite what happened, the full ownership I took of the situation actually increased the trust my commanding officer and master chief had in me. If I had tried to pass the blame on to others, I suspect I would have been fired—deservedly so. The SEALs in the troop, who did not expect me to take the blame, respected the fact that I had taken full responsibility for everything that had happened. They knew it was a dynamic situation caused by a multitude of factors, but I owned them all.

The U.S. Army and U.S. Marine conventional commanders took the debrief points as lessons learned and moved on. Having fought in Ramadi for an extended period of time, they understood something we SEALs did not: blue-on-blue was a risk that had to be mitigated as much as possible in an urban environment, but that risk could not be eliminated. This was urban combat, the most complex and difficult of all warfare, and it was simply impossible to conduct operations without some risk of blue-on-blue. But for SEALs accustomed to working in small groups against point targets, fratricide should never happen.

A very senior and highly respected SEAL officer, who before

joining the Navy had been a U.S. Marine Corps platoon commander in Vietnam at the historic Battle of Hue City, came to visit our task unit shortly after the incident. He told me that many of the Marine casualties in Hue were friendly fire, part of the brutal reality of urban combat. He understood what we had experienced and just how easily it could happen.

But, while a blue-on-blue incident in an environment like Ramadi might be likely, if not expected, we vowed to never let it happen again. We analyzed what had happened and implemented the lessons learned. We revised our standard operating procedures and planning methodology to better mitigate risk. As a result of this tragic incident, we undoubtedly saved lives going forward. While we were mistakenly engaged by friendly elements again many times during the rest of the deployment, we never let it escalate and were always able to regain control quickly.

But the tactical avoidance of fratricide was only part of what I learned. When I returned home from deployment, I took over Training Detachment One, which managed all training for West Coast SEAL platoons and task units in preparation for combat deployments. I set up scenarios where blue-on-blue shootings were almost guaranteed to happen. When they did, we, the training cadre, explained how to avoid them.

But more important, the commanders in training could learn what I had learned about leadership. While some commanders took full responsibility for blue-on-blue, others blamed their subordinates for simulated fratricide incidents in training. These weaker commanders would get a solid explanation about the burden of command and the deep meaning of responsibility: the leader is truly and ultimately responsible for *everything*.

That is Extreme Ownership, the fundamental core of what constitutes an effective leader in the SEAL Teams or in any leadership endeavor.

PRINCIPLE

On any team, in any organization, all responsibility for success and failure rests with the leader. *The leader must own everything in his or her world.* There is no one else to blame. The leader must acknowledge mistakes and admit failures, take ownership of them, and develop a plan to win.

The best leaders don't just take responsibility for their job. They take Extreme Ownership of everything that impacts their mission. This fundamental core concept enables SEAL leaders to lead high-performing teams in extraordinary circumstances and win. But Extreme Ownership isn't a principle whose application is limited to the battlefield. This concept is the number-one characteristic of any high-performance winning team, in any military unit, organization, sports team or business team in any industry.

When subordinates aren't doing what they should, leaders that exercise Extreme Ownership cannot blame the subordinates. They must first look in the mirror at themselves. The leader bears full responsibility for explaining the strategic mission, developing the tactics, and securing the training and resources to enable the team to properly and successfully execute.

If an individual on the team is not performing at the level required for the team to succeed, the leader must train and mentor that underperformer. But if the underperformer continually fails to meet standards, then a leader who exercises Extreme Ownership must be loyal to the team and the mission above any individual. If underperformers cannot improve, the leader must make the tough call to terminate them and hire others who can get the job done. It is all on the leader.

As individuals, we often attribute the success of others to luck or circumstances and make excuses for our own failures and the failures of our team. We blame our own poor performance on bad luck, circumstances beyond our control, or poorly performing subordinates—anyone but ourselves. Total responsibility for failure is a difficult thing to accept, and taking ownership when things go wrong requires extraordinary humility and courage. But doing just that is an absolute necessity to learning, growing as a leader, and improving a team's performance.

Extreme Ownership requires leaders to look at an organization's problems through the objective lens of reality, without emotional attachments to agendas or plans. It mandates that a leader set ego aside, accept responsibility for failures, attack weaknesses, and consistently work to build a better and more effective team. Such a leader, however, does not take credit for his or her team's successes but bestows that honor upon his subordinate leaders and team members. When a leader sets such an example and expects this from junior leaders within the team, the mindset develops into the team's culture at every level. With Extreme Ownership, junior leaders take charge of their smaller teams and their piece of the mission. Efficiency and effectiveness increase exponentially and a high-performance, winning team is the result.

APPLICATION TO BUSINESS

The vice president's plan looked good on paper. The board of directors had approved the plan the previous year and thought it could decrease production costs. But it wasn't working. And the board wanted to find out why. Who was at fault? Who was to blame?

I was brought on by the company to help provide leadership guidance and executive coaching to the company's vice president of manufacturing (VP). Although technically sound and experienced in his particular industry, the VP hadn't met the manufacturing goals set forth by the company's board of directors. His plan included the following: consolidate manufacturing plants to eliminate redundancy, increase worker productivity through an incentivized bonus program, and streamline the manufacturing process.

The problem arose in the plan's execution. At each quarterly board meeting, the VP delivered a myriad of excuses as to why so little of his plan had been executed. After a year, the board wondered if he could effectively lead this change. With little progress to show, the VP's job was now at risk.

I arrived on scene two weeks before the next board meeting. After spending several hours with the CEO to get some color on the situation, I was introduced to the VP of manufacturing. My initial assessment was positive. The VP was extremely smart and incredibly knowledgeable about the business. But would he be open to coaching?

"So, you're here to help me, right?" the VP inquired.

Knowing that, due to ego, some people bristle at the idea of criticism and coaching no matter how constructive, I chose to take a more indirect approach.

"Maybe not so much here to help *you*, but here to help the situation," I answered, effectively lowering the VP's defenses.

In the weeks leading up to the board meeting, I researched and examined the details of why the VP's plan had failed and what had gone wrong, and I spoke to the VP about the problems encountered in the plan's execution. He explained that the consolidation of manufacturing plants had failed because his distribution managers feared that increasing the distance between plants and distribution centers would prevent face-to-face interaction with the manufacturing team and reduce their ability to tweak order specifics. They surmised it would also inhibit their ability to handle rush-order deliveries. The VP dismissed his distribution managers' concerns as unfounded. In the event the need arose to adjust orders or customize, a teleconference or videoconference would more than suffice.

The VP also explained why the incentivized bonus structure

hadn't been put in place. Each time his plant managers and other key leaders were presented with the rollout plan, they pushed back with concerns: the employees wouldn't make enough money; they would leave for jobs with higher base salaries that didn't require minimum standards; recruiters would capitalize on the change and pull skilled workers away. When the VP pushed the manufacturing managers harder, they teamed up with the sales managers. The two groups opposed the VP's plan, claiming it was the company's reputation for skilled manufacturing that kept business coming in, and such a change would put the business at risk.

Finally, when it came to the VP's plan to streamline the manufacturing process, the pushback was universal and straight from the classic mantra of antichange: "We have always done it this way;" and "If it ain't broke, don't fix it."

"What does the board think of these reasons?" I asked, as we discussed the upcoming annual board meeting.

"They listen, but I don't think they really understand them. And they have been hearing the same reasons for a while now, so I think they are getting frustrated. I don't know if they believe them anymore. They sound like . . ."

"Excuses?" I finished the sentence for the VP, knowing the word itself was a big blow to his ego.

"Yes. Yes, they sound like excuses. But these are real and legitimate," insisted the VP.

"Could there be other reasons your plan wasn't successfully executed?" I asked.

"Absolutely," the VP answered. "The market has been tough. New technology advancements have taken some time to work through. Everyone got focused on some products that never really amounted to much. So, yes, there are a host of other reasons."

"Those all may be factors. But there is one most important reason why this plan has failed," I said.

"What reason is that?" the VP inquired with interest.

I paused for a moment to see if the VP was ready for what I had to tell him. The impact would be uncomfortable, but there was no way around it. I stated it plainly, "You. You are the reason."

The VP was surprised, then defensive. "Me?" he protested. "I came up with the plan! I have delivered it over and over. It's not my fault they aren't executing it!"

I listened patiently.

"The plant managers, the distribution and sales teams don't fully support the plan," he continued. "So how am I supposed to execute it? I'm not out there in the field with them. I can't make them listen to me." The VP's statements gradually became less emphatic. He soon realized what he was saying: he was making excuses.

I explained that the direct responsibility of a leader included getting people to listen, support, and execute plans. To drive the point home, I told him, "You can't *make* people listen to you. You can't *make* them execute. That might be a temporary solution for a simple task. But to implement real change, to drive people to accomplish something truly complex or difficult or dangerous— you can't *make* people do those things. You have to *lead* them."

"I did lead them," the VP protested. "They just didn't execute."

But he hadn't led them, at least not effectively. The measure of this was clear: he had been unsuccessful in implementing his plan.

"When I was in charge of a SEAL platoon or a SEAL task unit conducting combat operations, do you think every operation I led was a success?" I asked.

He shook his head. "No."

"Absolutely not," I agreed. "Sure, I led many operations that went well and accomplished the mission. But not always. I have been in charge of operations that went horribly wrong for a number of reasons: bad intelligence, bad decisions by subordinate leadership, mistakes by shooters, coordinating units not following the plan. The list goes on. Combat is a dangerous, complex, dynamic situation, where all kinds of things can go sideways in a hurry, with life and death consequences. There is no way to control every decision, every person, every occurrence that happens out there. It is just impossible. But let me tell you something: when things went wrong, you know who I blamed?" I asked, pausing slightly for this to sink in. "Me," I said. "I blamed me."

I continued: "As the commander, everything that happened on the battlefield was my responsibility. *Everything*. If a supporting unit didn't do what we needed it to do, then I hadn't given clear instructions. If one of my machine gunners engaged targets outside his field of fire, then I had not ensured he understood where his field of fire was. If the enemy surprised us and hit us where we hadn't expected, then I hadn't thought through all the possibilities. No matter what, I could never blame other people when a mission went wrong."

The VP contemplated this. After a thoughtful silence, he responded, "I always thought I was a good leader. I've always been in leadership positions."

"That might be one of the issues: in your mind you are doing everything right. So when things go wrong, instead of looking at yourself, you blame others. But no one is infallible. With Extreme Ownership, you must remove individual ego and personal agenda. It's all about the mission. How can you best get your team to most effectively execute the plan in order to accomplish the mission?" I continued. "That is the question you have to ask yourself. That is what Extreme Ownership is all about."

The VP nodded, beginning to grasp the concept and see its effectiveness.

"Do you think that every one of your employees is blatantly disobedient?" I said.

"No," the VP said.

"If so, they would need to be fired. But that doesn't seem to be the situation here," I continued. "Your people don't need to be fired. They need to be led."

"So what am I doing wrong as a leader?" asked the VP. "How can I lead them?"

"It all starts right here with you," I said. "You must assume total ownership of the failure to implement your new plan. You are to blame. And that is exactly what you need to tell the board."

"Tell the board that? Are you serious?" the VP asked in disbelief. "I don't mind taking a little blame, but this is not all my fault." Though beginning to see the light, he still resisted the idea of taking total responsibility.

"In order to execute this plan, in order to truly become an effective leader, you have to realize and accept total responsibility," I said. "You have to own it."

The VP was not yet convinced.

"If one of your manufacturing managers came to you and said, 'My team is failing,' what would your response be? Would you blame their team?" I asked.

"No," the VP admitted.

I explained that as the officer in charge of training for the West Coast SEAL Teams, we put SEAL units through highly demanding scenarios to get them ready for combat in Iraq and Afghanistan. When SEAL leaders were placed in worst-case-scenario training situations, it was almost always the leaders' attitudes that determined whether their SEAL units would ultimately succeed or fail. We knew how hard the training missions were because we had designed them.

In virtually every case, the SEAL troops and platoons that didn't perform well had leaders who blamed everyone and everything else—their troops, their subordinate leaders, or the scenario. They blamed the SEAL training instructor staff; they blamed inadequate equipment or the experience level of their men.

They refused to accept responsibility. Poor performance and mission failure were the result.

The best-performing SEAL units had leaders who accepted responsibility for everything. Every mistake, every failure or shortfall—those leaders would own it. During the debrief after a training mission, those good SEAL leaders took ownership of failures, sought guidance on how to improve, and figured out a way to overcome challenges on the next iteration. The best leaders checked their egos, accepted blame, sought out constructive criticism, and took detailed notes for improvement. They exhibited Extreme Ownership, and as a result, their SEAL platoons and task units dominated.

When a bad SEAL leader walked into a debrief and blamed everyone else, that attitude was picked up by subordinates and team members, who then followed suit. They all blamed everyone else, and inevitably the team was ineffective and unable to properly execute a plan.

Continuing, I told the VP, "In those situations, you ended up with a unit that never felt they were to blame for anything. All they did was make excuses and ultimately never made the adjustments necessary to fix problems. Now, compare that to the commander who came in and took the blame. He said, 'My subordinate leaders made bad calls; I must not have explained the overall intent well enough.' Or, 'The assault force didn't execute the way I envisioned; I need to make sure they better understand my intent and rehearse more thoroughly.' The good leaders took ownership of the mistakes and shortfalls. That's the key difference. And how do you think their SEAL platoons and task units reacted to this type of leadership?"

"They must have respected that," the VP acknowledged.

"Exactly. They see Extreme Ownership in their leaders, and, as a result, they emulate Extreme Ownership throughout the chain of command down to the most junior personnel. As a group they try to figure out how to fix their problems—instead of trying to figure out who or what to blame. For those on the outside looking in, like our training group—or the board in your case—the difference is obvious."

"And that is how I appear to the board right now—blaming everyone and everything else," the VP recognized.

"There is only one way to fix it," I told him.

For the next several days, I helped the VP prepare for the board meeting. At times, he slipped back into defensiveness, not wanting to accept blame. He felt in many ways that his knowledge exceeded that of many members of the board—and he was probably right. But that didn't change the fact that he was the leader of a team that was failing its mission. As we rehearsed the VP's portion of the board presentation, I was unconvinced that he truly accepted total responsibility for his team's failures. I told him that bluntly.

"I'm saying exactly what you told me to say," the VP retorted. "The reason that this mission was unsuccessful was my failure as a leader to force execution."

"That's the problem," I said. "You are saying it, but I'm not convinced you believe it. Look at your career. You have accomplished amazing things. But you certainly aren't perfect. None of us are perfect. You are still learning and growing. We all are. And this is a lesson for you: if you reengage on this task, if you do a stern self-assessment of how you lead and what you can do better, the outcome will be different. But it starts here. It starts at the board meeting when you go in, put your ego aside, and take ownership for the company's failure here. The board members will be impressed with what they see and hear, because most people are unable to do this. They will respect your Extreme Ownership. Take personal responsibility for the failures. You *will* come out the other side stronger than ever before," I concluded.

At the board meeting, the VP did just that. He took the blame for the failure to meet the manufacturing objectives and gave a solid no-nonsense list of corrective measures that he would implement to ensure execution. The list started with what *he* was going to do differently, not about what other people needed to do. Now, the VP was on his way to Extreme Ownership.

"Let's get it on." A SEAL turret gunner looks across his M2 .50-caliber heavy machine gun out Ogden Gate into enemy territory beyond. The giant tank-track vehicle (M88 Recovery Vehicle) blocking the entrance to Camp Ramadi was used to deter the enemy's most devastating weapon—the car bomb or VBIED with several thousand pounds of explosives driven by a suicide bomber. Beyond the gate, the threat in the city was immense—and no one felt that more than the lead turret gunner in the first Humvee during a daytime mounted patrol.

(Photo courtesy of the authors)

CHAPTER 2
No Bad Teams, Only Bad Leaders

Leif Babin

CORONADO, CALIFORNIA: BASIC UNDERWATER DEMOLITION/SEAL TRAINING

"It pays to be a winner!" shouted a much-feared blue-and-gold-shirted Navy SEAL instructor through the megaphone. It was night three into the infamous Hell Week of SEAL training. The students, in camouflage fatigues, were soaked to the bone and covered in gritty sand that chafed them until they were raw and bleeding. They shivered from the cold ocean water and cool wind of the Southern California night. The students moved with the aches and pains as only those who have suffered through seventy-two hours straight of nearly nonstop physical exertion can. Exhausted, over the previous three days they had slept for less than one hour total. Since Hell Week had begun, dozens of them had quit. Others had become sick or injured and were pulled from training. When this class had started Basic Underwater Demolition/SEAL Training (known as BUD/S)—the SEAL basic training course—several weeks before, nearly two hundred determined young men had eagerly begun. All dreamed of becoming a U.S. Navy SEAL, prepared for years, and came to BUD/S with every intention of graduating. And yet within the first forty-eight hours of Hell Week, most of those young men had surrendered to the brutal challenge, rung the bell three times—the signal for DOR, or drop on request—and walked away from their dream of becoming a SEAL. They had quit.

Hell Week was not a fitness test. While it did require some athletic ability, every student that survived the weeks of BUD/S training prior to Hell Week had already demonstrated adequate fitness to graduate. It was not a physical test but a mental one. Sometimes, the best athletes in the class didn't make it through Hell Week. Success resulted from determination and will, but also from innovation and communication with the team. Such training graduated men who were not only physically tough but who could also out-think their adversary.

Only a few years before, I had suffered through my own BUD/S class Hell Week on this very beach. We began our Hell Week with 101 students. When we finished only 40 of us remained. Some of the most gifted athletes in the class and loudest talking muscleheads had been first to quit. Those of us that had made it through realized we could push ourselves mentally and physically much further than most ever thought possible through the pain, misery, and exhaustion of days without sleep—precisely what Hell Week was designed to do.

Now I wore the blue-and-gold shirt of a SEAL instructor. Following two combat deployments to Iraq, I was assigned to our Naval Special Warfare Training Center to instruct the Junior Officer Training Course—our officer leadership program. In addition to my day job, I supported Hell Week as an instructor. As the officer in charge of this Hell Week shift, my job was to oversee the crew of BUD/S instructors who ran the training. The instructors were experts at their jobs of putting these students to the test. They were especially skilled at weeding out those who don't have what it takes to become a SEAL. For me, to observe Hell Week from the instructor perspective was a whole new experience.

The BUD/S students were grouped into teams—"boat crews" of seven men, established by height. Each seven-man boat crew was assigned an IBS—inflatable boat, small. An IBS was small by U.S. Navy terms but awfully large and heavy when carried by hand. These large rubber boats, black with a painted yellow rim, weighed nearly two hundred pounds and became heavier still when filled with water and sand. A relic from the Navy Frogmen (Underwater Demolition Team) days of World War II, the dreaded boats had to be awkwardly carried everywhere, usually upon the heads of the seven boat-crew members struggling underneath. On land, the boat crews carried them up and over twenty-feet-high sand berms and ran with them for miles along the beach. They carried them on the hard asphalt streets back and forth across Naval Amphibious Base Coronado, trying like hell to keep up with instructors leading the way. The boat crews even pushed, pulled, squeezed, and muscled the unwieldy boats through the ropes and over the telephone poles and walls of the notorious BUD/S obstacle course. Out on the Pacific Ocean, the boat crews paddled their boats through the powerful crashing waves, often capsizing and scattering wet students and paddles across the beach like a storied shipwreck. These damned rubber boats were the source of a great deal of misery for the men assigned to them. Each boat had a roman numeral painted in bright yellow on the front, indicating the boat crew number—all except the boat crew made up of the shortest men in the class, known as the "Smurf crew." They had a bright blue Smurf painted on the bow of their boat.

In each boat crew the senior-ranking man served as boat crew leader, responsible for receiving orders from the instructors and briefing, directing, and leading the other six members of the boat crew. The boat crew leader bore responsibility for the performance of his boat crew. And while each member of the boat crew had to perform, the boat crew leader—by his very position as leader— received the most scrutiny from the instructor staff.

During SEAL training (and really, throughout a SEAL's career) every evolution was a competition—a race, a fight, a contest. In BUD/S, this point was driven home by the SEAL instructors, who constantly reminded the students, "It pays to be a winner." When racing as a boat crew during Hell Week, the winning boat crew's prize for victory was to sit out the next race, earning a few brief minutes of respite from the grueling, nonstop physical evolutions. They weren't allowed to sleep, but just to sit down and rest were especially precious commodities. While it paid to be a winner, this rule had a corollary: it really sucked to be a loser. Second place, in the instructor's vernacular, was simply "the first loser." But bad performance—falling far behind the rest of the pack and coming in dead last—carried especially grueling penalties: unwanted attention from the SEAL instructors who dished out additional punishing exercises on top of the already exhausting Hell Week evolutions. Meanwhile, the victorious boat crew celebrated by sitting out the next race and, most important, not getting wet and cold for a few brief minutes.

The SEAL instructor cadre kept the students moving with constant boat crew races, giving detailed and intentionally complicated instructions to the boat crew leaders, who in turn briefed their men and executed the instructions as best they could in their exhausted state. The command went out from the SEAL instructor with the megaphone: "Boat crew leaders report!" The boat crew leaders left their boats and ran to take position, forming a smart line in front of the SEAL instructor, who laid out the specifics of the next race.

"Paddle your boats out through the surf zone, dump boat,* paddle your boats down to the next beach marker, then paddle them back into the beach, run up and over the berm and around the beach marker, then head-carry back to the rope station, then over the berm, and finish here," commanded the SEAL instructor. "Got it?"

The boat crew leaders raced back and briefed their boat crews. Then the race began. In place of the traditional "Ready, set, go," the SEAL command to begin was "Stand by . . . bust 'em!" And they were off.

In every race, there were standout performers. Throughout this particular Hell Week, one boat crew dominated the competition: Boat Crew II. They won or nearly won every single race. They pushed themselves hard every time, working in unison and operating as a team. Boat Crew II had a strong leader, and each of the individual boat crew members seemed highly motivated and performed well. They compensated for each other's weaknesses, helped each other, and took pride in winning, which had its rewards. After each victory, Boat Crew II enjoyed a few precious minutes of rest while the other boat crews toiled through the next race. Though Boat Crew II was still cold and exhausted, I saw smiles on most of their faces. They were performing exceptionally well; they were winning and morale was high.

Meanwhile, Boat Crew VI was delivering a standout performance of a different kind. They placed dead last in virtually every race, often lagging far behind the rest of the class. Rather than working together as a team, the men were operating as individuals, furious and frustrated at their teammates. We heard them yelling and cursing at each other from some distance, accusing the others of not doing their part. Each boat crew member focused

---

* turn the boat upside down, get everybody into the water, then right the boat and get back in.

on his own individual pain and discomfort, and the boat crew leader was no exception. He certainly recognized they were underperforming, but likely, in his mind and that of his boat crew, no amount of effort could change that. And their horrific performance was the result.

"Boat Crew Six, you better start putting out!" blared a SEAL instructor through his megaphone. Extra attention from the instructor staff had serious consequences. Our SEAL instructors were all over Boat Crew VI, dishing out punishment for their poor performance. As a result, the misery multiplied tenfold for Boat Crew VI. They were forced to sprint back and forth over the sand berm, down to the water to get wet and sandy, then bear-crawl on blistered hands and feet. Next they had to hold the boat at "extended arm carry," with their arms fully extended overhead supporting the full weight of the IBS until their shoulders were completely smoked. This punishment sapped every ounce of remaining strength from the already weary and demoralized boat crew. The boat crew leader, a young and inexperienced officer, was getting even more attention. As the leader, he bore the responsibility for his boat crew's poor performance. Yet he seemed indifferent, as though fate had dealt him a poor hand: a team of underperformers who, no matter how hard he tried, simply could not get the job done.

I kept my eye on the leader of Boat Crew VI. If he did not show substantial improvement in leadership ability, he would not graduate from the program. SEAL officers were expected to perform like everyone else, but more important, they were also expected to lead. So far, Boat Crew VI's leader was demonstrating performance that was subpar and unacceptable. Our SEAL senior chief petty officer, the most experienced and highly respected noncommissioned officer of the SEAL instructor cadre, took a keen interest in Boat Crew VI and their lackluster leader.

"You had better take charge and square your boat away, Sir," said Senior Chief to the Boat Crew VI leader. Senior Chief was a goliath of a man, with piercing eyes that instilled fear equally into terrorists on the battlefield and students in training. An exceptional and revered leader himself, he had mentored many young junior officers. Now, Senior Chief offered an interesting solution to Boat Crew VI's atrocious performance.

"Let's swap out the boat crew leaders from the best and the worst crews and see what happens," said Senior Chief. All other controls would remain the same—heavy and awkward boats, manned by the same exhausted crews, cold water, gritty and chafing sand, wearied men competing in challenging races. Only a single individual, the leader, would change.

Could it possibly make any difference? I wondered.

The plan was quickly relayed to the other SEAL instructors. "Boat crew leaders from Boat Crews Two and Six report," blared the SEAL instructor through the megaphone. The two boat crew leaders ran over and stood at attention. "You two will swap positions and take charge of the other's boat crew. Boat Crew Six leader, you're now the leader of Boat Crew Two. Boat Crew Two Leader, you're now the leader of Boat Crew Six. Got it?" said the SEAL instructor.

The boat crew leader from Boat Crew II was clearly not happy. I'm sure he hated to leave the team he had built and knew well. No doubt he was proud of their dominant performance. The new assignment to take charge of a poorly performing boat crew would be difficult and could potentially invite unwanted attention from the SEAL instructors. Still, he dared not try to argue the point with the instructor. With no choice, he accepted the challenging assignment with a look of determination.

Boat Crew VI's leader was obviously elated. It was clear he felt that only by the luck of the draw—and no fault of his own—had he been assigned to the worst boat crew of underperformers. In his mind, no amount of effort on his part could make Boat Crew

VI better. Now, the SEAL instructor directed him to take over Boat Crew II. His face revealed his inner conviction that justice was finally being done and his new assignment meant things would now be easy for him.

Having received the direction to swap places, each boat crew leader went to his new position in the opposite boat crew and stood by for the next race. As before, boat crew leaders were given instructions, and they in turn briefed their teams.

"Stand by . . . bust 'em!" came the command. And they were off.

We watched the boat crews sprint over the berm carrying their boats, then hurry down to the surf zone and into the dark water. They jumped into their boats and paddled furiously. Passing through the crashing waves, they dumped boat, got everyone back on board, and then paddled down the beach. The headlights from our instructors' vehicles caught the reflection of the yellow bands painted around the boats' rims. We could no longer see the boat numbers. However, two boats were ahead of the pack, almost neck and neck, with one vying for the lead. A half mile down the beach, as the instructors' trucks followed, the boat crews paddled back into shore. As the boats came in on the headlights, the numbers were clearly visible. Boat Crew VI was in the lead and maintained first place all the way across the finish line, just ahead of Boat Crew II. Boat Crew VI had won the race.

A miraculous turnaround had taken place: Boat Crew VI had gone from last place to first. The boat crew members had begun to work together as a team, and *won*. Boat Crew II still performed well, though they narrowly lost the race. They continued to challenge Boat Crew VI for the lead in the follow-on races. And each of these boat crews outperformed all the rest, with Boat Crew VI winning most of the races over the better part of the next hour.

It was a shocking turn of events. Boat Crew VI, the same team in the same circumstances only under new leadership, went from the worst boat crew in the class to the best. Gone was their cursing and frustration. And gone too was the constant scrutiny and individual attention they had received from the SEAL instructor staff. Had I not witnessed this amazing transformation, I might have doubted it. But it was a glaring, undeniable example of one of the most fundamental and important truths at the heart of Extreme Ownership: there are no bad teams, only bad leaders.

How is it possible that switching a single individual—only the leader—had completely turned around the performance of an entire group? The answer: leadership is the single greatest factor in any team's performance. Whether a team succeeds or fails is all up to the leader. The leader's attitude sets the tone for the entire team. The leader drives performance—or doesn't. And this applies not just to the most senior leader of an overall team, but to the junior leaders of teams within the team.

I reflected back to my own experience as a boat crew leader in BUD/S through the tribulations of Hell Week, where I had failed and should have done better and where I had succeeded. My boat crew at times had struggled to perform, until I figured out that I had to put myself in the most difficult position at the front of the boat and *lead*. That required driving the boat crew members hard, harder than they thought they could go. I discovered that it was far more effective to focus their efforts not on the days to come or the far-distant finish line they couldn't yet see, but instead on a physical goal immediately in front of them—the beach marker, landmark, or road sign a hundred yards ahead. If we could execute with a monumental effort just to reach an immediate goal that everyone could see, we could then continue to the next visually attainable goal and then the next. When pieced together, it meant our performance over time increased substantially and eventually we crossed the finish line at the head of the pack.

Looking back, I could have yelled a lot less and encouraged more. As a boat crew leader, I protected my boat crew from the instructor staff as much as I could. It was "us versus them," as I saw it. In protecting my boat crew, I actually sheltered a couple of perpetual underperformers who dragged the rest of the boat crew down. When Hell Week was over, talking to some of the other members of our boat crew, we realized we had carried along these mentally weak performers. They almost certainly would not have met the standards otherwise. That loyalty was misguided. If we wouldn't want to serve alongside our boat crew's weakest performers once we were all assigned to SEAL platoons in various SEAL Teams, we had no right to force other SEALs to do so. The instructors were tasked with weeding out those without the determination and will to meet the high standards of performance. We had hindered that.

Ultimately, how my boat crew performed was entirely on me. The concept that there were no bad teams, only bad leaders was a difficult one to accept but nevertheless a crucial concept that leaders must fully understand and implement to enable them to most effectively lead a high-performance team. Leaders must accept total responsibility, own problems that inhibit performance, and develop solutions to those problems. A team could only deliver exceptional performance if a leader ensured the team worked together toward a focused goal and enforced high standards of performance, working to continuously improve. With a culture of Extreme Ownership within the team, every member of the team could contribute to this effort and ensure the highest levels of performance.

Watching these events now unfold as a BUD/S instructor, I knew that as difficult a challenge as Hell Week was for these students, it was only training. These young boat crew leaders could not fully comprehend the burden of leadership for which they would soon be responsible as SEAL officers on the battlefield. As combat leaders, the pressure on them would be immense, beyond their imagination.

Only months before this very Hell Week, I had been a SEAL platoon commander in Ramadi, Iraq, leading combat missions into the most violent, enemy-held areas of the city. We'd been in more firefights than I could count, against a well-armed, experienced, and highly determined enemy. Death lurked around the corner at any moment. Every decision I (and the leaders within our platoon and task unit) made carried potentially mortal consequences. We had delivered a huge impact on the battlefield, killed hundreds of insurgents, and protected U.S. Soldiers and Marines. I was proud of those triumphs. But we had also suffered immense tragedy with the loss of the first Navy SEAL killed in combat in Iraq, Marc Lee. Marc was an incredible teammate, an exceptional SEAL warrior with an amazing sense of humor that kept us laughing through the darkest of times. He was shot and killed in the midst of a furious firefight in one of the largest single battles fought by U.S. forces in South-Central Ramadi. Marc was my friend and brother. I was his commander, ultimately responsible for his life. Yet I had received only a minor gunshot wound that day, while Marc was struck and killed instantly. I had come home and he had not. This was devastating beyond measure.

I grieved too for Mike Monsoor, from Task Unit Bruiser's Delta Platoon, who, while not a member of my platoon, was also a friend and brother. Mike had jumped on a grenade to save three of his teammates. Mike was loved and respected by all who knew him. Like Marc, we deeply mourned his loss.

On the same day Marc Lee had been killed, another beloved SEAL from Charlie Platoon, Ryan Job, had been shot in the face by an enemy sniper. He was gravely wounded and we weren't sure he would live. Yet Ryan, tough as nails, had survived, although his wound left him permanently blind. Still, Ryan's drive and determination were unstoppable. He married the girl of his dreams and, after medically retiring from the Navy, enrolled in a college program and earned a business degree, graduating with a 4.0 GPA. Despite being blind, Ryan successfully reached the 14,410-foot summit of Mount Rainier and personally bagged a trophy bull elk (using a rifle fitted with a specially designed scope with a camera for a spotter).* Ryan was an exceptional SEAL, a wonderful teammate and a friend who inspired all who knew him. Though he had as much right as anyone to be bitter about the hand life dealt him, he was not. We laughed continuously every time we got together. Ryan and his wife were expecting their first child, and he could hardly contain his excitement. But just when I thought that the men of Charlie Platoon and Task Unit Bruiser and their families who had suffered and endured so much were safe from the specter of death, Ryan Job died in recovery from a surgery to repair his combat wounds—wounds he had received under my charge. No words can fully describe the hammer blow that this news dealt—agony beyond comprehension.

As their platoon commander, the loss of Marc and Ryan were a crushing burden that I would bear for the rest of my days. I knew that Mike's platoon commander in Delta Platoon felt the same way. And, as commander of Task Unit Bruiser, Jocko carried this burden for all. And yet as difficult as this was for me, I knew I could not ever fully understand how devastating the loss of these fine men was to their families and closest friends. In the months and years ahead, it was my duty to help them and support them as best I could.

As I stood watching these young boat crew leaders—not yet SEALs—I knew they could not possibly grasp the responsibilities

---

* Ryan was afforded these opportunities at spectacular outdoor adventures through the amazing work of Camp Patriot (www.camppatriot.org), a nonprofit organization for wounded veterans.

in store for them as future SEAL officers and combat leaders. Sure, BUD/S training was tough. Hell Week was a kick in the nuts. But nobody was striving to kill them. Decisions in training here weren't life or death. Boat Crew races did not lead to memorial services. There was no pressure that wrong decisions might spark an international incident, which could instantly make the evening news or front-page newspaper headlines, with negative repercussions on the entire war effort, just as it had been for us in Iraq.

When these inexperienced soon-to-be SEAL officers graduated from BUD/S, I put them through our five-week-long Junior Officer Training Course, a program focused on their leadership development. I did my utmost to pass onto them everything I wish someone had taught me prior to leading in combat. In the final weeks of each course, we ran the Marc Lee and Mike Monsoor Memorial Run, a five-mile, uphill course that climbed to the top of the huge cliffs of Point Loma and finished at Fort Rosecrans National Cemetery, where both Marc and Mike are buried. In that serene setting overlooking the Pacific Ocean, most fitting for these two noble warriors, I gathered the class of junior officers around the headstones and told them about Marc and Mike. To me, it was deeply important to tell their stories so that the legacies of Marc Lee and Mike Monsoor could carry on. It also served as a stark realization to these future SEAL combat leaders of just how immense their responsibilities were and how deadly serious the burden of command.

As they went forth to serve as officers and leaders in SEAL platoons and beyond, all responsibility and accountability rested on their shoulders. If their platoons underperformed, it was up to them to solve problems, overcome obstacles and get the team working together to accomplish the mission. Ultimately, they must fully accept that there truly are no bad teams, only bad leaders.

PRINCIPLE

About Face: The Odyssey of an American Warrior, by Colonel David Hackworth, U.S. Army (Retired) influenced many frontline leaders in the SEAL Teams and throughout the military. The lengthy memoir details Colonel Hackworth's military career, combat experiences in Korea and Vietnam, and his myriad of leadership lessons learned. Although a controversial figure later in life, Hackworth was an exceptional and highly respected battlefield leader. In the book, Hackworth relates the philosophy of his U.S. Army mentors who fought and defeated the Germans and Japanese in World War II: "There are no bad units, only bad officers."* This captures the essence of what Extreme Ownership is all about. This is a difficult and humbling concept for any leader to accept. But it is an essential mind-set to building a high-performance, winning team.

When leaders who epitomize Extreme Ownership drive their teams to achieve a higher standard of performance, they must recognize that when it comes to standards, as a leader, *it's not what you preach, it's what you tolerate*. When setting expectations, no matter what has been said or written, if substandard performance is accepted and no one is held accountable—if there are no consequences—that poor performance becomes the new standard. Therefore, leaders must enforce standards. Consequences for failing need not be immediately severe, but leaders must ensure that tasks are repeated until the higher expected standard is achieved. Leaders must push the standards in a way that encourages and enables the team to utilize Extreme Ownership.

The leader must pull the different elements within the team

---

* *About Face: The Odyssey of an American Warrior,* by Colonel David Hackworth, U.S. Army (Retired) and Julie Sherman.

together to support one another, with all focused exclusively on how to best accomplish the mission. One lesson from the BUD/S boat crew leader example above is that most people, like Boat Crew VI, want to be part of a winning team. Yet, they often don't know how, or simply need motivation and encouragement. Teams need a forcing function to get the different members working together to accomplish the mission and that is what leadership is all about.

Once a culture of Extreme Ownership is built into the team at every level, the entire team performs well, and performance continues to improve, even when a strong leader is temporarily removed from the team. On the battlefield, preparation for potential casualties plays a critical role in a team's success, if a key leader should go down. But life can throw any number of circumstances in the way of any business or team, and every team must have junior leaders ready to step up and temporarily take on the roles and responsibilities of their immediate bosses to carry on the team's mission and get the job done if and when the need arises.

Leaders should never be satisfied. They must always strive to improve, and they must build that mind-set into the team. They must face the facts through a realistic, brutally honest assessment of themselves and their team's performance. Identifying weaknesses, good leaders seek to strengthen them and come up with a plan to overcome challenges. The best teams anywhere, like the SEAL Teams, are constantly looking to improve, add capability, and push the standards higher. It starts with the individual and spreads to each of the team members until this becomes the culture, the new standard. The recognition that there are *no bad teams, only bad leaders* facilitates Extreme Ownership and enables leaders to build high-performance teams that dominate on any battlefield, literal or figurative.

APPLICATION TO BUSINESS

"I love this concept of Extreme Ownership," the CEO said. "We could really use some at my company. We have a fairly solid team, but I have some key leaders that lack Extreme Ownership. I'd like to bring you in to work with us."

The CEO and founder of a financial services company had observed a presentation I gave to a group of senior corporate executives. Intrigued by the concept of Extreme Ownership, he had approached me afterward to engage in conversation.

"Happy to help," I replied.

To better understand the dynamics of his team and the particular challenges of his company and industry, I spent some time with the CEO in discussions via phone, visited his company offices, and met with his leadership team. I then conducted a leadership program for the company's department heads and key leaders.

The CEO opened the program and introduced me to those in the room, explaining why he had invested in this training.

"We aren't winning," the CEO stated plainly. A new product rollout the company had recently launched had not gone well, and the company's books were in the red. Now the company stood at a pivotal junction. "We need to take on these concepts like Extreme Ownership, which Leif is going to talk to you about today, so that we can get back on track and win." The CEO then left the room all to me, his senior managers, and department heads.

After presenting some background on my combat experience and how the principle of Extreme Ownership was critical to the success of any team, I engaged the department heads and managers in discussion.

"How can you apply Extreme Ownership to your teams to succeed and help your company win?" I asked.

One of the company's key department leaders, the chief technology officer (CTO), who built the company's signature products, exhibited a defensive demeanor. He was not a fan of Extreme Ownership. I quickly recognized why. Since the new product line had been his baby, taking ownership of the disastrous rollout was humbling and difficult. The CTO was full of excuses for why his team had failed and for the resulting damage to the company's bottom line. He shamelessly blamed the failed new-product rollout on a challenging market, an industry in flux, inexperienced personnel within his team, poor communication with the sales force, and lackluster customer service. He also blamed the company's senior executive team. The CTO refused to take ownership of mistakes or acknowledge that his team could perform better, though the CEO had made it clear they must all improve or the company might fold.

I told the BUD/S boat crew leader story to the group, how Boat Crew VI turned their performance around under new leadership, and I outlined the concept that there are no bad teams, only bad leaders.

"During my own training and performance in BUD/S as a boat crew leader," I told them, "I can remember many times when my boat crew struggled. It was easy to make excuses for our team's performance and why it wasn't what it should have been. But I learned that good leaders don't make excuses. Instead, they figure out a way to get it done and win."

"What was the difference between the two leaders in the boat crew leader example?" asked one of the managers, in charge of a critical team within the company.

"When Boat Crew Six was failing under their original leader," I answered, "that leader didn't seem to think it was possible for them to perform any better, and he certainly didn't think they could win. This negative attitude infected his entire boat crew.

As is common in teams that are struggling, the original leader of Boat Crew Six almost certainly justified his team's poor performance with any number of excuses. In his mind, the other boat crews were outperforming his own only because those leaders had been lucky enough to be assigned better crews. His attitude reflected victimization: life dealt him and his boat crew members a disadvantage, which justified poor performance. As a result, his attitude prevented his team from looking inwardly at themselves and where they could improve. Finally, the leader and each member of Boat Crew Six focused not on the mission but on themselves, their own exhaustion, misery, and individual pain and suffering. Though the instructors demanded that they do better, Boat Crew Six had become comfortable with substandard performance. Working under poor leadership and an unending cycle of blame, the team constantly failed. No one took ownership, assumed responsibility, or adopted a winning attitude."

"What did the new boat crew leader do differently?" asked another of the department heads.

"When the leader of Boat Crew Two took charge of Boat Crew Six, he exhibited Extreme Ownership to the fullest," I explained. "He faced the facts: he recognized and accepted that Boat Crew Six's performance was terrible, that they were losing and had to get better. He didn't blame anyone, nor did he make excuses to justify poor performance. He didn't wait for others to solve his boat crew's problems. His realistic assessment, acknowledgment of failure, and *ownership* of the problem were key to developing a plan to improve performance and ultimately win. Most important of all, *he believed winning was possible.* In a boat crew where winning seemed so far beyond reach, the belief that the team actually could improve and win was essential."

I continued: "The new leader of Boat Crew Six focused his team on the mission. Rather than tolerate their bickering and infighting, he pulled the team together and focused their collective efforts on the single specific goal of winning the race. He established a new and higher standard of performance and accepted nothing less from the men in his boat crew."

"Why do you think Boat Crew Two, which had lost its strong leader, continued to perform well, even with the far less capable leader from Boat Crew Six?" asked another department leader.

"Extreme Ownership—good leadership—is contagious," I answered. "Boat Crew Two's original leader had instilled a *culture* of Extreme Ownership, of winning and how to win, in every individual. Boat Crew Two had developed into a solid team of high-performing individuals. Each member demanded the highest performance from the others. Repetitive exceptional performance became a habit. Each individual knew what they needed to do to win and did it. They no longer needed explicit direction from a leader. As a result, Boat Crew Two continued to outperform virtually every other boat crew and vied with Boat Crew Six for first place in nearly every race."

I detailed how the original leader of Boat Crew VI joined Boat Crew II thinking life would be easy for him. Instead, he had to seriously step up his game to keep up with such a high-performance team. For him, the greatest lesson of that day was learned: he witnessed a complete turnaround in the performance of his former team as he watched a new leader demonstrate that what seemed impossible was achievable through good leadership. Though he had failed to lead effectively to that point, the original leader of Boat Crew VI learned and implemented that humbling lesson. Ultimately, he graduated from BUD/S training and had a successful career in the SEAL Teams.

"In summary," I told them, "whether or not your team succeeds or fails is all on you. Extreme Ownership is a concept to help you make the right decisions as a key leader so that you can win."

The chief technology officer bristled. "We *are* making the right decisions," he said. He was serious.

Surprised at his statement, I responded, "You've all admitted that as a company you aren't winning."

"We may not be winning," said the CTO resolutely, "but we're making the right decisions."

"If you aren't winning," I responded, "then you aren't making the right decisions." The CTO was so sure he was right, so content to make excuses and shift blame for his own mistakes and failures, that he made ludicrous claims to avoid taking any ownership or responsibility.

Just like the original boat crew leader in Boat Crew VI, this CTO exhibited the opposite of Extreme Ownership. He took no meaningful action to improve his performance or push his team to improve. Worse, he refused to admit that his own performance was subpar and that he and his team could do better. His CEO had stated plainly that the company's performance must improve substantially. But the CTO was stuck in a cycle of blaming others and refused to take ownership or responsibility. He had become what a good friend from my own BUD/S class and SEAL qualification training dubbed the "Tortured Genius." By this, he did not mean the artist or musician who suffers from mental health issues, but in the context of ownership. No matter how obvious his or her failing, or how valid the criticism, a Tortured Genius, in this sense, accepts zero responsibility for mistakes, makes excuses, and blames everyone else for their failings (and those of their team). In their mind, the rest of the world just can't see or appreciate the genius in what they are doing. An individual with a Tortured Genius mind-set can have catastrophic impact on a team's performance.

After lengthy discussion with the department heads and managers, many of them came to understand and appreciate Extreme

Ownership. But not the CTO. After the workshop concluded, I met with the company's CEO to debrief.

"How did things go?" he asked.

"The workshop went well. Most of your department heads and key leaders took on board this concept of Extreme Ownership," I replied. "You have one major issue, though."

"Let me guess," replied the CEO. "My chief technology officer."

"Affirmative," I responded. "He resisted the concept of Extreme Ownership at every turn." I had seen this before, both in the SEAL Teams and with other client companies. In any group, there was always a small number of people who wanted to shirk responsibility. But this CTO was a particularly serious case.

"Your CTO might be one of the worst 'Tortured Geniuses' I have seen," I said.

The CEO acknowledged that his CTO was a problem, that he was difficult to work with and other department leaders in the company had major issues with him. But the CEO felt that because the CTO's experience level and knowledge were critical to the company, he couldn't possibly fire him. It also seemed the CTO felt he was above reproach.

"I can't tell you to fire anyone," I responded. "Those are decisions only you can make. But what I can tell you is this: when it comes to performance standards, *It's not what you preach, it's what you tolerate.* You have to drive your CTO to exercise Extreme Ownership—to acknowledge mistakes, stop blaming others, and lead his team to success. If you allow the status quo to persist, you can't expect to improve performance, and you can't expect to win."

A week later, I followed up with a phone call to the CEO to see how his team was doing.

"Some folks are really embracing this concept of Extreme Ownership," he said enthusiastically. "But the chief technology officer continues to be a problem." The CEO related how, upon my departure, the CTO had barged into his office and warned that the concept of Extreme Ownership had "negative repercussions." This was laughable.

"There are no negative repercussions to Extreme Ownership," I said. "There are only two types of leaders: effective and ineffective. Effective leaders that lead successful, high-performance teams exhibit Extreme Ownership. Anything else is simply ineffective. Anything else is *bad leadership.*"

The CTO's performance and the performance of his team illustrated this in Technicolor. His abrasiveness affected his entire team and other departments in the company that had difficulty working with him. The CEO understood. His company wasn't winning, and he cared too much about the company he had built and the livelihood of his other employees to allow the company to fail. They must do better.

He let the CTO go.

A new CTO came on board with a different attitude—a mindset of Extreme Ownership.

With this change in the leadership of the company's technology team, other departments began to work together with success, and that teamwork played a key role as the company rebounded. Once failing and struggling to survive, the company was now back on a path toward profitability and growth. Their success illustrated once again that leadership is the most important thing on any battlefield; it is the single greatest factor in whether a team succeeds or fails. A leader must find a way to become effective and drive high performance within his or her team in order to win. Whether in SEAL training, in combat on distant battlefields, in business, or in life: there are no bad teams, only bad leaders.

Iraqi soldiers help a wounded comrade away from danger during a firefight in the Mala'ab District of Ramadi on a joint operation with U.S. Soldiers, Marines, and SEALs of Task Unit Bruiser.

(Photo courtesy of the authors)

CHAPTER 3

Believe

Jocko Willink

SHARKBASE, CAMP RAMADI, IRAQ: QUESTIONING THE MISSION

This makes no sense, no sense at all, I thought as I read through the mission statement from higher command. We were to execute missions "by, with, and through Iraqi security forces." Unlike my first deployment to Iraq where SEALs worked almost exclusively with our own SEAL Team and other U.S. or NATO special operations units, my SEAL task unit had now been directed to work with conventional forces. But not just any conventional forces—Iraqi conventional forces.

The SEALs in Task Unit Bruiser were like a professional sports team, exceptionally well trained to perform at the highest level. We knew each other so well that we could anticipate each other's thoughts and moves. We could recognize each other's silhouettes on patrol in the darkness. This was the result of years of training, not only in BUD/S, the basic SEAL training course from which we all had graduated, but in the year-long training cycle that the entire task unit had gone through together. That workup consisted of training and practicing as a team: in desert, urban and maritime environments in vehicles, boats, planes, helicopters, and on foot. We had fired thousands of rounds through our vast arsenal of weapons, until we could do so with the highest degree of accuracy while under substantial pressure. We had trained for hundreds of hours, iteration after iteration, drill after drill, until we could operate not just as a group of individuals, but as a team—a synchronized machine, maneuvering with precision and efficiency through the challenges of chaotic battlefields.

As SEALs, we kept ourselves in peak physical condition so that we could execute tough missions and meet the extreme physical demands of combat. We did hundreds of pull-ups and push-ups, ran for miles, lifted heavy weights, swam long distances in the open ocean—all to prepare for combat. During our training cycle, in the precious few hours we didn't have a scheduled training evolution, we were in the gym physically pushing ourselves through punishing, high-intensity workouts. If there was no gym at our training location, we'd be out on the road for a hard run, in the parking lot dragging or flipping heavy tires, or on the mats in fierce grappling and jiu-jitsu contests—whatever we could do to stay strong and conditioned. Each man was expected to maintain that high level of physical conditioning so that he could pull his weight and never falter on an operation. We had to be ready to carry a wounded comrade in full, heavy combat gear to safety across rugged terrain. As a critical part of our culture, we constantly challenged each other to tests of physical strength.

We also had some of the best gear in the world: encrypted radios, night-vision goggles, infrared lasers, lights and markers, uniform Kevlar vests and helmets. In the hands of operators who knew how to use this gear, the tactical advantage over the enemy was huge.

Now I was being told that Task Unit Bruiser—my friends, my *brothers,* these highly trained and motivated men—would have to fight alongside conventional Iraqi Army soldiers, arguably some of the *worst* combat troops in the world. Most Iraqi soldiers were poor, uneducated, untrained, undernourished, and unmotivated. With dire economic conditions across Iraq, many simply joined for a paycheck. When the going got tough, they often deserted (as we later witnessed).

All of the soldiers had, to their credit, risked their lives to be part of the Iraqi Army. Often their families were targeted by terrorists, their lives threatened while the soldier deployed to fight in a distant Iraqi city. Of course, there were some better soldiers among them. But the competent and capable Iraqi soldier was the rare exception, not the rule. The vast majority of soldiers in the Iraqi Army, as fighting men, were far below the standard expected of any military, and certainly far below what was needed to take on and defeat Iraq's growing insurgency.

Back in 2003, the U.S.-led Coalition Provisional Authority disbanded Saddam Hussein's Iraqi Army completely. It then had to be rebuilt from the ground up. The new Iraqi Army's training was disorganized, ad hoc, and scattered, at best. Some Iraqi soldiers had almost no training. Officers often bribed or bought their way into their rank. Young enlisted Iraqi soldiers' primary goal was survival, not victory. Physically, they were weak. Most Iraqi soldiers were incapable of doing even a few push-ups or jumping jacks. Tactically, they were dangerous and unsound, regularly violating basic safety procedures.

Worse, some of the Iraqi soldiers had questionable loyalty to the coalition and to the new government of Iraq. Some Sunni soldiers remained loyal to Saddam. But most Iraqi soldiers were Shiites, and many of these saw Muqtada al-Sadr, the fiery cleric hostile to Americans and closely allied with Iran, as a national hero. Every so often, reports surfaced of Iraqi soldiers who turned their weapons on their U.S. Army or Marine Corps advisors. With that knowledge, how could trust be built?

In addition to poor training, the Iraqi soldiers were barely equipped for a camping trip, much less combat operations. Some wore sneakers or sandals. Their uniforms were a mix-and-match collection of military clothing in American, Soviet, or Middle Eastern camouflage. The variety of clothing made it hard to distinguish friend from foe—especially in an environment where the enemy also wore paramilitary uniforms and gear.

Iraqi soldiers' web gear (or load-bearing equipment) consisted of tattered canvas Soviet-era chest rigs with AK-47 magazine pouches that often fell apart. The weapons they carried were a mix of rifles confiscated from insurgents, many of them poorly made Iraqi or Chinese copies of the AK-47. Most were in poor shape and far below the standards of the original Russian design. It was not uncommon to find the weapons rusted to the point that the sites could not be adjusted. Their technology generally stopped at their weapon. They had no night-vision goggles, no lasers, no radios. In fact, very few even had a simple flashlight. Their body armor was ancient with questionable effectiveness.

Task Unit Bruiser was charged with getting our Iraqi soldiers equipped, organized, and, most important, trained and ready to fight the insurgents who seemed to be increasingly effective against U.S. military forces. In less-hostile areas of Iraq, this meant building training programs on secure bases and running Iraqi soldiers through basic soldiering skills and finally some advanced infantry tactics before taking them out on patrol in enemy territory.

But this was Ramadi, the epicenter of the insurgency and the decisive battle for Anbar Province. There was fighting to be done, outposts to protect, and enemy fighters to capture and kill. To pull Iraqi soldiers from the battlefield for training beyond a day or two was simply impossible.

Our mission as SEALs was to go into hostile territory with

these ragtag Iraqi soldiers and fight against hardcore insurgent *mujahideen* fighters determined to kill as many of us as they could. Now, SEALs are known to run to the sound of the guns. But running to the sound of guns is much easier when a SEAL is surrounded by other SEALs; when we know the man covering our "six" (or backside) is someone who has been through the same training, has the same gear, and speaks the same language— someone we *trust*. For a SEAL to put his life in the hands of someone he doesn't know—a person he has barely worked with, who is not well trained, undisciplined, speaks a different language, and whose trustworthiness is doubtful—is asking a hell of a lot. In the SEAL Teams, the bond of our brotherhood is our strongest weapon. If you take that away from us, we lose our most important quality as a team.

When our SEALs in Task Unit Bruiser learned that they would be allowed to conduct combat operations only alongside Iraqi soldiers, they were livid and completely against the idea. We knew that the dangers in Ramadi from the enemy were already extremely high. There was no need to increase the risk to our force. Yet that is exactly what we were being directed to do.

Even my initial reaction was *Hell no*. It just wasn't worth the risk. Why would we go into combat without every possible advantage, much less a self-inflicted distinct disadvantage? I didn't believe that this mission made sense. I didn't believe it was smart. I didn't believe it would be successful. To imagine a firefight alongside Iraqi soldiers with such inferior training and questionable loyalty seemed outrageous, perhaps even suicidal. But as Task Unit Bruiser's commander, I knew my actions and mind-set carried great weight among my troops. These were my orders, and for me to lead, I had to believe. So I kept my doubts to myself as I asked the simple question: *Why?*

Why would the U.S. military leadership on the ground in Iraq and back in America—from Baghdad to the Pentagon to the White House—task Navy SEALs, other Special Operations, and U.S. Army and Marine Corps units with such a high-risk mission? I had seen how difficult combat could be with the best people by my side. Why make it harder?

I knew I had to adjust my perspective, to mentally step back from the immediate fight just outside the wire and think about this question from a strategic level, as if I were one of those generals in Baghdad or back at the Pentagon. Sure, they were far from the front lines, but certainly, they had the same goal we did: to win.

That led to another question: What was winning? It certainly wasn't winning in the traditional military sense of the word. There would be no surrender from this enemy we fought against. There would be no peace treaty signed. Winning here meant only that Iraq would become a relatively secure and stable country.

So I asked myself: *How can we prepare the Iraqi soldiers to handle security in their own country?* They needed to start somewhere. If there wasn't time to train Iraqi soldiers off the battlefield in a secure environment on base, then they would have to learn by doing, through OJT (on the job training). If the Iraqis never reached a level of skill at which they could defend their country from terrorist insurgents, then who would defend it? The answer was all too clear: us, the U.S. military. We would be stuck here securing their country for them for generations.

The disparity between the capability of the poorly trained, ill-equipped, and unmotivated Iraqi soldiers and that of the determined, well-equipped, and highly effective insurgent fighters they were up against was gigantic. Virtually every time an American outpost in Ramadi was handed over to the control of Iraqi soldiers, insurgents attacked and overran their position, killing dozens of Iraqi troops and sometimes the U.S. Marine or Army advisors assigned to them. The Iraqi soldiers were no match for the insurgents. It would take generations of training to get the Iraqi soldiers to the level needed to overcome and defeat such an aggressive enemy. Even then, such lackluster soldiers would likely never be capable of fighting and defeating a serious adversary. For those of us on the front lines of this conflict, it was clear that there were many senior U.S. military officers who, far removed from direct interaction with Iraqi soldiers, did not understand the Iraqi Army's true lack of capability. They were simply terrible, and no amount of training would make them *excellent* soldiers; but perhaps we could make them *good enough*.

As I thought about this, I realized that there was something that we—Task Unit Bruiser and other U.S. and coalition forces— could do. These Iraqi troops, or *jundhis,** as they called themselves in Arabic, may never be good enough to take on a well-equipped and determined enemy. But they could be good enough to handle a less substantial enemy. We could ensure the current enemy fit into that category by reducing the insurgents' ability to wage war. In addition to building the Iraqi Army's capability through training and combat-advising on the battlefield, we (our SEALs and U.S. forces) would have to crush the insurgency and lower its capability to a point where Iraqi soldiers and police would at least have a chance to maintain a relative peace by themselves—a chance to win. In order to do that, our Task Unit Bruiser SEALs needed to get outside the wire, onto the battlefield, and inflict serious damage on insurgent fighters. But we couldn't operate unless our combat missions received approval through our chain of command. The SEAL task unit that had been in Ramadi for the months prior to our arrival had told us they planned a number of combat operations that consisted of only SEALs—without Iraqi soldiers. Almost all of those operations had been denied

---

* Meaning soldiers

approval. In order to receive that approval, I knew we must take Iraqi soldiers with us on every operation. They were our ticket to leave the base, push into enemy territory, and unleash fury upon the insurgents.

With that, I understood, and I believed. Now, I had to ensure that my troops understood and believed.

I called for a meeting and pulled all the SEAL operators from Task Unit Bruiser together into the briefing room.

"Alright fellas," I said. "You've heard the rumors. Every operation we conduct will include Iraqi soldiers." There were mutterings of obscenities and loud exhales of disgust. I repeated: "Every mission we undertake we will fight alongside *jundhis*." The room cut loose again, this time with louder disagreement and curses. The consensus from our SEALs, the frontline troops who would execute our missions, was clear: "This is garbage."

I cut the not-so-subtle protest short: "I understand. The battlefield here in Ramadi is dangerous. It's difficult. Why make it even harder by forcing us to fight alongside Iraqi soldiers?" *Damn right*, nodded much of the room in agreement.

"Well, let me ask you something," I continued. "If the Iraqi military can't get to a point where they can handle security in their own country, who is going to do it?"

The room fell silent. I drove the point home by restating the question: "I say again, if the Iraqi military can't handle the security in this country, who is going to do it?" I had their attention, and they knew the answer. But to ensure everyone clearly understood the strategic importance of *why* we were being directed to do this, I made it perfectly clear: "If Iraqi soldiers can't do it, there is only one group that will—us. If we don't get these guys up to speed we will have this mission next year and the year after and the year after. The U.S. military will be stuck here for generations. It will be up to our sons and our sons' sons to secure Iraq."

I could see that, although there was still resistance to the idea of working with Iraqi soldiers, they were beginning to see this mission from a strategic perspective.

I continued: "Like you, I understand that no matter how much we train them, the Iraqi Army will never come close to achieving the standards we set for ourselves. But we will help them get better. And there is something else we can do to help them. We will close with and destroy the enemy on the streets of Ramadi to reduce the insurgents' military capability and lower the level of violence. When the enemy is beaten, then the Iraqi Army can take over security duties for themselves."

I saw some heads nod in agreement.

"But to do that," I said, "we have to get each mission—each operation—approved. And if we want our missions approved, we must have Iraqi soldiers with us on every operation. Does anyone not understand this?"

The room was quiet. Everyone understood. They didn't have to jump for joy at the thought of fighting alongside Iraqi soldiers on a dangerous battlefield. But they did have to understand why they were doing it so that they could believe in the mission.

Afterward, I spoke to my key leaders in greater detail about why this mission was important. Unlike the previous SEAL task unit, I told my officers and chiefs they were not to submit *any* concept of operations (CONOPS)—a document that lays out the basic idea of an operation for approval by higher headquarters—without Iraqi soldiers as part of our force.

"What about all the unilateral* operations you did on your last deployment?" Leif asked me. "Didn't they make a difference?" The other platoon commander and both platoon chiefs waited for my response.

"Yes. We did a whole lot of unilateral DAs† in Iraq two years

---

* SEAL only
† direct-action capture/kill raids

ago," I answered. "And since that time, coalition forces across Iraq have continued to do them. But, here are the facts: in the last two years, enemy attacks are up three hundred percent. Three hundred percent! This place is on a downward spiral. We've got to do something different if we want to win."

"Every one of your operations will have Iraqi soldiers," I told them. "These Iraqi soldiers are our means to do something different—our ticket to operate. We will get them up to speed. We will prepare them the best we can. We will fight alongside them. And we will crush the enemy until even the Iraqi Army will be able to fight them on their own. Any other questions?"

There were no more questions. The most important question had been answered: Why? Once I analyzed the mission and understood for myself that critical piece of information, I could then believe in the mission. If I didn't believe in it, there was no way I could possibly convince the SEALs in my task unit to believe in it. If I expressed doubts or openly questioned the wisdom of this plan in front of the troops, their derision toward the mission would increase exponentially. They would never believe in it. As a result, they would never commit to it, and it would fail. But once I understood and believed, I then passed that understanding and belief on, clearly and succinctly, to my troops so that they believed in it themselves. When they understood why, they would commit to the mission, persevere through the inevitable challenges in store, and accomplish the task set before us.

Most of the operators accepted my explanation. Not every member of Task Unit Bruiser was convinced immediately. We had to reinforce the importance of combat-advising Iraqi soldiers continuously.

Through the course of the deployment, our SEALs conducted every major operation with Iraqi soldiers. Often the Iraqi soldiers did things that were stupid and dangerous. On one combat operation, an Iraqi soldier accidentally squeezed the trigger of his AK-47 rifle and blasted a dozen rounds of fully automatic fire into the floor next to the SEAL operators standing near him. The bullets missed some of our SEALs by inches. On another operation, Leif and his SEAL combat advisors had to rip the rifles out of the hands of Iraqi soldiers who, while under fire, ran from the enemy contact while shooting their AK-47s backward over their heads, with other SEALs and Iraqi soldiers downrange from them—incredibly foolish. Another time, Iraqi soldiers on patrol with our SEALs were engaged by enemy fighters. An Iraqi soldier was hit, and his comrades abandoned him in the street and ran for cover. Two SEALs had to run through a hailstorm of enemy fire across an open street (what we called a "Medal of Honor" run) to retrieve the wounded Iraqi soldier and drag him to cover while bullets impacted all around them.

The Iraqi soldiers frustrated the hell out of our SEALs who trained and fought alongside them. But they also proved useful in ways we hadn't anticipated. A SEAL breacher might use a sledgehammer or explosive charge to open a gate—an effective method, though extremely loud—which let everyone in the neighborhood know we were there. Our Iraqi soldiers knew how the doors and gates were secured and would quietly pop them open by hand with little effort. They also could tell the bad guys from the good. To our American eyes, when unarmed enemy fighters were hiding among the civilian populace, we often couldn't tell the difference. But our Iraqi soldiers could discern dress, mannerisms, and Arabic accents that were different from that of the local populace. Their local and cultural knowledge were advantageous in helping us better understand and identify the enemy.

Over the next six months, we took Iraqi soldiers right into the thick of some of the biggest battles for the city of Ar Ramadi. Several of them were killed in action. Others were wounded. Despite

the grumblings from Task Unit Bruiser, a certain base level of camaraderie formed between our SEALs and their Iraqi counterparts
through the blood, sweat, and tears of difficult combat operations.

Through the success of the U.S. Army 1st Armored Division
Ready First Brigade Combat Team's Seize, Clear, Hold, Build strategy, enemy fighters were forced out of their former safe havens
within Ramadi. Because we included Iraqi soldiers with us on
every operation, our chain of command approved all of our plans
to push deep into dangerous enemy territory in support of this
strategy. That enabled us to hammer enemy fighters with deadly
effect, making those areas a little safer for the U.S. Soldiers and
Marines that built the permanent combat outposts and lived and
patrolled out of them, forcing the insurgents out of their former
strongholds. As a result, the local people ceased passive support
of the insurgents and instead switched sides to support U.S. and
Iraqi forces. Over time, the level of violence decreased dramati-
cally, as did the insurgents' military capability. By the end of our
deployment, the area was secure enough to enable our Iraqi Army
units to begin operations under their own command and control:
patrolling into the city, engaging the enemy, and capturing or killing insurgents. That portion of the mission was a success by any
measure.

PRINCIPLE

In order to convince and inspire others to follow and accomplish
a mission, a leader must be a *true believer* in the mission. Even
when others doubt and question the amount of risk, asking, "Is it
worth it?" the leader must believe in the greater cause. If a leader
does not believe, he or she will not take the risks required to overcome the inevitable challenges necessary to win. And they will
not be able to convince others—especially the frontline troops
who must execute the mission—to do so. Leaders must always operate with the understanding that they are part of something

greater than themselves and their own personal interests. They must impart this understanding to their teams down to the tactical-level operators on the ground. Far more important than training or equipment, a resolute belief in the mission is critical for any team or organization to win and achieve big results.

In many cases, the leader must align his thoughts and vision to that of the mission. Once a leader believes in the mission, that belief shines through to those below and above in the chain of command. Actions and words reflect belief with a clear confidence and self-assuredness that is not possible when belief is in doubt.

The challenge comes when that alignment isn't explicitly clear. When a leader's confidence breaks, those who are supposed to follow him or her see this and begin to question their own belief in the mission.

Every leader must be able to detach from the immediate tactical mission and understand how it fits into strategic goals. When leaders receive an order that they themselves question and do not understand, they must ask the question: why? Why are we being asked to do this? Those leaders must take a step back, deconstruct the situation, analyze the strategic picture, and then come to a conclusion. If they cannot determine a satisfactory answer themselves, they must ask questions up the chain of command until they understand why. If frontline leaders and troops understand *why,* they can move forward, fully believing in what they are doing.

It is likewise incumbent on senior leaders to take the time to explain and answer the questions of their junior leaders so that they too can understand why and believe. Whether in the ranks of military units or companies and corporations, the frontline troops never have as clear an understanding of the strategic picture as senior leaders might anticipate. It is critical that those senior leaders impart a general understanding of that strategic knowledge— the *why*—to their troops.

In any organization, goals must always be in alignment. If goals aren't aligned at some level, this issue must be addressed and rectified. In business just as in the military, no senior executive team would knowingly choose a course of action or issue an order that would purposely result in failure. But a subordinate may not understand a certain strategy and thus not believe in it. Junior leaders must ask questions and also provide feedback up the chain so that senior leaders can fully understand the ramifications of how strategic plans affect execution on the ground.

Belief in the mission ties in with the fourth Law of Combat: Decentralized Command (chapter 8). The leader must explain not just what to do, but *why*. It is the responsibility of the subordinate leader to reach out and ask if they do not understand. Only when leaders at all levels understand and believe in the mission can they pass that understanding and belief to their teams so that they can persevere through challenges, execute and win.

APPLICATION TO BUSINESS

"This new compensation plan is terrible," said one of the midlevel managers. "It will drive our best salespeople away." The rest of the class agreed.

Toward the end of a short leadership-development program for the company's midlevel managers, my discussions with the class had revealed a major issue that created stress and fragmentation among the ranks of the company.

Corporate leadership had recently announced a new compensation structure for their sales force. The new plan substantially reduced compensation, especially for low-producing salespeople.

"What's the issue?" I asked the group.

"It's hard enough to keep salespeople here; this doesn't help!" one manager responded.

"They don't get how hard it is in this market," said another, referring to corporate senior leadership. "This new compensation plan will push people to our competitors."

"Some of my folks have already heard rumors about it; they don't like it at all. And I can't convince them otherwise. I don't believe in it myself!" another responded.

I asked them all a simple question: "Why?"

"Why what?" one of the managers responded.

"Why is your leadership making this change?" I asked.

"Hell if I know!" one manager stated emphatically, which brought laughs from the group.

I smiled and nodded. Then I asked again: "OK, but *why* do you think they are implementing this plan? Do you think they want to push your best salespeople out the door? Do they want those salespeople to go to your competitors? Do you think they actually want the company to lose money and fail?"

The room was quiet. The managers—most of whom respected their bosses and maintained good relationships with the company's corporate leadership—knew their leaders were smart, experienced, and committed to the success of the company. The problem was that no one could understand why this new plan had been implemented.

"Has anyone asked?" I questioned them.

The room fell silent. Finally the class clown blurted out, "I'm not asking. I like my job!" Laughter erupted from the room.

I smiled and let them settle down. "Understandable," I replied. "So the CEO, is she unreasonable? Would she actually fire someone for asking the question?"

The group of managers mumbled, "No."

"What is it then?" I asked.

Finally, one of the more senior managers spoke up with a serious answer: "I'd feel pretty stupid asking. Our CEO is smart and has a lot of experience. She gets this business."

"OK," I shot back. "So you're all just scared to look stupid?"
Heads nodded in a universal *yes*.

I nodded as well, now more fully understanding the issue. No one wants to look stupid, especially in front of the boss. "Let me ask you this," I continued. "When you can't explain the reason behind this new compensation plan to your sales force, how does that make you look?"

"Stupid and scared," the class clown responded.

"Exactly!" I shot back, in jest. But I knew a simple, easy way to solve the problem had been uncovered.

That afternoon I swung by the CEO's office. She was meeting with the company's president of sales.

"How is the workshop going?" the CEO inquired.

"It's going pretty well," I said. "You have a solid crew of managers."

"Absolutely. They are a great group," replied the CEO.

"How is your relationship with them?" I asked.

"Oh, I think it is very strong with most of them. Some of the newer ones I don't know all that well yet, but as a whole, I have a good relationship with our managers," the CEO answered.

"Do they ever confront you on anything or ask questions?" I asked.

The CEO thought for a few seconds. "Not really," she acknowledged. "I think they get the business, and I think they know what we are trying to do. So there really isn't much that they would need to confront me on. I've been in this game a long time. I wouldn't be here today if I didn't know what I was doing. They know that and I think they respect that. Experience counts for a lot in this business. But I think if they had an issue, they would certainly bring it up to me."

A common misperception among military leaders or corporate senior executives, this was an example of a boss who didn't fully comprehend the weight of her position. In her mind, she was fairly laid back, open to questions, comments, and suggestions from people. She talked about maintaining an "open-door policy." But in the minds of her sales managers, she was still *The Boss*: experienced, smart, and most important, powerful. That position demanded a high level of reverence—so high, in fact, that for an employee to question her ideas seemed disrespectful. None of them were comfortable questioning her, even though none of the midlevel managers actually worried about losing their jobs because they asked a question. But they were certainly worried about looking bad in front of The Boss.

"I'm not sure they are as comfortable confronting you or opening up to you as you think," I stated bluntly.

"Really?" The CEO asked with a slightly puzzled face.

"Let me give you an example that came up today," I replied. "The new sales compensation plan."

"What about it? Don't they like it?" the CEO asked with surprise.

"It's not that they don't like it," I answered. "I don't think they get it."

"Don't get it? The plan isn't really that complex. In fact, it is simple," said the CEO, preparing to give me the quick explanation.

"It's not that they don't get what the plan is," I said. "You're right: it is simple. It reduces overall compensation for sales staff, especially for the low producers."

"Exactly. What's the issue with that?" the CEO said. She was right. Even I, without experience in this particular field, had no trouble understanding the basic concept of the new compensation plan.

"The issue is not that they don't understand the plan, but that they don't understand *why* the plan is being implemented. They don't believe in it. They think this plan will drive away good salespeople, who will look for and possibly find better compensation plans at your competitors," I explained.

The CEO now got a little defensive. "Then they clearly don't understand what I am doing with the business," she stated. "When we cut compensation, especially on the low-producing salespeople, that savings reduces cost. When I reduce cost for salespeople, it reduces our overhead. With overhead reduced, I can lower the price of our products. That will allow our bigger producers to bring in even more business. Sure, the new compensation plan is punitive toward our bottom people, but those bottom people really don't move the needle in our business. If some of them leave, it won't impact our business. In fact, it will allow some of our better producers to expand into those accounts and increase sales. So there is opportunity for our sales force to do even better."

"That makes a lot of sense," I replied.

"It absolutely does," said the CEO. She explained how she had made this move before in a tough market. "It almost always helps. It might reduce the overall size of our sales force, but it will increase our volume in the long run. A smaller, more effective sales force also reduces overhead: lower health care costs, fewer desks, fewer computers to buy, greater efficiency. It is a win-win."

"That sounds brilliant. There is only one problem with it," I said.

"What's that?" the CEO asked, incredulous.

"Your midlevel managers don't understand those points— they don't understand *why*—and so they don't believe in the strategy. If they don't believe, neither will your sales force. If this plan rolls out and those executing it don't believe in it, your plan is far more likely to fail."

"So what can I do to make them believe?" asked the CEO.

"It's easy," I explained. "Just tell them *why*."

The CEO finally understood what she needed to do.

For my training with the midlevel managers the next day, the

CEO made an appearance and kicked things off with a short presentation.

"Good morning, everyone," she began. "Jocko pointed out to me that you all had some issues with the new compensation plan. What don't you like?"

After a few moments of silence, one of the more senior managers finally mustered the courage to speak up. "Cutting into our sales team's take-home pay hurts," said the manager. "It may drive some of them elsewhere, and that could hurt us in the long run."

The CEO smiled. She explained the details of the strategy behind the plan: the increased volume, the reduced overhead, the greater capture of existing accounts when handled by higher producing salespeople. The managers quickly saw the connection and understood the benefits of the plan.

"Does anyone have any questions?" the CEO finished. No one spoke up. "Seriously. Does anyone have any questions? Don't be afraid to ask. I obviously didn't make this clear to you. And unfortunately, none of you asked!" she jabbed.

"No, I think we get it now," one of the managers replied.

"Do you think you can explain it to your sales force in a manner that they will understand?" asked the CEO.

"I do," a manager answered. "But I still think some of the low producers will be upset."

"I'm sure some of them will be," the CEO replied. "As I said, that is part of the strategy here. The ones I want you to focus on here are the big producers and those that you think have the potential to become big producers. I have done this before; we will get results. Anyone else have anything?"

The room, now loosened up by the straight-shooting conversation with the CEO, relaxed and broke into some small talk before the CEO went on her way. The class continued.

"What do you think?" I asked the class.

"That is exactly what we needed," said one manager.

"Now I get it," remarked another.

"I wish we would have known that all along," a third manager stated.

"Let me ask you another question: Who is to blame for the CEO not explaining this to you in more detail?" I asked.

The managers in the room remained silent. They knew the answer and nodded as they acknowledged a topic that I had covered in detail earlier.

"That's right," I said, "you! That is what Extreme Ownership is all about. If you don't understand or believe in the decisions coming down from your leadership, it is up to you to ask questions until you understand how and why those decisions are being made. Not knowing the *why* prohibits you from believing in the mission. When you are in a leadership position, that is a recipe for failure, and it is unacceptable. As a leader, you must believe."

"But the boss should have explained this to us, right?" one manager asked.

"Absolutely. I explained that to her, and, sure enough, she came down here and did just that. But she's not a mind reader. The CEO can't predict what you won't get or understand. She's not perfect; none of us are. Things are going to slip through the cracks from time to time. It happens. I made all kinds of mistakes when I led SEALs. Often, my subordinate leadership would pick up the slack for me. And they wouldn't hold it against me, nor did I think they were infringing on my 'leadership turf.' On the contrary, I would thank them for covering for me. Leadership isn't one person leading a team. It is a group of leaders working together, up and down the chain of command, to lead. If you are on your own, I don't care how good you are, you won't be able to handle it."

"So we let the boss down when we didn't ask questions and communicate with her," said one of the quieter managers in the back of the room.

"Yes, you did," I confirmed. "People talk about leadership requiring courage. This is exactly one of those situations. It takes
courage to go to the CEO's office, knock on her door, and explain
that you don't understand the strategy behind her decisions. You
might feel stupid. But you will feel far worse trying to explain to
your team a mission or strategy that you don't understand or
believe in yourself. And, as you pointed out, you are letting the
boss down because she will never know that her guidance is not
being promulgated properly through the ranks. If you don't ask
questions so you can understand and believe in the mission, you
are failing as a leader and you are failing your team. So, if you ever
get a task or guidance or a mission that you don't believe in, don't
just sit back and accept it. Ask questions until you understand
why so you can believe in what you are doing and you can pass
that information down the chain to your team with confidence, so
they can get out and execute the mission. That is leadership."

Bruiser SEALs take the high ground, South-Central Ramadi. Charlie Platoon's point man and lead sniper, Chris Kyle, observes smoke from Team Bulldog, Bravo Company, (B/1-37) Abrams tanks' 120mm main gun impacts in the distance. The Soldiers of Team Bulldog, an exceptional combat unit, continuously braved treacherous IED-laden roads to bring the thunder from their M1A2 Abrams tanks in support of Charlie Platoon SEALs. Bulldog's courageous efforts saved SEAL lives and systematically beat back the insurgency from one of the most dangerous areas of Ramadi. SEALs and Soldiers formed an unbreakable bond that remains to this day.

(Photo courtesy of the authors)

CHAPTER 4
Check the Ego

Jocko Willink

CAMP CORREGIDOR, RAMADI, IRAQ: WELCOME TO RAMADI

Enemy tracer rounds were zipping overhead as I raced up the stairs to the third-story rooftop of our tactical operations center (TOC) building. Our camp was under attack. I hadn't even had time to fasten my body armor. When the shooting started, I grabbed my helmet and rifle, slung my load-bearing equipment over my shoulders, and headed for the roof. SEALs were arriving by the dozen, some in flip-flops with only shorts and T-shirts under their body armor, but helmets on and weapons at the ready.

Just across the river, in the darkness, enemy fighters had unleashed heavy volleys of machine gun fire on two separate U.S. outposts and the American Soldiers were returning fire with a vengeance. The bright glow of tracer fire was evident in both directions. Another group of enemy fighters had engaged our camp and were hammering our TOC building with gunfire from the far bank of the Euphrates River.

But they hadn't counted on the response. Within minutes, every Navy SEAL in Task Unit Bruiser and several of our non-SEAL support personnel were on the rooftop shooting back. Some SEALs had brought their M4 rifles, others M79 40mm grenade launchers, others their Mk48 and Mk46 belt-fed machine guns. We unleashed incredible volleys of fire back at the enemy fighters' muzzle flashes. I directed an M79 gunner to put some 40mm illumination rounds up so we could better identify our targets.

Leif was on the rooftop right next to me, shooting and directing fire. The SEAL just beside him unloaded two full hundred-round belts through his machine gun, spewing spent shell casings across the rooftop that bounced with a metallic *clink*. Everybody was shooting, having a hell of a time. There was much laughter as guys unloaded what was clearly a ridiculous amount of gunfire at the enemy. Soon, the enemy fighters were either dead or retreating and their attack subsided. The SEAL machine gunner looked around with a smile.

"This is my third deployment to Iraq," said the SEAL machine gunner, excitedly. "And that's the first time I've ever fired my machine gun in combat." It was his first day on the ground in Ramadi.

A few of us had been here for a week, including Leif, some of the other key leaders, and me. But most of Task Unit Bruiser's SEALs had arrived only that day. As much fun as we had shooting from the rooftop, this was a wake-up call for everyone in Task Unit Bruiser. This was Ramadi, a total war zone and the most violent place in Iraq. For those of us who had deployed to Iraq previously, it was a realization that this time would be different— and a lot more dangerous. Welcome to Ramadi.

Throughout 2005 and 2006, the vast and volatile Al Anbar Province was the most dangerous place in Iraq, accounting for the majority of U.S. casualties in Operation Iraqi Freedom. Of all the places in Anbar, the city of Ar Ramadi was the most deadly.

Located on the Euphrates River, Ramadi, with four hundred thousand residents, was the capital of Anbar Province and the epicenter of the violent Sunni insurgency. The city was strewn with rubble-pile buildings, burned-out hulks of twisted metal that had once been vehicles, and walls marred by bullet holes. Giant bomb craters from IEDs* dotted the main roads through town. Thousands of heavily armed Sunni insurgent fighters loyal to al Qaeda in Iraq controlled some two-thirds of the geographic area of the city. U.S. forces couldn't even begin to penetrate these areas without sustaining massive casualties. Al Qaeda in Iraq claimed the city as the capital of their caliphate.

Valiant U.S. Army Soldiers and Marines ran convoys and patrols along the deadly, heavily IED'ed roads. They conducted cordon and search operations into enemy territory and engaged in fierce fighting. Most of the several thousand U.S. troops in Ramadi were located on large secure bases outside the city itself. But along the main road through the city, a string of isolated U.S. Marine and Army outposts were constantly under attack.

The level of determination and sophistication from insurgent fighters in Ramadi was alarming—far beyond what any of us in Task Unit Bruiser had seen on previous deployments. Several times a week, groups of twenty or thirty well-armed enemy fighters launched hellacious attacks on U.S. forces. These were well-coordinated, complex attacks executed simultaneously on multiple U.S. outposts separated by several kilometers. They were hardcore *muj*.

Many enemy attacks followed a similar pattern. Each began with a sudden barrage of accurate, devastating machine gun fire from multiple directions, which hammered the American sentry posts and forced those on guard to take cover. Then, while Soldiers

---

* IED, or improvised explosive device, the deadly roadside bombs that accounted for roughly 70–80 percent of U.S. casualties in Iraq in 2006.

or Marines were hunkered down, deadly RPG-7 shoulder-fired rockets were launched in rapid succession, impacting with violent noise and lethal shrapnel. Next, mortars (fired from some distance away) rained down inside the walls of the coalition compound, often impacting with alarming accuracy. All this was done in an effort to take out the sentries or force them to keep their heads down long enough so they couldn't return fire, while the enemy launched their final and most devastating weapon: the VBIED suicide bomber driving a large truck or vehicle filled with several thousand pounds of explosives.* If the truck made it past the concrete barriers, past the Marine or Army sentries that would engage them, and inside the compound, the results could be catastrophic—as deadly as the most powerful U.S. Tomahawk missile launched from a Navy warship or Joint Direct Attack Munition (JDAM) guided bomb dropped from U.S. aircraft.

These enemy attacks were well coordinated and viciously executed. The Sunni jihadi militants were far more capable than those I had previously seen in Iraq two years before and eager to wipe out the American outposts, leaving dozens of Marines or Soldiers dead and many more wounded. But those fearless Marine and Army sentries held their ground every time and beat the insurgents back. Instead of taking cover to save themselves, the young Marines and Soldiers who manned the watchtowers and sentry posts courageously stood fast and returned fire with deadly accurate machine gun fire of their own. Their selfless stands almost always prevented those VBIEDs from entering all the way into compound. The VBIED might explode in a massive fireball and concussion, but the enemy could not get close enough to U.S. forces, protected behind sandbags and concrete barriers.

---

* what the U.S. military called a vehicle-borne improvised explosive device, or VBIED

The Marines and Soldiers fought off those attacks with such frequency that they almost became commonplace—just another day in Ramadi.

In Task Unit Bruiser, we were confident and perhaps even a little cocky. But I tried to temper that confidence by instilling a culture within our task unit to never be satisfied; we pushed ourselves harder to continuously improve our performance. I reminded our troops that we couldn't take the enemy for granted, that we could never get complacent. With all that in mind, the boys of Task Unit Bruiser were fired up and eager to prove themselves as we deployed to Ar Ramadi in the spring of 2006.

Immediately upon arrival, we were humbled by the violence of the battlefield and the incredible heroism of conventional U.S. Soldiers and Marines of the 2nd Brigade Combat Team, 28th (2-28) Infantry Division. Our SEALs had the benefit of much more advanced training and all the finest weapons, lasers, optics, and gadgetry that the enormous Special Operations Command budget could buy. But we were in awe of the Soldiers and Marines who manned the outposts in enemy territory and were daily locked in a deadly struggle against a fierce and determined enemy. When the 1st Armored Division's Ready First Brigade Combat Team arrived to replace 2-28 a month into our deployment, again we developed a deep respect and admiration for these brothers-in-arms and were proud to serve alongside them. Every one of the conventional units* we worked with had seen extensive combat; all had lost troops, and suffered many more wounded. These Soldiers and Marines were the real deal. They epitomized the term "warrior."

The enemy was also strong and incredibly capable. They were deadly and efficient, always watching, analyzing, and looking for

---

* Now called General Purpose Forces.

weaknesses to exploit. If U.S. forces were to win in Ramadi, I saw right away that all of us—U.S. conventional Army and Marine units and Special Operations units like our SEALs in Task Unit Bruiser—had to work together and support each other. Unfortunately, there were a small number of U.S. special operations units, including some SEALs, who viewed themselves as a cut above regular U.S. Army Soldiers and Marines and would only operate independently. That cockiness produced some conventional Army and Marine commanders who didn't like special operations units. But if U.S. forces were to win this difficult fight here in Ramadi, we would all need to check our egos and work together.

From our earliest arrival, we established the precedent that in TU Bruiser we would treat our Army and Marine brothers-and sisters-in-arms with nothing but the highest professional respect and courtesy. SEAL units are sometimes known for long hair and sloppy uniforms. But to conventional units, appearance was a measure of professionalism. In Task Unit Bruiser, I insisted that our uniforms be squared away and our haircuts military regulation. We sought ways to work together with these units in support of one another. The goal was simple: secure and stabilize Ramadi. With this attitude of humility and mutual respect, we forged strong relationships with the Army and Marine battalions and companies that owned the battlespace in and around Ramadi. We took great risks to patrol deep into enemy territory to provide sniper support and protect friendly troops in the streets. Those Soldiers and Marines, in turn, constantly put their troops at risk to come help us with heavy fire support—M1A2 Abrams tanks and M2 Bradley Fighting Vehicles—and casualty evacuations when we needed it.

After a month on the ground in Ramadi, Task Unit Bruiser had made a mark. We had figured out how to position ourselves on the high ground where we could do the most damage to enemy fighters and best support the U.S. Army and Marine units operating in the city. When the enemy rallied to attack, SEAL snipers sprung into action and engaged with precision sniper fire, killing large numbers of well-armed *muj* fighters and routing their attacks. As enemy activity escalated, so did SEAL aggression. Once our SEAL elements were discovered, our positions transitioned from clandestine sniper hide sites into fortified fighting positions. SEAL machine gunners joined in the fight, hammering enemy fighters with hundreds of rounds from their belt-fed machine guns. Other SEALs lobbed 40mm high-explosive grenades and launched our own shoulder-fired rockets at the enemy. Rapidly, the number of enemy fighters killed at the hands of our Task Unit Bruiser SEALs grew to unprecedented levels. Every bad guy killed meant more U.S. Soldiers, Marines, and SEALs survived another day; they were one day closer to returning home safely to their families. Every enemy fighter killed also meant another Iraqi soldier, policemen, or government official survived, and more Iraqi civilians lived in a little less fear of al Qaeda in Iraq and their insurgent allies. We fought an evil enemy, perhaps as evil as any the U.S. military had faced in its long history. These violent jihadis used torture, rape, and murder as weapons to ruthlessly terrorize, intimidate, and rule over the civilian populace who lived in abject fear. The American public and much of the Western World lived in willful naïveté of the barbaric, unspeakable tactics these jihadis employed It was subhuman savagery. Having witnessed this repeatedly, in our minds and those of the people who suffered under their brutal reign, the *muj* deserved no mercy.

For our relatively small group of about thirty-six SEALs, the number of enemy fighters killed on a daily basis drew attention from the upper echelons of our chain of command. As Task Unit Bruiser continued to operate with awesome lethality, some other units across Iraq wanted in on the action in Ramadi.

One particular group of advisors from another part of Iraq had similar capability to our SEALs in Ramadi and worked alongside a well-trained Iraqi Army unit. Unlike most Iraqi soldiers, these troops were equipped with good gear including some of the best rifles, scopes, lasers, night-vision goggles, and body armor in Iraq. With the right training and the right equipment, these Iraqi soldiers' skill level and operational capabilities far exceeded any of the other Iraqi Army units we worked with in Ramadi. Because of their superior training and high level of visibility with U.S. top military brass, this Iraqi unit and their U.S. advisors had a great deal of leeway to operate wherever and however they wanted. When they got wind of the action in Ramadi, they quickly gained approval to move there and get to work.

When the new unit arrived, they were sent to Camp Corregidor Forward Operating Base on the eastern side of the city. Camp Corregidor was owned and operated by the U.S. Army 101st Airborne Division's First Battalion, 506th Parachute Infantry Regiment—the legendary "Five-O-Sixth" made famous by Stephen Ambrose's book *Band of Brothers* (which became an HBO miniseries). The book followed a single company's heroic efforts in the European campaign against Nazi Germany in World War II. Those brave men had set a high standard, and the modern-day Soldiers of the 1/506th carried on that tradition with pride and added to their historic legacy.

The 1/506th Battalion was commanded by a U.S. Army lieutenant colonel, an extremely smart, charismatic, and professional officer who set the standard for military leaders. He was one of the finest battlefield commanders with whom I had the honor to serve. The colonel commanded with subtle intensity that was complemented with a genuinely kind and easygoing attitude. He was an incredible leader; and leading men in the violent battle in Ramadi demanded every ounce of leadership possible.

Camp Corregidor was combat living defined. Everything was difficult there. A fine, powderlike sand, which U.S. troops called "moon dust," caked buildings, equipment, weapons, vehicles, clothing, and skin. But that was the least of the problems. Camp Corregidor bordered one of the most dangerous areas of Ramadi, called the Mala'ab District. The camp was under constant attack from mortars, machine guns, and rockets.

The colonel expected the highest level of discipline from his 1/506th Soldiers; he knew that slacking here, even when just going to the chow hall for lunch, could result in horrific wounds and death. Discipline in such a situation started with the little things: high-and-tight haircuts, a clean shave every day, and uniforms maintained. With that, the more important things fell into place: body armor and helmets worn outdoors at all times, and weapons cleaned and ready for use at a moment's notice. Discipline created vigilance and operational readiness, which translated to high performance and success on the battlefield.

We sent Task Unit Bruiser SEALs from Delta Platoon to live and work out of Camp Corregidor to train and combat-advise Iraqi soldiers there and support the 1/506th Band of Brothers. When the SEAL element arrived, they humbly took on the same habits as their 1/506th hosts. Despite more relaxed grooming standards SEALs typically enjoy elsewhere, the SEALs at Camp Corregidor cropped their hair short, shaved every day, and even donned the same ACU (army combat uniform) camouflage as their Army counterparts. This overt sign of camaraderie endeared the SEALs to the Soldiers of the 1/506th. These Soldiers had been in a bloody fight for nearly six months, and the SEALs treated them with professionalism and respect. The Army returned that respect, and a bond quickly formed between Soldiers and SEALs.

Our SEALs had been working out of Camp Corregidor for several weeks, carrying out dangerous operations with courage, skill, and effectiveness when the new unit arrived. At first, the SEAL platoon commander at Camp Corregidor was concerned at the arrival of the new well-trained Iraqi unit and their American advisors. He called me on the field-expedient telephone and confided, "This unit that just arrived likely has a much better capability than us. They have a lot of experience. Their Iraqis' skill level is far and above our conventional *jundhis*. They have much better gear and good weapons; and their Iraqis even have a sniper capability."

I replied, "That's good. I'm glad there are Iraqi soldiers that have progressed that far. If you show them the ropes and get them familiar with the battlespace, they will be a great asset."

"I don't know," the SEAL platoon commander replied. "I'm worried these guys will be better than us and take over our mission. Maybe I should just let them figure it out on their own," he said.

I quickly realized what was going on. As good as this platoon commander was, his ego was being threatened. In an environment like Ramadi, trying to figure things out for yourself could easily get you killed. This was no place for ego.

"No. Don't even think about that. Listen: the enemy is outside the wire," I told my SEAL platoon commander bluntly.

Our enemies were the insurgents lurking in the city of Ramadi, not other coalition forces "inside the wire" on the U.S. bases with us. We had to all work together toward the same goal of defeating that insurgency. We couldn't let ego get in the way.

I continued, "This new advisor unit—these are Americans and good Iraqis, possibly the best Iraqis; you do whatever you can to help these guys. If they outperform your team and take your mission, good. We will find you another one. Our mission is to defeat this insurgency. We can't let our egos take precedence over doing what is best to accomplish that."

"Got it, boss," said the platoon commander. A smart and humble warrior, he quickly recognized his viewpoint was wrong and changed his attitude. It was immaterial which units did what or who conducted the most operations. It was about the mission and how we could best accomplish it and win. The platoon commander and his element of SEALs had been bravely fighting hard. They had been in dozens of firefights in the few weeks they had been at Corregidor and could use all the help they could get from another capable unit.

While the SEAL platoon commander quickly put his ego in check, unfortunately, there were other egos getting in the way. As the new unit began to interact with the SEALs and the 1/506th personnel, some of their attitudes raised eyebrows. A few of them did not carry themselves with the same humility as the Band of Brothers 1/506th Soldiers and our SEALs did on Camp Corregidor. A handful of the troops from the new unit flaunted an undisciplined appearance. Some had mustaches and goatees with long hair. They wore dirty baseball caps and cutoff T-shirts with mismatched uniforms. Now, some military units on remote, isolated bases might ease their grooming standards in order to fit in with the local populace or with the foreign military units they are working with. In some cases, such an appearance might even be required. But here in Ramadi, in close proximity with conventional forces on bases owned and operated by the Army and Marine Corps, this was bound to cause friction.

In the minds of some of the members of this new unit, they were above conforming to the colonel's strict grooming policies. But that alone was an issue that could be overcome. After all, a clean uniform does not a good soldier make. But the problems didn't stop there. Some of the unit's U.S. advisors did not address the

1/506th Soldiers with professionalism and respect. They talked down not only to rank Soldiers but also to senior leaders. Considering virtually every rifleman in the 1/506th had more combat experience than most of the men in this unit ever would, this was especially shocking.

To make matters worse, the new unit made it clear that they had little interest in listening to advice or learning from the SEAL platoon commander and his men. After weeks of sustained combat operations in one of the worst sectors of Ramadi, our SEALs had learned lessons that saved lives. From specific gear needed to how much ammunition to carry, to the amount of water needed for missions, to effective tactics and communications plans, the SEALs had learned a great deal about conducting operations with 1/506th in this specific area. When they attempted to pass this valuable information on to the new unit, their advice was shunned. Overconfidence was risky in such a hostile environment, a mistake most often made by warriors who had never truly been tested.

Because of the thousands of well-armed insurgents and the extreme violence that engulfed Ramadi, every U.S. unit had to carefully coordinate plans and be ready to support each other. Here the constant threat from a large-scale enemy attack, with the potential to overwhelm and annihilate a small group of U.S. troops, was very real. That meant everyone had to share operational details of plans as much as they could in order to ensure synchronized efforts. From large battalion-size operations to simple logistics convoys, it was essential to coordinate and keep other units informed in order to give everyone the greatest chance of survival and prevent fratricide. Yet, when planning their missions, this new unit working in 1/506th battlespace refused to disclose their plans, locations, timelines, or other operational details. They didn't think they needed to inform the colonel of their plans. This meant they intended to go out into the colonel's battlespace, among his units, rely on his support when things went sideways, and conduct operations without fully coordinating. When the 1/506th battalion operations officer confronted them and asked for the plan detailing their first mission, the new unit's leader told him, "We'll tell you later on a need-to-know basis."

When the 1/506th tactical operations center (TOC) inquired about the unit's specific planned location for a mission, (a standard practice to prevent friendly units operating in the area from accidently engaging them, and enabling the 1/506th TOC to send help to their location when needed) the unit's leader provided a four-digit grid (from the military grid reference system). This meant that the unit's troops could be located anywhere within a thousand-meter grid square—all but worthless to the 1/506th TOC. Earlier, we had learned some tough lessons in information sharing, or lack thereof, that had resulted in fratricide. In such a dangerous operating environment with large numbers of well-armed enemy fighters and multiple friendly units maneuvering in the same battlespace, such lack of coordination could well mean a death sentence.

The SEAL platoon commander soon reported back to me on the friction between the new unit and the 1/506th Soldiers. My advice was simple: "Give them what they need and try to help them if you can, but it sounds like they will make their own bed."

Unfortunately, the platoon commander was not able to help and the situation did not improve. In less than two weeks, the colonel directed the unit to leave Camp Corregidor. With such impressive operational capability, they should have been a big contributor to the fight. But the colonel and his troops simply could not risk working with a group where some members' egos prevented them from ever fully integrating with the 1/506th battalion. As a result, the unit had to watch the historic Battle of Ramadi from afar as Delta Platoon SEALs and 1/506th Soldiers took the fight to the enemy in the Mala'ab, killing scores of insurgents and helping to accomplish the strategic objectives of securing and stabilizing the city.

PRINCIPLE

Ego clouds and disrupts everything: the planning process, the ability to take good advice, and the ability to accept constructive criticism. It can even stifle someone's sense of self-preservation. Often, the most difficult ego to deal with is *your own*.

Everyone has an ego. Ego drives the most successful people in life—in the SEAL Teams, in the military, in the business world. They want to win, to be the best. That is good. But when ego clouds our judgment and prevents us from seeing the world as it is, then ego becomes destructive. When personal agendas become more important than the team and the overarching mission's success, performance suffers and failure ensues. Many of the disruptive issues that arise within any team can be attributed directly to a problem with ego.

Implementing Extreme Ownership requires checking your ego and operating with a high degree of humility. Admitting mistakes, taking ownership, and developing a plan to overcome challenges are integral to any successful team. Ego can prevent a leader from conducting an honest, realistic assessment of his or her own performance and the performance of the team.

In the SEAL Teams, we strive to be confident, but not cocky (see chapter 12). We take tremendous pride in the history and legacy of our organization. We are confident in our skills and are eager to take on challenging missions that others cannot or aren't willing to execute. But we can't ever think we are too good to fail or that our enemies are not capable, deadly, and eager to exploit our weaknesses. We must never get complacent. This is where controlling the ego is most important.

APPLICATION TO BUSINESS

Leif Babin

"I've got an immediate fire that's causing us a big issue, and I need some help with this," said the voice mail. "Please give me a call as soon as you can."

The voice mail was from Gary, a midlevel manager in the operations department of a corporation with which Jocko and I had worked through our company, Echelon Front. We had developed a twelve-month leadership program for the corporation. Every few weeks, we traveled to their corporate headquarters for training with a class of a dozen midlevel managers from various departments. In addition to the classroom sessions, we provided coaching and mentorship to help our course participants apply what they learned in class to their everyday leadership challenges.

Jocko and I had spoken to Gary by phone several times over the past few months and helped him solve some minor leadership dilemmas and build a more effective team. He was a hard worker, dedicated to his job and his team, and he was eager to learn. It was rewarding to watch him grow as a leader over the months of our course. As a result, he had much greater confidence in himself to make the decisions that would help his team more effectively execute their mission. Now he had a major issue—a serious leadership challenge that was pressing. I was eager to help.

I quickly gave him a call to find out what had happened and what I could do.

"How you doing, Gary?" I asked when he picked up the phone.

"Not too good," Gary responded. "We just had a major issue on one of our critical projects."

"What happened?" I asked. I couldn't hope to match Gary's

expertise in this industry. But I could help him solve his leadership challenges, improve communication, and run a more effective team.

"Our drilling superintendent made a call on his own to swap out a critical piece of equipment," said Gary. "He totally violated our standard operating procedures. I have told him before how I wanted this done, and he completely blew me off!" Gary was angry.

Obviously, Gary's ego had been bruised by the fact that the drilling superintendent hadn't cleared the decision through him.

"This was something he knew he should have run through me," Gary continued, "and he blatantly did not. He made the wrong call, and that set our completion date back several days, costing our company serious capital." In this industry, each day lost on the project could cost hundreds of thousands of dollars.

"Tell me about your superintendent," I said. "Why do you think he would do that?"

"No idea," said Gary. "He knows he has to run that call through me. But he's been in this business way longer than I have, and he's got a ton of experience. Sometimes he looks at me, and his face says *What the hell do you know?* I'm sure he thinks he knows better than me."

"Perhaps he was just pushing the envelope to see what he could get away with," I replied. "Which can escalate if you let it go."

"That's part of the problem. I'm worried about how he will respond to my critique," said Gary. "With his years of knowledge and experience, he is a critical member of this team. We can't afford to lose him. If I call him out, he is going to blow up at me and the friction between us is likely to get even worse than it already is. And you know the climate in this industry. With his experience, he can find another job tomorrow if he wants to."

"That means you will have to check your ego in order to

have a constructive discussion with him and get this under control," I responded.

"Let's think through this," I continued. "Do you think he deliberately tried to shut down drilling operations and cost the company money?"

"No," admitted Gary. "I'm sure he thought he was doing what was best for the immediate situation as it presented itself."

"At the tactical level, on the front lines where the guys in the field execute the mission," I said, "it is critical that the troops grasp how what they do connects to the bigger picture. Your superintendent may not have really understood how his failure to follow procedure and get approval for these changes would result in hundreds of thousands of dollars lost. Do you think that is possible?"

"Definitely. He has exceptional hands-on knowledge of drilling, but he doesn't really deal with the big picture," Gary replied. His anger subsided and his bruised ego diminished as he realized the superintendent had probably not been willfully insubordinate. He now began to understand the reasons the superintendent made the decisions he did.

"As a leader, it is up to you to explain the bigger picture to him—and to all your front line leaders. That is a critical component of leadership," I replied.

But Gary was still concerned about how to deal with his drilling superintendent—and the superintendent's ego. "How can I communicate this to him without ruffling his feathers and getting him all pissed off at me?" asked Gary. "If I confront him about this, our communication will get even worse than it already is."

"That is another critical component of leadership," I quickly replied. "Dealing with people's egos. And you can do so by using one of the main principles we have taught you during our course: Extreme Ownership."

Gary responded, "Ownership of what? He's the one that

screwed this up, not me." It was clear Gary's ego was getting in the way of the solution to this problem.

"Ownership of everything!" I answered. "This isn't his fault, it's *yours*. You are in charge, so the fact that he didn't follow procedure is your fault. And you have to believe that, because it's true. When you talk to him, you need to start the conversation like this: 'Our team made a mistake and it's my fault. It's my fault because I obviously wasn't as clear as I should have been in explaining why we have these procedures in place and how not following them can cost the company hundreds of thousands of dollars. You are an extremely skilled and knowledgeable superintendent. You know more about this business than I ever will. It was up to me to make sure you know the parameters we have to work within and why some decisions have got to be run through me. Now, I need to fix this so it doesn't happen again.'"

"Do you think that will work?" asked Gary, sounding unconvinced.

"I'm confident it will," I replied. "If you approached it as *he* did something wrong, and *he* needs to fix something, and *he* is at fault, it becomes a clash of egos and you two will be at odds. That's human nature. But, if you put your own ego in check, meaning *you* take the blame, that will allow him to actually see the problem without his vision clouded by ego. Then you both can make sure that your team's standard operating procedures—when to communicate, what is and isn't within his decision-making authority—are clearly understood."

"I wouldn't have thought to take that tact," Gary admitted.

"It's counterintuitive," I said. "It's natural for anyone in a leadership position to blame subordinate leaders and direct reports when something goes wrong. Our egos don't like to take blame. But it's on us as leaders to see where we failed to communicate effectively and help our troops clearly understand what their roles and responsibilities are and how their actions impact the bigger strategic picture.

"Remember, it's not about you," I continued. "It's not about the drilling superintendent. It's about the mission and how best to accomplish it. With that attitude exemplified in you and your key leaders, your team will dominate."

PART II

THE LAWS OF COMBAT

Bruiser SEALs clear target buildings in central Ramadi. Ruthless insurgents could be waiting behind every door or firing from every window or rooftop. Enemy mortars, rifles, machine guns, RPG-7 rockets, and IEDs made every clearance a challenge.

(Photo courtesy of the authors)

CHAPTER 5

Cover and Move

Leif Babin

SOUTH-CENTRAL RAMADI, IRAQ: COVERING THE FLANK

"So what are we doing?" asked our leading petty officer.

The clock was ticking and every second counted. There were no good options. Each one could have deadly consequences. But I had to make a call.

As SEALs, we often protected the troops in the streets with our snipers and machine gunners in a type of operation we called "sniper overwatch." By taking the high ground in buildings and positioning SEAL snipers where they could best observe and engage enemy fighters maneuvering to attack, we could eliminate threats and disrupt insurgent attacks before they could fully materialize. This helped mitigate the substantial risks to U.S. and Iraqi troops patrolling the streets, enabled them to more safely accomplish their mission, and ensured more U.S. Soldiers and Marines came home alive to their families back in the States.

The U.S. Army's Ready First Brigade Combat Team (1st Armored Division) adopted a radical and innovative strategy to take back Ramadi from the malevolent clutches of the insurgency—Seize, Clear, Hold, Build. It called for U.S. forces to penetrate into the most dangerous enemy-held neighborhoods, push back insurgent fighters, and construct permanent U.S. combat outposts from which to base further operations. Iraqi soldiers were brought in to take part in the effort. Once a foothold was established in enemy territory, the next step required a show of force in enemy controlled areas and engagement with the Iraqi populace in the neighborhood. Though the battles raged around them, hundreds of thousands of civilians lived in the city and simply tried to survive. Securing the people and protecting them from the brutal jihadi fighters that hid among them was the key to victory. Integral to the success of this strategy were cordon and search operations—clearing through city blocks house by house. Often executed during daylight hours, these operations could be treacherous for the U.S. Army Soldiers, Marines, and Iraqi troops as they cordoned off neighborhoods (or sectors) and moved street to street, building to building through some of the most violent areas of the city.

On one particular operation, Team Bulldog (U.S. Army Bravo Company, 1st Battalion, 37th Armored Regiment) planned a large cordon and search operation in a particularly dangerous area of South-Central Ramadi spanning several blocks from their base located in the heart of enemy territory, a combat outpost called COP Falcon. Such an operation required some one hundred Soldiers on the ground, supported by armor—M1A2 Abrams Main Battle Tanks and M2 Bradley Fighting Vehicles—with their substantial firepower. Additional forces from the battalion were brought in to reinforce Team Bulldog in this effort.

Through dozens of dangerous combat operations, we had built an excellent working relationship with the U.S. Soldiers and tankers of Team Bulldog. Bulldog's company commander was one of the finest combat leaders I have known. He and his Soldiers were exceptional warriors. Our SEALs had tremendous respect and admiration for their courage and fighting spirit as they lived everyday under constant attack, right in the heart of dangerous enemy territory. Our SEAL elements worked out of COP Falcon and from there pushed even deeper into al Qaeda battle space. When we were ferociously attacked by insurgents, which was often, the company commander personally mounted up in his tank, rallied his troops, and brought the thunder with the main guns of Team Bulldog's M1A2 Abrams tanks to bear on our behalf. He and his Bulldog Soldiers were an outstanding group, eager to close with and destroy the enemy, and we loved them for it.

On this particular cordon and search operation, our SEALs from Charlie Platoon and Task Unit Bruiser would provide sniper overwatch, while our SEAL combat advisors would manage a platoon of Iraqi soldiers participating in the clearance on the ground. Jocko teamed up with the Army battalion's operations officer, who would help manage the clearance, while Jocko would provide command and control as well as coordination of our SEAL elements supporting the operation.

In planning, we decided to set up two separate SEAL sniper overwatch positions several hundred meters apart to cover the U.S. Army and Iraqi Army cordon and search teams as they entered buildings block by block across the sector. The first SEAL sniper overwatch position, OP1, led by Charlie Platoon's assistant officer-in-charge, would take position in a large four-story apartment building some three hundred meters to the east of COP Falcon to protect the northern flank of the cordon and search teams. I would lead a second SEAL sniper overwatch position, OP2, of eight SEALs and seven Iraqi soldiers. We planned to take position about one kilometer southeast of COP Falcon along the southern flank of the cordon and search teams. The area was heavily IED'ed.

At 0200 local time (or two o'clock in the morning), those of us in OP2 stepped off via foot patrol from COP Falcon into the dark and dangerous Ramadi streets. Empty at this hour, all appeared quiet. But in this neighborhood, enemy fighters could be waiting around every corner. The other SEAL overwatch team, OP1, would depart an hour later, since their position was very near the friendly combat outpost and it was one they knew well, having utilized this position before. My team, OP2, had much farther to travel, and not having been in any of the buildings in the immediate area, we would need more time to establish a good position. On the patrol in, I served as patrol leader positioned second from the front, just behind the point man. We moved as quietly as possible through the streets, weapons trained at every angle, watching for enemy, ready for contact at all times. We took great care to avoid debris, such as trash piles on the street or other suspicious items, being deliberate in where we stepped, as the threat from IEDs was substantial. Each man carried a heavy load of weapons, ammunition, and water, in anticipation of what we knew could likely be a big and lengthy fight come daylight.

This urban war zone was straight out of a Hollywood set for a World War II movie, like the ones we watched growing up: walls riddled with bullet holes, burnt-out cars in the streets, rubbled buildings, and bomb craters. It was surreal to be in a place filled with such violence and destruction. We continued our patrol down the dusty, trash-covered streets, weapons bristling in all directions. Our patrol snaked through alleyways, avoiding the rare operating streetlamp (most had been shot out or didn't have electrical power), and maneuvered the best we could around packs of mangy street dogs whose barking could give away our position. We planned to utilize a two-story house as our OP2 overwatch position and thought it would provide a clear view to cover the cordon and search teams' southern flank.

After a twenty-minute patrol without incident we arrived at the location. Just outside the walled compound, the entire element took up security positions around the gate. With weapons covering, we boosted a couple of our Iraqi soldiers over the wall. They quickly unbolted the gate from the inside and then let the rest of us in. SEAL shooters and Iraqi soldiers swiftly but quietly flowed into the compound and moved toward the house's front door. Iraqi soldiers knocked and instructed the family inside to open up. A bewildered Iraqi man answered the door and complied. SEALs quickly cleared the compound, checking each room, a second-story balcony, the rooftop, and the interior courtyard for threats. Once clear, we set security positions.

The house provided a decent view in one direction along the main road. In the other direction, however, it offered little vantage point except from an exposed balcony. It was also difficult to place key security positions without exposing personnel to attack from surrounding buildings. Our OP2 snipers brought these significant concerns to me and our platoon's leading petty officer (LPO)—one of my most trusted leaders. We were in a bind.

"We could take the building next door and maintain a security contingent there," the LPO offered. It was a great idea, and we decided to pursue that option.

Leaving a team in place, we sent a clearance team to the adjacent building. But what they found was not encouraging: the vantage point was no better. Positioning adequate security forces in two different buildings would spread us extremely thin, especially in such a dangerous neighborhood crawling with heavily armed *muj*. With this option not practical, I talked things over with the LPO. It was still dark, but sunrise was not far off, and the first call to prayer would soon echo from the mosque minarets and awaken the city. Time was running out to get into position, especially as the cordon and search teams of Army Soldiers, our SEAL advisor teams and Iraqi soldiers would commence their operation soon and were depending on our sniper overwatch team to cover them.

"No options are good," I lamented. "But our least bad option is to pull everyone back to our original building and secure that position as best we can." The LPO agreed and immediately executed the plan. We knew the position had substantial vulnerabilities, but we would have to do all we could to mitigate such risks. Our SEAL snipers took positions to best protect the troops on the ground, and then we placed the rest of our team in positions to protect the snipers, one of whom was somewhat exposed on the balcony. With the position set, OP2's SEAL radioman made a call to our other SEAL sniper overwatch, OP1, reporting our position. We then checked in on Team Bulldog's net and passed our location to Jocko, who was with Team Bulldog at COP Falcon, so he could coordinate with the other troops on the ground.

"Aaaaalllllllaaaaaaaaaaahhhhhuu Akbar . . ." echoed the first call to prayer from the minaret loudspeakers of mosques throughout the city, signaling the dawning of the day. Soon, the first rays of light painted the eastern horizon, and South-Central Ramadi began to awaken. Even in this war-torn city, some semblance of normal life carried on. People emerged from their houses. Cars and trucks backed out of driveways and made their way down city streets. Shepherd boys drove their herds of sheep down the road to graze along the fertile banks of the Euphrates River. The sun rose with searing heat which would crescendo midday to baking temperatures of over 115 degrees Fahrenheit.

Over the radio, the Soldiers of Team Bulldog signaled their cordon and search operation was under way. Dozens of Soldiers (including the SEAL advisor and Iraqi soldier clearance team) moved out from COP Falcon accompanied by armored firepower from Abrams tanks and Bradley vehicles. From our position hundreds of meters away, OP2 could hear the heavy grind of tank tracks on pavement and the rev of their powerful gas turbine engines. I checked in with Jocko via radio, as he moved out with the cordon and search team. All was proceeding according to plan.

In such a nasty neighborhood, it didn't take long for enemy fighters to mount an attack. The first attempts came from the north. OP2 could hear the report of big rifles as OP1's SEAL snipers hammered a couple of armed insurgents moving to attack. Soon, our OP2 snipers observed three enemy fighters with AK-47s and an RPG rocket maneuvering through the streets toward the clearance teams. SEAL snipers engaged, hitting two of the three and sending the third running for cover. With those shots, the enemy had a good indication of where we were. Within the hour, the first bursts of *muj* machine gun fire snapped over the heads of the two SEALs positioned on the balcony. It was only the beginning, as the enemy sporadically engaged our building and probed our position. We knew their attacks would no doubt grow bolder as they pinpointed our position and the day progressed.

The cordon and search operation proceeded with sporadic gunfire and a few warning shots fired. The SEAL sniper overwatch positions were able to help thwart any major attacks before they could materialize. The vigilant Team Bulldog Soldiers with their tanks at the ready were also a substantial deterrent. Within about two hours of sunrise, the Army Soldiers along with Jocko and the small team of SEAL combat advisors with their Iraqi soldiers had cleared every building in the sector. Having accomplished their mission, they all moved safely back to COP Falcon. It had been a relatively smooth operation, which, in such a dangerous neighborhood right in the heart of South-Central Ramadi, was somewhat miraculous. No American or Iraqi soldiers had been wounded or killed. That was also a testament to good planning and execution by the U.S. forces involved and a tribute to the effectiveness of the SEAL sniper overwatch teams.

With the cordon and search force back at COP Falcon, both SEAL overwatch teams—OP1 and OP2—had accomplished our objectives. Our standard operating procedure (SOP) dictated we remain in position until nightfall and then patrol back to base under cover of darkness, when we could more safely move through the dangerous streets. A small element patrolling in broad daylight through enemy territory presented serious risk of almost certain contact. Enemy machine guns, RPG-7 shoulder-fired rockets, and IEDs could be utilized to deadly effect. But for OP2, remaining in our current position also presented great risks. The building we held had substantial tactical vulnerabilities. The enemy knew where we were, and there was a high probability that with enough time, enemy fighters would mount a serious attack. Should they do so, we might very well take significant casualties and even find our position overrun by determined enemy fighters at close quarters.

This presented quite a leadership dilemma. Again, I discussed options with my trusted LPO: "We can stay where we are and wait until nightfall. Or we can quickly break out of here and foot-patrol back to COP Falcon. Or we could call in the Bradleys* for extract, though that could take some time." Bradley Fighting Vehicles provided protection from small-arms fire behind their armored plating, and they brought significant firepower with a 25mm chain gun and 7.62mm coaxial machine gun. But they required some time to coordinate—to brief crews and drive to our position. Bradleys were loud and the bad guys would hear them coming from some distance. This option would also expose the U.S. Soldiers that crewed the vehicles to the substantial IED threat, as the roads in the vicinity of our position were extremely dangerous and had not been swept by the IED-clearance teams. This could very well result in an IED strike—a deadly explosive buried in the road, which might kill or seriously wound the Soldiers inside. Were this to happen, it would require sending even more vehicles and troops in harm's way to extract casualties and downed vehicles.

---

* M2 Bradley Fighting Vehicles could carry six soldiers each

Calling in the Bradleys meant waiting for perhaps another half hour and would put Team Bulldog Soldiers in significant danger. It would also endanger us riding in the vehicles through heavily IED'ed streets. If we stayed in position until dark in accordance with SOP, we would almost certainly have to fend off increasingly violent enemy attacks for another eight to ten hours. Should those attacks exploit the significant weaknesses of our defenses, we might be pinned down and unable to depart without calling in massive fire support and putting more forces at even greater risk to bail us out.

If we pulled out on foot immediately and quickly patrolled back to COP Falcon, we would probably get shot at. But it would likely be a hasty attack that the *muj* wouldn't have enough time to coordinate for maximum effectiveness. We could help mitigate that risk by moving quickly and utilizing misdirection in the streets and alleyways to prevent the enemy from predicting our exact route back to COP Falcon so they couldn't set an ambush. Still, any gunfire we received no matter how hasty could certainly kill or horribly wound any of us.

No options were good options. We had to choose the least bad option.

"So what are we doing, L-T?"* asked the LPO. Time was ticking.

I had to make a call. "We're pulling out," I decided. It was the least bad option. "Let's get packed up quick and break out of here as soon as we can."

"Roger that," said the LPO. He passed the word to the rest of OP2, and everybody quickly gathered up their gear and double-checked to ensure nothing was left behind. Our OP2 radioman contacted OP1, the other sniper overwatch team, to tell them we were moving back on foot to the combat outpost. We also notified

---

* "L-T": a common nickname in the U.S. Navy SEAL Teams for the junior officer rank of U.S. Navy Lieutenant.

Team Bulldog's Soldiers back at COP Falcon, where Jocko and a few of our SEALs with the clearance team had returned.

For OP1, only a short three-hundred-meter patrol from COP Falcon, there was no such dilemma about what to do. They had an easy foot patrol back to COP Falcon, covered by COP Falcon's nearby tanks and heavy machine guns the entire way. OP1 radioed to us in OP2 that they too were pulling out. But OP1 made the mistake of not telling Jocko, which meant he could not coordinate the movement.

"Roger that," our OP2 radioman responded to OP1's call. He relayed the information to the LPO and me. With our focus entirely on getting OP2 moving out in a hurry, we thought little of it. Every minute that passed by gave enemy fighters more time to coordinate a serious attack on our position. Within a few minutes, everyone was ready. We quickly briefed the team and emphasized that we needed to move fast.

"Let's do this," was the consensus. Everybody knew we would likely get in a gunfight. But we wanted that gunfight to be on our terms, not the enemy's.

With everything ready, we broke out of the building and emerged onto the street, our weapons pointed in all directions, ready for a fight. We quickly moved out and made our way through the streets, covering and moving as a team past Iraqi citizens who stared at us with some surprise. When aggressive men with guns pointed their weapons at them, the locals knew to keep their distance. Anyone who didn't avoid interfering with a heavily armed SEAL squad was certainly looking for trouble. Rapidly, we pushed past parked cars and piles of trash. Threats were everywhere in this urban environment. Every gate, door, and alleyway that we passed, the distant intersections down the street at ground level, and above us from every rooftop, balcony, and upstairs window—each presented the possibility of well-armed *muj* fighters ready to inflict horrible wounds or death upon us.

Our tactic, which we had trained for, practiced, and utilized, was a fundamental one we called "Cover and Move." Within our OP2 squad, we had four elements of smaller teams. One team covered, their weapons trained on threats, while the other team moved. Then those teams reversed roles. In this way, the teams leapfrogged in bounds, constantly utilizing Cover and Move to ensure we were prepared to fend off an attack as we maneuvered through the streets.

For about five hundred meters, OP2 moved along steadily, making our way back toward COP Falcon. Then all hell broke loose. Fully automatic gunfire erupted from the rear of the patrol. Insurgent fighters had followed us and heavily engaged us with AK-47s and PKC belt-fed machine guns, and rounds smashed into nearby walls and kicked up dust in the street right at our feet.

Immediately, we responded with withering gunfire of our own. Our SEAL machine gunners were an awesome sight to behold, fearlessly laying down fire with deadly accuracy, even as enemy rounds impacted all around them. Like a well-oiled machine, we executed a "center peel" maneuver: a coordinated tactic where two columns systematically alternate shooting at the enemy and moving away in a safe direction until able to break contact. I lobbed a few 40mm grenades over the heads of our patrol and onto enemy positions to help keep their heads down as we bounded back. Our overwhelming fire quickly repulsed the enemy attack, and we continued to a street corner that provided additional cover, moving in a hurry toward COP Falcon. Those courageous SEAL machine gunners had provided the cover fire that enabled us to move safely through the maelstrom. Within minutes, we covered the remaining distance to the COP and made our way past the Abrams tank guarding the entrance. We pushed past the concertina wire and concrete barriers into the relative safety of the U.S. Army combat outpost. We were breathing hard after running and gunning in the late morning heat with heavy gear. But we had all survived without a scratch. The LPO and I smiled and laughed at each other. We had just gotten ourselves into a solid gunfight on the street, hammered the enemy, and brought everyone back unscathed. It was awesome. We were fired up.

But already back at COP Falcon was our platoon chief. He had been with the cordon and search force and had returned earlier with Jocko and the rest of our small team of SEALs and the Iraqi soldiers. Chief wasn't happy. He pulled me aside.

"What the hell were you guys doing out there?" the chief asked sternly.

"What do you mean?" I asked, immediately getting defensive.

The chief was a hell of a battlefield leader—extraordinary in a gunfight. With a long career of nearly twenty years, he was the most experienced SEAL in the task unit, and we highly valued his guidance and mentorship. Never one to shy away from a fight, he was courageous and always eager to close with and destroy the enemy. So why now was he critical of us, particularly my leadership on the battlefield?

"What are you talking about?" I said.

"Why didn't you leave the other SEAL sniper overwatch position—OP1—in place to cover your movement back here to COP Falcon?" the chief asked.

I thought about that for a moment. My initial defensiveness wore off. He was right.

"No reason," I replied, understanding that his logic was absolutely correct. I realized my error. "I was so focused on our own squad's dilemma, I didn't think to coordinate with the other team, OP1, to work together. We absolutely should have." This was the first rule in Jocko's Laws of Combat: Cover and Move. I had broken it. We had used Cover and Move within my own immediate OP2 team, but I had forgotten about the greater team and support available. We had operated independently, failing to support or help each other. Had we left OP1 in place, they would have had an excellent vantage from the high ground and could have covered our OP2 movement much of the way as we patrolled through the dangerous streets back to COP Falcon. Once at the COP, we (OP2) could have provided additional cover for OP1 as they returned to COP Falcon.

It was foolishness not to work together. Though we were working in small teams with some distance between us we weren't on our own. We were all trying to accomplish the same mission. The enemy was out there working against us—all of us. It was essential that we support each other and work together. One element must cover so that the other element could move. Our OP2 had gotten lucky this time around, damn lucky. But my chief knew, and I now recognized, that we had taken a needless and foolish risk. We should have utilized every strength and tactical advantage possible against these ruthless enemy fighters occupying Ramadi. The most important tactical advantage we had was working together as a team, always supporting each other.

It was a rude awakening for me. I had become so immersed in the details, decision points, and immediate challenges of my own team that I had forgotten about the other team, what they could do for us and how we might help them.

Going forward I never forgot my chief's guidance. We utilized the principle of Cover and Move on every operation: all teams working together in support of one another. That realization and the lesson learned implemented no doubt saved lives, greatly reduced casualties and enabled us to more effectively accomplish our mission and win.

PRINCIPLE

Cover and Move: it is the most fundamental tactic, perhaps the only tactic. Put simply, Cover and Move means teamwork. All elements within the greater team are crucial and must work together to accomplish the mission, mutually supporting one another for that singular purpose. Departments and groups within the team must break down silos, depend on each other and understand who depends on them. If they forsake this principle and operate independently or work against each other, the results can be catastrophic to the overall team's performance.

Within any team, there are divisions that arise. Often, when smaller teams within the team get so focused on their immediate tasks, they forget about what others are doing or how they depend on other teams. They may start to compete with one another, and when there are obstacles, animosity and blame develops. This creates friction that inhibits the overall team's performance. It falls on leaders to continually keep perspective on the strategic mission and remind the team that they are part of the greater team and the strategic mission is paramount.

Each member of the team is critical to success, though the main effort and supporting efforts must be clearly identified. If the overall team fails, everyone fails, even if a specific member or an element within the team did their job successfully. Pointing fingers and placing blame on others contributes to further dissension between teams and individuals. These individuals and teams must instead find a way to work together, communicate with each other, and mutually support one another. The focus must always be on how to best accomplish the mission.

Alternatively, when the team succeeds, everyone within and supporting that team succeeds. Every individual and every team within the larger team gets to share in the success. Accomplishing the strategic mission is the highest priority. Team members, departments, and supporting assets must always Cover and Move—help each other, work *together,* and support each other to win. This principle is integral for any team to achieve victory.

APPLICATION TO BUSINESS

"Those guys are horrible," said the production manager. He described a subsidiary company, owned by their parent corporation, on which his team depended to transport their product. "They can't get their jobs completed on schedule. And that prevents us from doing our jobs." Clearly, there were major issues between his field leaders—the frontline troops of his team—and those of the subsidiary company.

Jocko and I stood before the class of a dozen midlevel managers seated at tables forming a U-shape in a conference room of the company's corporate headquarters. In the second session of a twelve-month leadership-training program, our presentation and discussion centered on the Laws of Combat. We solicited from each of the class participants specific leadership challenges that they currently faced. Jocko and I set about to help them solve these challenges through the application of the SEAL combat leadership principles they had just learned.

The production manager explained that his team struggled to minimize downtime in their production—the times when they had to cease making product. These disruptions occurred for a variety of reasons, but they stopped product from moving to market, and every hour and day of downtime cost the company huge revenues and substantially impacted the bottom line. With his crew just getting up and running, there had been a steep learning curve. The production manager's team maintained an average downtime that was much worse than the industry standard. Such a glaring discrepancy was a major detriment to the company's profits. As a result, the production manager was under scrutiny and intense pressure to reduce downtime. The subsidiary company on which his production team depended became the major scapegoat to blame.

"We spend a lot of our time waiting on them [the subsidiary

company], and that causes big problems and delays for us," said the production manager. "Those delays are impacting production and costing our company serious revenue."

"How can you help this subsidiary company?" I asked the production manager.

"I can't!" he replied. "They don't work for me. We don't work for the same bosses. They are a different company." While he was right that they were a different company, both companies fell under the leadership of the same parent corporation.

"Besides," he added with indifference, "they aren't *my* problem. I've got my own team to worry about."

"It sounds like they *are* your problem," I responded.

"In that sense," he agreed, "I guess they are."

"What's worse," continued the production manager, now on a roll of bashing the subsidiary company, "because corporate owns them, we are forced to use their services."

"What you just called the worst part should be the best part," Jocko responded. "You are both owned by the same corporation, so you both have the same mission. And that is what this is about—the overall mission, the overall team. Not just your team, but the whole team; the entire corporation—all departments within your company, all subsidiary companies under the corporation, outside contractors, the whole enterprise. You must work together and support each other as *one team*."

"The enemy is out there," I said, pointing out the window to the world beyond. "The enemy is all the other competing companies in your industry that are vying for your customers. The enemy is not in here, inside the walls of this corporation. The departments within and the subsidiary companies that all fall under the same leadership structure—you are all on the same team. You have to overcome the 'us versus them' mentality and work together, mutually supporting one another."

Just as I had on the battlefield in Ramadi years before, the production manager was now so focused on his own department and its immediate tasks that he couldn't see how his mission aligned with the rest of the corporation and supporting assets, all striving to accomplish the same strategic mission. As I had done after some constructive guidance from my chief, the production manager must now be willing to take a step back and see how his production team's mission fit into the overall plan.

"It's about the bigger, strategic mission," I said. "How can you help this subsidiary company do their job more effectively so they can help you accomplish your mission and you can all win?"

The production manager pondered this. He was still skeptical.

"Engage with them," directed Jocko. "Build a personal relationship with them. Explain to them what you need from them and why, and ask them what you can do to help them get you what you need. Make them a part of your team, not an excuse for your team. Remember the stories Leif and I have told about relying on other units to support us? Those Army and Marine Corps units we worked with were not under our control. We had different bosses. But we depended on them and they depended on us. So we formed relationships with them and worked together to accomplish the overall mission of securing Ramadi. That's Cover and Move. You need to do the same thing here: work together to win."

The production manager was a driven leader who wanted his team to perform at the highest level. Now, he began to understand true teamwork. The proverbial lightbulb went off in his head, and his attitude completely changed: if he wasn't working together with this subsidiary company, then he was failing his team.

Over the next weeks and months, the production manager made every effort to positively engage with the subsidiary company, to communicate with them, and establish a better working relationship. He came to more fully understand the myriad challenges that impacted their timelines and caused delays and what he could do on his end to help mitigate those issues. It wasn't that they were "horrible," as he had initially surmised. They were operating with limited resources and limited manpower. Once he accepted that they weren't out to sabotage his team, he realized that there were steps that he and his team could take to help the subsidiary company become more efficient and fill in gaps that had caused their delays. Instead of working as two separate entities against each other, they began to work together.

With this shift in mind-set, the production manager's encouragement enabled his field leaders to see the subsidiary company employees in a different light: not as adversaries but as critical resources part of the same greater team. Most important, the production team began to work with the subsidiary company's field team. Within a few months, the production team's field leaders encouraged key personnel from the subsidiary company to sit in on their coordination meetings. Very soon, the "us versus them" mentality had all but disappeared. They had broken through the silos and no longer worked against each other. The production team's downtime radically improved to industry leading levels. They now worked together as one team—Cover and Move.

Band of Brothers: Iraqi soldiers and U.S. Military Transition Team advisors, SEALs from Task Unit Bruiser, and U.S. Army Soldiers from 1/506th, 101st Airborne (Task Force Red Currahee) use smoke grenades to mask their movement from enemy shooters, on patrol in Ramadi.

(Photo courtesy of the authors)

CHAPTER 6
Simple

Jocko Willink

COMBAT OUTPOST FALCON, RAMADI, IRAQ: INTO THE FRAY

WHOOM!

A massive explosion shook the walls of the building I was sitting in right in the middle of Combat Outpost (COP) Falcon. Adrenaline shot from my core, down my arms, into my hands. Seconds later, another explosion rocked the compound. Soon the word spread: mortars. Insurgents had lobbed 120mm mortar rounds smack-dab into the center of COP Falcon with deadly accuracy. "One-twenties" were vicious. Each massive projectile carried twenty-plus pounds of high explosives wrapped in a half-inch-thick steel jacket designed to throw jagged pieces of shrapnel in all directions, causing catastrophic wounds and death. The rounds had wounded several American Soldiers at COP Falcon, one critically, who later succumbed to his injuries. A third 120mm mortar round hit the roof of the building I was in, but thankfully for the Soldiers nearby, it didn't explode: it was a dud. The mortars were alarmingly accurate, proving once again that the insurgents we were fighting were highly capable. As daylight dawned on this early morning, it was a grim reminder that this was dangerous territory, and we were sitting right in the middle of it.

The night before, Leif and his SEALs from Task Unit Bruiser's Charlie Platoon had inserted from U.S. Marine Corps Small Unit Riverine Craft (SURC) boats manned by a great crew of highly motivated Marines. Charlie Platoon's SEALs, accompanied by an expert team from the 2nd U.S. Marine Air-Naval Gunfire Liaison Company (ANGLICO) with which they often worked closely, a small Army sniper team, and a partner force of Iraqi Soldiers had hopped from the SURC boats onto the riverbank. They quietly sneaked into this enemy-controlled neighborhood—one of the most violent areas of Ramadi. Our SEALs were the first U.S. boots on the ground. They led the opening salvo of this massive operation involving hundreds of U.S. Soldiers, tanks, and aircraft to establish a combat outpost, literally in the center of enemy-controlled territory. Within minutes of their arrival, Charlie Platoon had killed an armed insurgent fighter patrolling the neighborhood in the early morning darkness. SEALs then seized and cleared the building complex that was to become COP Falcon and held it for a few hours into the night while SEAL snipers provided cover for the dozens of U.S. Army tanks and vehicles that followed the IED clearance teams along the road into the area. I had ridden in with the U.S. Army battalion Task Force 1-37 Bandits (1st Battalion, 37th Armored Regiment, 1st Armored Division) in an M2 Bradley Fighting Vehicle early in the morning before the sun had risen, to link up with Leif and Charlie Platoon. My job was command and control of our SEALs. I would coordinate their efforts with Task Force Bandit's Soldiers.

Shortly after our arrival, Charlie Platoon's SEALs turned the buildings they had cleared and occupied over to the U.S. Army company commander of Team Bulldog and other Soldiers of Task

Force 1-37 Bandit. Then Leif and most of the SEALs pushed out to a building a few hundred yards down the road to set up another sniper position. I remained at COP Falcon to coordinate their movements providing overwatch for the Army combat engineers as they built COP Falcon into a defensible position. This required extensive planning, coordination and hours of intense labor to haul and emplace some 30,000 sandbags, over 150 concrete barriers, and hundreds of yards of concertina wire. It had been a long night. The jarring impact of the deadly mortars was our morning wake-up call.

There had been intermittent small-arms fire throughout the night, but no serious firefights. The mortars were the first real attack that did damage and inflicted casualties. Not that it slowed down the operation. The courageous Army engineers had a job to do and they kept working, swinging hammers and operating heavy machinery even as bullets flew; they were brave Soldiers, to a man. As the hot Iraqi sun rose above the dusty city streets and people awakened, so did the bulk of the enemy fighters. I soon heard the loud report of SEAL sniper rifles from Charlie Platoon's position on the high ground in a four-story apartment building a few hundred meters down the street. Leif relayed to me via radio that his SEAL snipers had engaged enemy fighters maneuvering to attack COP Falcon.

But building the combat outpost in enemy territory was only the beginning. There was more to be done. One of the primary objectives in placing this combat outpost in the heart of enemy territory was to show the local populace that we, the coalition of American and Iraqi soldiers, were here to stay and that we did not fear the al Qaeda insurgents who had controlled most of Ramadi unchecked for years. This could not be accomplished by sitting and hiding inside heavily reinforced bases. The troops had to go out and *into* the neighborhoods surrounding the COP. They had to conduct a type of operation so straightforward its name requires almost no explanation: a presence patrol. It required a group of soldiers to push into enemy-held areas to establish their presence among the populace. In this situation, the mission called for a combined operation including Iraqi and American Soldiers working together.

A U.S. Army officer from a military transition team (teams of U.S. Soldiers or Marines built and deployed to train and combat-advise Iraq soldiers, known as MiTTs) planned to lead a group of Iraqi soldiers out into the neighborhood. The MiTT leader was very excited to get out on patrol with his Iraqi soldiers and test their mettle. He had been working and training with them for several months in another city in northern Iraq and had conducted some fairly benign patrols and combat operations with them. But this was Ramadi. There would be nothing easy or benign about patrolling into these neighborhoods. Here, the enemy was determined, well armed, and ready. They would be waiting to attack and kill any U.S. Soldier, SEAL, Marine, or Iraqi soldier that they could. My immediate discussions with the MiTT leader revealed he did not fully appreciate the dangers that lay in store. I was also concerned that his Iraqi soldiers might not yet be ready for the intense street fighting that was likely to take place in this sector of Ramadi. So I assigned a small group of our SEALs to accompany him and his Iraqi soldiers as command and control to help coordinate any help should they need it.

I stood with one of Charlie Platoon's young SEAL officers, who would lead the SEAL element accompanying the Iraqi soldiers, as the MiTT leader strolled over to us and pulled out his battle map to brief us on the route he intended for the patrol. He outlined a path that snaked through the treacherous city streets and stretched clear across South-Central Ramadi over to the next U.S. combat outpost to the east, COP Eagle's Nest. This was nearly two kilometers through some of the most hostile territory in Iraq held by a determined and vicious enemy. None of the roads had been cleared by the U.S. minesweeping teams, so no doubt massive IEDs lay buried along the route. That meant U.S. armored vehicles and firepower could not get to the patrol along much of the leader's planned path without putting the vehicles at huge risk should he and his Iraqis (and now our SEALs) get pinned down.

Beyond that, his planned route passed through battlespace owned by different American units, including two U.S. Army companies, another Army battalion, and a U.S. Marine Corps company. Each had unique standard operating procedures and utilized separate radio nets. That would mean coordinating with all these units prior to launch and setting up contingency plans for help should something go wrong. The amount of water needed for such a long trek in the Iraqi summertime heat that exceed 115 degrees Fahrenheit, along with the massive amount of ammunition required to penetrate so deeply into enemy territory added up to far more than anyone could effectively fight with or carry. Even in a much more permissive or peaceful environment, the MiTT leader's plan for the patrol across battlespace owned by different units would be extremely complex. To try to accomplish this in the worst neighborhoods of Ramadi—the most hazardous battlefield in Iraq—was just plain crazy.

I listened to the plan. When I understood the overall idea and the complexity it involved, I finally commented, "Lieutenant, I appreciate your motivation to get out there and get after it. But perhaps—at least for these first few patrols—we need to simplify this a little bit."

"Simplify?" asked the MiTT leader incredulously. "It is just a patrol. How complex can it get?"

I nodded my head respectfully. "I know it's *just* a patrol," I said. "But there are some risks that can compound when working in an environment like this."

"It's nothing I haven't trained these Iraqis on," he responded confidently.

While I appreciated his confidence, I knew it was hard for the lieutenant to fully grasp the complexities of the mission he was planning when he had not executed missions in such a hostile environment.

"I know you have trained them well, and I'm sure your Iraqi soldiers are a good group," I said, knowing it was likely they had never been in a serious firefight together. "But let's look at what you have here: this route will take you through three separate battlespace owners—two Army and one Marine Corps. It will take you into areas that are known to be heavily IED'ed, which will make any type of support, like CASEVAC* or fire support from tanks, extremely risky. They may not even be able to get to you at all. Even though you have worked extensively with these Iraqi soldiers, my SEALs haven't worked with them at all. So, do you think—at least for this first patrol—we can simplify this a little by cutting down the distance and keeping the entire patrol inside battlespace owned by this company, Team Bulldog?"

"That will only be a few hundred meters out," the MiTT leader objected.

"I know," I replied. "I know it seems short, but let's just keep it simple to start, and we can expand as we get more experience." I knew that one real operation in this environment for the MiTT leader would convince him that simplicity was key. After some further discussion, the MiTT leader agreed to a much shorter, simpler route.

Soon after, the MiTT leader, his Iraqi soldiers, and a small contingent of SEALs gathered around to go through an OPORD

---

* casualty evacuation

(operations order, the pre-mission brief that explains the details of the operation to the members of the team). It was this Iraqi element's first patrol in Ramadi, and despite the mortars that had hit and wounded several U.S. Soldiers, and the constant sound of gunfire in the background, they didn't seem too concerned. Neither did the MiTT leader. Neither, for that matter, did my SEAL element leader. Everyone seemed pretty nonchalant about the patrol. I knew that contact with the enemy was highly likely—if not imminent.

After the brief they split up to do some final preparations: grab water, check ammo and weapons, and go over individual instructions. I went in and covered the route again with the SEAL element leader, noting landmarks such as easily recognizable buildings, unique intersections, water towers, and mosque minarets, which could be used as reference points. We also looked at the battle map, with an overlay of numbers assigned to every building in this sector of the city. The young SEAL officer and I reviewed the building numbers of prominent buildings in the area so we could better communicate both the patrol's position and the position of the enemy, should we need to do so.

The combined element then mustered to form up and begin the patrol. I had already coordinated with Leif to have his element of SEALs, in their sniper overwatch position in the four-story building three hundred meters outside the perimeter of COP Falcon, cover the movement of the presence patrol. With precision sniper fire, machine guns, rockets, and an elevated fighting position, Leif's element could effectively protect the movement of the patrol through the streets. That would help mitigate the risk of enemy attack. I watched closely the attitude of the troops getting ready to head out. It wasn't real for them yet. Finally, I walked up to the young SEAL leader, looked him in the eye, and said, "You are going to get contacted out there. It will happen quick. Stay sharp. Understand?"

My serious tone impacted the young SEAL lieutenant, who nodded slowly and confirmed, "Got it, Sir. Will do."

With that, I stepped back and watched the patrol head out the gate of COP Falcon and into enemy territory. Curious as to how long it might take for enemy fighters to attack, I pressed START on my stopwatch as the patrol stepped off. This was the first overt presence patrol into this section of South-Central Ramadi by Coalition Soldiers in months, perhaps years. Task Unit Bruiser's Delta Platoon, working in an adjacent sector across the city, had for the past two months been attacked by enemy fighters on almost every single patrol.

I monitored the radio at COP Falcon, tracking the patrol's progress. Suddenly, gunfire rang out, echoing across the city blocks.

Da-da-da-da-da-da-da, sounded an enemy AK-47 in the near distance.

Bu-bu-bu-bu-bu-bu-bu-bu-bu-bu-bu-bu-bu, a SEAL machine gunner answered. It was immediately joined by dozens of other weapons that let loose a hellacious barrage of fire, which confirmed to me that these were my SEALs in contact. There was no other unit that unleashed such fury when the shooting started. I looked at my watch. It had been twelve minutes since the patrol stepped off from COP Falcon.

From my position at the COP, I listened to the radio calls. They were broken and jumbled, weakened by the thick concrete walls of city buildings that radio waves could not always penetrate. The shooting continued. It was a substantial firefight. Volleys of gunfire rattled back and forth between the patrol and enemy fighters. More garbled communications. I recognized the voice of the SEAL element leader with the patrol but couldn't make out what he was saying. Leif, on the high ground with direct line of site to both of us, had good radio communications both with the SEAL leader on the ground with the patrol and with me. Leif received a situational update from the patrol. He and the young SEAL element leader both communicated with a clear, calm voice, despite the chaos of the situation, just like we had trained. Leif relayed the report to me: two friendlies wounded, need CASEVAC and fire support.

In order to quickly get tanks and CASEVAC vehicles out to help the patrol, I needed to get direct radio communications with the SEAL officer in the patrol and confirm their position. I quickly sprinted to the top of the largest building on COP Falcon, stood up, and extended my radio antenna for maximum reception.

I keyed up my radio to try and reach the patrol: "Redbull,* this is Jocko."

"Go Jocko," responded the SEAL leader with the patrol in a calm voice. We now had direct radio communications.

"What do you got?" I asked.

"Two wounded. Need CASEVAC. And fire support," he responded. Just as he had been taught: simple, clear, concise information—exactly what was needed.

"Roger. Confirm your location," I said.

"Building J51†," he replied.

"Are all your troops in J51?" I asked.

"Affirm. All friendly troops in J51," he confirmed.

"Roger. Tanks and CASEVAC inbound," I notified him.

I sprinted back down to the first floor into the makeshift TOC where Team Bulldog's company commander stood waiting for the information he needed to get his troops and tanks moving out.

---

* our call SEAL sign at the time in that particular battlespace
† J51, spoken in the phonetic alphabet as "Juliette Five-One."

"What's going on out there, sir?" the company commander asked. "What do they need?"

Calmly, I relayed to him the critical info: "They need fire support and CASEVAC in vicinity of building J51. All friendly personnel are consolidated inside building J51. There are two wounded." I stepped to the huge battle map hanging on the wall next to us and guided my finger to building fifty-one on the map. "Right here," I said and pointed to ensure everybody was clear.

"Got it, sir," answered the company commander. "I'll take a section of tanks* and an M113† to building J51. All friendlies are located in that building. Two wounded."

"Check," I replied, confirming he had all information correct.

He quickly flew out the door toward his tank, briefed his troops, and personally mounted up. He and his men would brave the dangerous IED-laden streets to get to the SEALs, American MiTT advisors and Iraqi troops pinned down under enemy attack. They would do their utmost to save the lives of their wounded.

Meanwhile, from the vantage point of Leif's overwatch position, his SEAL snipers and machine gunners engaged numerous enemy fighters as they rallied to join the attack on the patrol. The powerful sniper rifles our SEALs used made a distinct *crack* as they engaged multiple enemy fighters sneaking toward the friendly patrol hunkered down in building J51. As insurgent fighters rallied to attack the patrol, SEAL machine gunners from the overwatch position joined in and laid down a barrage of fire, beating back the enemy assault.

Within minutes, Team Bulldog's tanks and M113 arrived at building J51. At the sight of the tanks, most of the enemy fighters quickly disappeared into the urban landscape, hiding their weap-

---

* two M1A2 Abrams Main Battle Tanks with heavy firepower
† M113 Armored Personnel Carrier used to evacuate casualties

ons to blend in among the civilian populace. The two casualties were Iraqi soldiers. Both had been shot; one while crossing the street had been abandoned by his fellow Iraqi soldiers who fled to cover. Luckily for him, two SEALs risked their lives to run out into the street through a hail of enemy gunfire and drag him to safety. Both casualties were evacuated. One Iraqi soldier survived, the other unfortunately died from his wounds. Under the cover of the tanks firepower, the rest of the patrol exited building J51 and fell into a column formation, bracketed by the two Abrams tanks, one fore and one aft, like a scene from World War II. Together, they moved back toward COP Falcon. As Team Bulldog's tank covered the rear, an insurgent fighter with an RPG-7 rocket rounded a corner to take a shot at the patrol. But before he could fire the rocket, Team Bulldog's company commander, sitting in the turret of his tank, plugged him in the chest with a .50-caliber machine gun.

When the patrol made it back to COP Falcon, I met them as they entered the compound. Making eye contact with the young SEAL leader in the patrol, I gave him an approving nod that, without words, said: *Well done; you kept your composure and you made clear calls. You got the help you needed and kept the rest of your team alive.* The SEAL leader nodded back: he understood.

The MiTT leader was clearly shaken up. It had been his first serious firefight—his first real test as a leader. Luckily, he had our SEAL element with him, which helped ensure his patrol's survival. Fortunately, he had agreed to keep his mission simple, to minimize complexity for the inevitable contingencies that could arise. It was a worst-case scenario. Had this gunfight happened where he had originally planned to go—much deeper into enemy territory, out of the range of COP Falcon, with separate supporting Army or Marine elements that had different radio frequencies and different operating procedures—it would likely have been catastrophic. If they had made this patrol more difficult and complex than it already was, the MiTT leader and all his Iraqi soldiers might have been killed.

I gave the MiTT leader a different nod than the one I gave the SEAL leader. This nod said, *That's why we keep it simple.* The MiTT leader looked back at me. He didn't say a word, but his eyes communicated to me clearly, *I know that now. I understand.*

PRINCIPLE

Combat, like anything in life, has inherent layers of complexities. Simplifying as much as possible is crucial to success. When plans and orders are too complicated, people may not understand them. And when things go wrong, and *they inevitably do go wrong,* complexity compounds issues that can spiral out of control into total disaster. Plans and orders must be communicated in a manner that is simple, clear, and concise. Everyone that is part of the mission must know and understand his or her role in the mission and what to do in the event of likely contingencies. As a leader, it doesn't matter how well you feel you have presented the information or communicated an order, plan, tactic, or strategy. If your team doesn't get it, you have not kept things simple and you have failed. You must brief to ensure the lowest common denominator on the team understands.

It is critical, as well, that the operating relationship facilitate the ability of the frontline troops to ask questions that clarify when they do not understand the mission or key tasks to be performed. Leaders must encourage this communication and take the time to explain so that every member of the team understands.

Simple: this principle isn't limited to the battlefield. In the business world, and in life, there are inherent complexities. It is critical to keep plans and communication simple. Following this rule is crucial to the success of any team in any combat, business or life.

APPLICATION TO BUSINESS

"I don't have any idea what this means," the employee said as he held up a piece of paper that was supposed to explain his monthly bonus. "Point eight-four," he continued. "I have no idea what that number means. What I do know is that my bonus for this month was $423.97. But I have no idea why. Last month I made $279 bucks. Don't know why. I did the same amount of work; produced about the same amount of units. But for some reason, I got short-changed last month. What the hell?"

"Are they trying to get you to focus on one aspect of your job?" I inquired.

"Honestly, I have no idea," he replied. "I mean, I'm happy for the bonus, but I don't know what they want me to focus on."

I spoke to several other assembly technicians in this division on a visit to the manufacturing plant of a client company. Over and over again, I heard similar answers. People weren't sure what they should be focused on. They had no idea how their bonuses were calculated or why they were being rewarded or penalized in pay each month.

The next day I met with the chief engineer and plant manager. They were both extremely smart and passionate about the company and took a lot of pride in their products. They also recognized that there was a disconnect.

"We definitely are not maximizing our efficiency with our production staff," said the plant manager, her frustration evident.

"No doubt about it," explained the chief engineer. "We have a relatively small line of products here. There are some nuances, but they are all similar to produce. We thought we could ramp up production when we created the bonus plan, but it hasn't really worked."

"Yeah," added the plant manager, "there is real opportunity to make significant money through the bonus plan, but the employees on the line don't seem to adapt and focus to take advantage of it."

"Explain to me how the bonus system works," I said.

"OK. It's a little tricky," warned the plant manager.

"That's fine, I'm sure it can't be too hard," I replied, knowing that excessive complexity was one of the major problems of any SEAL unit (or any military unit) on the battlefield. It was essential to keep things simple so that everyone on the team understood.

"Honestly, it is pretty complex," the plant manager answered, "as there are a lot of different aspects that we needed to work in to ensure that the different facets of production were accounted for."

"Well maybe you could just give me the basics then," I requested.

The plant manager began: "OK. So it all starts off with a base level of productivity. Now, as you know, we have six different units that we assemble here, each with varying levels of complexity. So what we did was give them a weight. Our most commonly produced model sets the standard with a weight of 1.0. Our most complex model is weighted 1.75 and the simplest model is a .50, with the other models weighted somewhere in between based on the level of difficulty in assembly."

"Of course, those are what we call the 'base weights,'" added the chief engineer. "Depending on the orders we get for various models, we sometimes need to increase production of certain models, so we have a variable weight curve, which means the weight can be adjusted up or down depending on the specific demand at anytime."

"This is where we had to get crafty: we then take the total weighted number of units produced and we have a tiered efficiency metric," the plant manager said, clearly proud of the complex system they had developed. She explained in intricate detail how the variable tier system worked, stratified based on the number of people that made bonus in each tier every month.

"That way, a certain level of competitiveness is inspired and we prevent ourselves from paying out too many bonuses, which we feel would decrease their impact," concluded the plant manager.

But it didn't end there. She went into greater detail on how the efficiency metric was then compared to the employee's previous six-month tiered breakout and how an employee who maintained the top 25 percent stratification could receive an additional percentage on their bonus.

On top of that, they factored in the quality of the product. The chief engineer and the plant manager outlined a list of common faults, breaking these out as either "hold faults," which could be corrected, or "fatal faults," which rendered a unit unusable. For each fault and type of fault registered, a graduated weight system multiplied by a certain factor reduced an employee's potential bonus. A similar multiple added to the bonus for employees who had no registered faults in the units they produced. While the senior management expressed pride in the bonus system they had created, it was staggeringly complex.

I was quiet for a few moments. Then, I asked, "That's it?"

"Well," answered the plant manager, "there are several other little nuanced factors that we do calculate for—"

"Really?" I questioned, surprised that they didn't catch my sarcasm. "I'm kidding. That is crazy."

"Crazy? What's crazy?" she asked defensively.

They were so close to the bonus plan, so emotional and passionate about it, that they didn't recognize the vast complexity of it. They didn't see their own "fatal fault" in the confusing and elaborate scheme they had created, one that no one in the team understood.

"That is an extremely complex plan, *too* complex. I think you really need to simplify," I said.

"Well, it is a complex environment. Perhaps if we drew it out for you, you would understand it," the chief engineer responded.

"It doesn't matter if I understand it," I responded. "What matters is that *they* understand it—your production team. And not in some theoretical way. They need to understand it to a point that they don't need to be thinking about it to understand it. It needs to be on the top of their minds all the time."

"But we have to make sure we incentivize them in the right direction," said the chief engineer.

"Exactly," echoed the plant manager. "We have got to take the variables into account so that they are constantly pushed or pulled the right way."

They had each very clearly put extensive time and effort into the bonus plan and now tried desperately to defend their efforts despite its glaring overly complex deficiency.

"How well is this bonus plan working to incentivize them now?" I asked. "You just told me they aren't taking advantage of it, so they aren't being effectively incentivized to do anything differently or to move in any direction. Your plan is so complex that there is no way that they can mindfully move in the direction that would increase their bonus. Even when they use operant conditioning on rats, the rats have to understand what they are being punished or rewarded for. If there is not a strong enough correlation between the behavior and the reward or the punishment, then behavior will never be modified. If the rats don't know why they received a sugar pellet or why they were just given an electric shock, they will not change."

"So our people are rats?" the chief engineer said jokingly.

I laughed—it was funny—but then I replied, "No, not at all. But all animals, including humans, need to see the connection between action and consequence in order to learn or react appropriately. The way you have this set up, they can't see that connection."

"Well, they could see it if they looked and took the time to figure it out," replied the production manager.

"It certainly is possible that they *could*. But they *don't*. People generally take the path of least resistance. It is just in our nature. Let me ask you this: What kind of quantifiable lift have you gotten out of this incentive plan?" I asked.

"You know, honestly we haven't seen any real, meaningful pickup," the production manager admitted. "Definitely not as much as we thought we would."

"This actually isn't surprising to me," I said. "Your plan violates one of the most important principles we adhered to in combat: simplicity. When young SEAL leaders in training look at targets for training missions, they often try to develop a course of action that accounts for every single possibility they can think of. That results in a plan that is extraordinarily complex and very difficult to follow. While the troops might understand their individual pieces of the plan, they have a hard time following all the intricacies of the grand scheme. Perhaps they can even get away with that a few times if everything goes smoothly, but remember: the enemy gets a vote."

"The enemy gets a vote?" the plant manager repeated, questioning what that meant.

"Yes. Regardless of how you think an operation is going to unfold," I answered, "the enemy gets their say as well—and they are going to do something to disrupt it. When something goes wrong—and it eventually does—complex plans add to confusion, which can compound into disaster. Almost no mission ever goes according to plan. There are simply too many variables to deal with. This is where simplicity is key. If the plan is simple enough, everyone understands it, which means each person can rapidly adjust and modify what he or she is doing. If the plan is too complex, the team can't make rapid adjustments to it, because there is no baseline understanding of it."

"That makes sense," the chief engineer said.

"We followed that rule with everything we did," I continued. "Our standard operating procedures were always kept as simple as possible. Our communication plans were simple. The way we talked on the radio was as simple and direct as possible. The way we organized our gear, even the way we got a head count to ensure we had all of our people was broken down into the simplest possible method so we could do it quickly, accurately, and easily at any time. With all this simplicity embedded in the way we worked, our troops clearly understood what they were doing and how that tied in to the mission. That core understanding allowed us to adapt quickly without stumbling over ourselves."

"I can see how that would be a huge advantage," said the plant manager.

"OK then," I concluded. "We have nothing to lose. The best way to make your bonus plan work is to go back to the drawing board and try to figure out a new model for compensation, with two or three—no more than four—areas to measure and grade upon."

The chief engineer and the plant manager accepted the mission I laid out for them and headed back to their office to get to work.

The next day, I walked into the office. They had the plan written up on their dry-erase board. It had only two parts: (1) weighted units; (2) quality.

"That's it?" I inquired, this time without sarcasm.

"That's it," the plant manager replied. "Very simple. You produce as many units as you can. We will still adjust the weights of the units based on demand, but we will set the weights on Monday and let them stay there until Friday. That still gives us time the next week to make adjustments and change weights if demand spikes on a certain unit. And we are going to post the weights of each unit out there on the bulletin board so that every employee on the line sees it, knows it, and is thinking about it. The quality piece we will measure each month. Anyone with a quality score of ninety-five percent or higher will receive a fifteen percent increase in their bonus."

"I like it," I replied. This plan was much easier to communicate and much easier to understand. "When you need to adjust it, you will be able to do so with ease."

That afternoon, I watched as the chief engineer and the plant manager discussed the plan with the team leads and the afternoon shift. The response was great.

The employees now had a good understanding of what it was they needed to do to earn their bonus. As a result, the bonus now truly incentivized behavior and could thereby make the company more productive.

In the coming weeks, the plant manager and chief engineer reported an almost immediate increase in productivity. More employees focused their energy on what product would make them more money, which was of course aligned with the goals of the company. There were secondary effects as well. As the higher-producing employees strove harder to increase their bonuses, the lower-producing workers were left with less orders to fulfill. Within a month, the company let go the four employees with the lowest bonus scores, who had long been the weakest performers and had dragged the entire team down. Now, the company no longer needed them, as the rest of the crew had drastically increased their efficiency.

The most impressive thing about this improvement in performance was that it did not come from a major process change or an advance in technology. Instead, it came through a leadership principle that has been around for ages: Simple.

"Frogman on the roof," was the radio call that let friendly forces know SEALs were on the high ground. Here, SEAL machine gunner Marc Lee engages insurgents with lethal machine gun fire as another SEAL assesses the situation and a SEAL grenadier scans for targets.

(Photo courtesy of Todd Pitman)

CHAPTER 7
Prioritize and Execute

Leif Babin

SOUTH-CENTRAL RAMADI, IRAQ: THE HORNET'S NEST

All day, murderous bursts of machine gun fire hammered our position, shattering windows and impacting interior walls, each round with the violence and kinetic energy of a sledgehammer wielded at full force. Some of the incoming rounds were armor-piercing and punched through the thick concrete of the low wall surrounding the rooftop. All our element of SEALs, EOD bomb technicians and Iraqi soldiers could do under such accurate enemy fire was hit the deck and try not to get our heads shot off. Rounds snapped inches above us, and shards of glass and concrete fragments rained down everywhere.

"Damn! Some of these bastards can shoot!" yelled a SEAL operator pressed as close to the floor as humanly possible. We couldn't help but laugh at our predicament.

RPG-7 rockets followed in rapid sequence of three or four, exploding with tremendous concussion against the exterior walls. Hunkered down inside the building, we were separated from the bone-jarring explosions and deadly shrapnel by a foot or so of concrete. One errant RPG rocket missed its mark and sailed high over the building, trailing across the hazy, cloudless Iraqi summer sky like a bottle rocket on an American Fourth of July. But if just one of those rockets impacted a window, it meant red-hot fragments of jagged metal ripping through just about every man in the room.

Despite the onslaught, we held our position in the large four-story apartment building. When the fury of the attack subsided, our SEAL snipers returned fire with devastating effect. As armed enemy fighters maneuvered through the streets to attack, SEAL snipers squeezed off round after round with deadly accuracy, confirming ten enemy fighters killed and a handful more probable kills.

As the platoon commander, in charge of the entire element, I made my way from room to room on each floor to get a status check and make sure none of our guys were hit. Gathering information on our snipers' engagements, I passed situational reports over the radio to the U.S. Army's TOC in the distant friendly combat outpost.

"You guys good?" I asked, ducking into a room with SEAL snipers and machine gunners manning positions, while others took a break.

"Good to go," came the response.

In another room, I checked in with our SEAL platoon chief. Just then, enemy fire poured through the windows bracketing his position as he pressed against the corner wall. He laughed and gave me a thumbs-up. Chief was a badass. SEAL machine gunners came looking for work, and we directed their fire at the enemy's location; the gunners quickly hammered the enemy position with an accurate barrage of 7.62mm link.

One SEAL gunner, Ryan Job, eagerly employed his big machine gun with deadly accuracy. He fearlessly stood in the window braving incoming enemy rounds as he unleashed three to five round bursts of his own into insurgent positions. A group of armed insurgents tried to sneak up even closer to us using the concealment of a sheep pen to hide their movement. Ryan hammered them and beat back their attempt before it could even materialize. The sheep in the pen took some casualties in the crossfire.

"Damn," I told him. "Those sheep just took heavies."

"They were *muj* sheep," Ryan laughed.

I lobbed several 40 mm high-explosive grenades at a doorway where Chief had seen enemy fighters engaging us. *Whoomph!* sounded the explosion, as one round landed right inside the doorway with a fiery blast. That should keep their heads down for a little while at least.

Long before dawn broke that morning, before the day's first call to prayer echoed from the minaret speakers of the many mosques across South-Central Ramadi, our group of Charlie Platoon SEALs, our EOD operators (who were very much a part of our platoon), an interpreter, and Iraqi soldiers had stealthily foot-patrolled under the cover of darkness through the dusty, rubble-strewn streets. We had "BTF'ed in," as our chief called it. BTF stood for "Big Tough Frogman," an unofficial mantra adopted by Charlie Platoon. BTF entailed taking on substantial physical exertion and great risk and persevering by simply being a Big Tough Frogman. Pushing deep inside enemy territory was a BTF evolution. We knew it likely meant a gunfight was in store for us—what chief called a "Big Mix-It-Up." Our routine for most of these operations, in chief's terminology, was this: "BTF in, Big Mix-It-Up, BTF out." Then, once back on base, we'd hit the mess hall for "Big Chow."

We had patrolled out of COP Falcon in the early morning darkness through the densely packed urban neighborhood of two-story houses, adjoining compound walls, and heavy-duty metal gates. We "BTF'ed in" on foot for about 1.5 kilometers, carrying our heavy gear and substantial firepower, into another violent, enemy-held neighborhood of the city—an area firmly in the grasp of a brutal insurgency. Driven back from the areas to the east and the west, enemy fighters chose to stand and fight for this dirty patch of ground in the city's geographic center. We took position in a building just up the street from a mosque that frequently rallied the call to jihad from its minaret speakers to the hundreds of well-armed *muj* that occupied this area.

Not long before, off this very street, a large force of enemy fighters had attacked a squad of U.S. Marines and pinned them down for several hours before they could evacuate their wounded. Two weeks before, only a half block to the south, that street witnessed the destruction of a heavily armored U.S. mine-clearance vehicle by the massive blast of an IED. Nearly a dozen American tanks and armored vehicles had been destroyed in this section of the city. The "vehicle graveyard" back at Camp Ramadi became the final resting place for their charred wreckage. The burned-out hulks of blackened, twisted metal stood as a stark reminder of the intensity of violence in the streets and the many wounded and killed.

Our SEAL platoon had chosen this particular building for its commanding views of the area. Most important, it was right in the enemy's backyard. Here, insurgent fighters had enjoyed complete safe haven and freedom of movement. The frequent and intense onslaught of enemy machine gun fire and RPG rockets now served as a testament that our presence here was most unwelcome.

We had stirred up a hornet's nest, but it was exactly where we wanted to be. Our plan: go where the bad guys would least expect us in order to seriously disrupt their program, kill as many enemy fighters as we could, and decrease their ability to attack nearby U.S. Army and Marine combat outposts. We wanted the enemy to know that they no longer could enjoy safe haven here. This neighborhood was no longer theirs. We owned this ground.

Pushing this far into enemy territory carried tremendous risks. Though the nearest U.S. combat outpost was not more than 1.5 kilometers or so in a straight-line distance from our position, the extreme IED threat and heavy enemy presence could render any support we needed from tanks or armored vehicles extremely hazardous and difficult, if not impossible. Although our Army brethren would come to our aid if we called, we knew we would be putting them at great risk to do so. It was a tactic we had learned from the U.S. Marine companies stationed along the main route through the city: unless we had an urgent casualty, we would hold our position hunkered down right where we were. We would not call in vehicles or additional troops and put them at risk unless we took serious casualties and absolutely needed them.

The apartment building our SEAL platoon now occupied provided an excellent tactical position. With a higher vantage point above the buildings around us, its thick concrete walls provided some protection from enemy fire. There was only one problem: the building had only one entrance and exit from the second story—a narrow stairway leading down to the street. There was no way of watching the entrance or the street surrounding it during daylight without exposure to enemy fire. This meant the enemy could possibly emplace IEDs near the entrance while we were inside and detonate them on us as we exited. We had heard stories of how this had happened to a Marine sniper team and other American units during our tour. To counter the threat, my chief and I considered occupying a house across the street that would allow us to watch the entrance. But we didn't have the manpower. With no viable alternative, it was a vulnerability we were forced to accept. To mitigate the risk of an IED being planted at the doorstep, the EOD operators studied the area in detail around the exit door and planned a meticulous sweep for explosives prior to our anticipated departure later that night.

The onslaught of heavy enemy fire continued frequently throughout the day, with periods of intense violence and periods of calm. Enemy fighters attacked from multiple directions, and SEAL snipers engaged and killed many of them. Our SEAL machine gunners returned fire into enemy positions with devastating effect. Other SEALs fired LAAW (light anti-armor weapon) rockets and 40mm grenades at enemy fighters hiding behind concrete walls. Even the Iraqi soldiers, typically far more focused on self-preservation, joined in the fight and returned fire with their AK-47s and PKC belt-fed machine guns. As the day faded and the sun dipped below the horizon, the attacks diminished. Gunfire and explosions subsided. With the darkness an eerie quiet descended upon Ramadi, broken only by the evening call to prayer that echoed across the dusty rooftops.

Our SEAL platoon and Iraqi soldiers packed our gear and prepared to depart. Remembering the vulnerability of the single exit to the street, our two EOD bomb technicians went to work. Peering over the second story balcony through their night-vision goggles they scanned the area around the exit door and the surrounding street littered with trash and potholes, in some places scarred by the craters of previous IED blasts. But something was out of place; something looked different than when they had scanned the area in the early morning darkness before dawn. An otherwise unobtrusive item lay against the building wall only feet from the exit door, covered with a plastic tarp. Just a tiny sliver of a smooth, cylindrical object peeked out from under the edge of the tarp.

"Something looks suspicious," an EOD operator relayed to me. It was most unwelcome news, as the stairway to the street was our only easy means of departure.

I called a huddle with chief, our leading petty officer (LPO), and our platoon junior officers. "We need to figure another way out of here," I said. That was no easy task.

From the second story, three sides of the building offered a near-twenty-foot drop from a window or balcony straight down to the street. We had no rope. Jumping with all our gear and heavy equipment was likely to result in serious injury, and that same street had at least one explosive device. We had to assume there were more.

Somebody suggested a children's cartoon prison escape method: "What if we tie bed sheets together and climbed down from the third-story windows onto the rooftop next door?" It was a harebrained idea, but under the circumstances, an option that had to be seriously considered.

The fourth and remaining wall of the second story was solid concrete with no windows, doors, or openings. We certainly couldn't go around it or over it. But we could go through it.

"Looks like it's time to BTF," said the LPO. It meant we were about to tackle another serious feat of strength and toughness that would challenge us to our physical limits. But Charlie Platoon took great pride in accomplishing such feats. "Let's get our sledgehammer on!"

We always carried a sledgehammer with us to make entry through locked doors and windows when necessary. The LPO called for the "sledge" and went to work. He began swinging the hammer with full force against the concrete wall, each swing impacted with a loud, head-jarring *THWACK!* He and a handful of other SEALs rotated every few minutes as they hammered through the thick wall. It was painfully slow, back-breaking work. We needed a hole big enough for operators with rucksacks and heavy gear to walk through onto the flat rooftop of the one-story building next door.

In the meantime, our EOD operators carefully went to work

on the IED planted at our doorstep. Through meticulous investigation, they uncovered two 130mm rocket projectiles whose nose cones were packed with Semtex, a plastic explosive. Had they not discovered the device—and had we triggered it—the massive explosion and deadly shrapnel could have wiped out half our platoon. We couldn't leave this IED here to kill other U.S. Soldiers, Marines, or innocent Iraqi civilians. So EOD carefully set their own explosive charge on it to set it off (or "blow it in place") where it lay. Once prepared, the EOD operators notified me and waited for the command to "pop smoke" and ignite the time fuse that would initiate the charge.

After a solid twenty minutes of furious sledgehammering, the LPO and his rotating crew of BTF SEALs finally broke through the concrete wall. They were winded and sweating profusely in the sweltering heat, but we now had an alternate exit that would enable us to circumvent the IED threat.

Everyone double-checked their gear to ensure we left nothing behind, then we lined up next to the jagged hole in the wall and made ready to exit the building.

"Stand by to break out," I said over the intersquad radio. SEALs and Iraqi soldiers shouldered their rucksacks. "Pop smoke," I passed to the waiting EOD techs. One popped smoke while the other started a stopwatch that counted down to detonation. We now had only a few minutes to get everyone to a safe distance from what would be a significant blast. Swiftly, we pushed through the jagged hole in the concrete and onto the flat, dusty rooftop of the adjacent building. SEAL shooters fanned out, scanning for threats, weapons trained on the darkened windows and rooftops of the higher buildings surrounding us. Tactically, this was a hell of a bad position: a wide-open rooftop with no cover, surrounded by higher buildings all around, deep in the enemy's backyard after having taken heavy fire all day.

"We need a head count; make sure we got everybody," I said

to the LPO. The LPO had already positioned himself for this and was making it happen. Suddenly, a SEAL moving along the edge of the rooftop just steps ahead of me crashed through the roof and fell twenty feet to the ground, landing hard with a loud smack on the concrete.

Holy shit! I thought, standing just behind him. This was crazy. What had appeared in the darkness to be the edge of the rooftop was actually only a plastic tarp covered with dust. In an instant, things had spiraled into mayhem.

The SEAL lay on the ground groaning in pain. We called down to him and tried to contact him via his radio.

"Hey, you alright?" I asked him. There was no response. The SEALs up ahead immediately tried to find a way down to him, but the door to the only stairway leading down from the rooftop was blocked by a gate of heavy iron bars, chained and locked.

This was *bad*. Dreadfully exposed on a wide-open rooftop with no cover, we were completely surrounded by higher, tactically superior positions in the heart of an extremely dangerous, enemy-controlled area. Large numbers of enemy fighters had total freedom of movement here, had attacked us throughout the day, and knew our location. Even worse, the clock was ticking on an explosive charge that would set off a huge IED blast, throwing deadly metal fragments (or "frag") in all directions. Our SEAL element did not yet have a full head count to ensure all our personnel were out of the building. And now, one of our SEALs lay helplessly alone and unable to defend himself on the most dangerous street of the nastiest, enemy-held area in Ramadi and we couldn't get to him. His neck or back might be broken. His skull could be fractured. We had to get a SEAL corpsman—our combat medic—to him immediately. But we could not even reach him without breaking through a locked iron gate to get to the street below. The massive pressure of the situation bore down on me. This was a hell of a dilemma, one that could overwhelm even the most competent leader. How could we possibly tackle so many problems at once?

Prioritize and Execute. Even the greatest of battlefield leaders could not handle an array of challenges simultaneously without being overwhelmed. That risked failing at them all. I had to remain calm, step back from my immediate emotional reaction, and determine the greatest priority for the team. Then, rapidly direct the team to attack that priority. Once the wheels were in motion and the full resources of the team were engaged in that highest priority effort, I could then determine the next priority, focus the team's effort there, and then move on to the next priority. I could not allow myself to be overwhelmed. I had to relax, look around, and make a call. That was what Prioritize and Execute was all about.

Through dozens of intense training scenarios throughout the previous year, our SEAL platoon and task unit had rehearsed in chaotic and difficult situations. That training was designed to overwhelm us, to push us far outside our comfort zone, and force us to make critical decisions under pressure. Amid the noise, mayhem, and uncertainty of the outcome, we had practiced the ability to remain calm, step back from the situation mentally, assess the scenario, decide what had to be done, and make a call. We had learned to Prioritize and Execute. This process was not intuitive to most people but could be learned, built upon, and greatly enhanced through many iterations of training.

Here, I recognized our highest priority, and I gave the broad guidance to execute on that priority with a simple command: "Set security!" Though I, like everyone else in our platoon, wanted desperately to help our wounded man lying in the street below, the best way for us to do that was by occupying the strongest tactical position to defend ourselves. With threats all around and above us, we needed SEAL shooters in covering positions with weapons ready to engage any enemy threat to the men on the exposed rooftop, those SEALs and others still exiting the building, and the wounded man lying helpless in the street below.

Chief immediately stepped in and started directing shooters flowing through the hole in the wall and onto the rooftop. "Give me some guns over here!" he shouted.

Within moments, we had weapons, and in particular machine gunners, in key covering positions and had security set.

Second, the next priority: find a way down to get everyone off the exposed rooftop and get to our wounded man. To accomplish this, the SEALs up front needed a SEAL breacher to break through the locked iron gate to a stairwell that led down to the street. All the training had imparted the instinct of Prioritize and Execute on the whole platoon. The entire team would simultaneously assess problems, figure out which one was most important with minimal direction from me, and handle it before moving on to the next priority problem. And the SEALs up front who could see the locked gate got the job done with no direction needed. With a simple "breacher up" call, a breacher quickly moved forward and went to work on the gate to break through.

Third, the next priority: ensure a full head count of all personnel and confirm they had exited the building to a safe distance from the imminent explosion.

"Head count," I called to the LPO. Despite the immediate chaos around him, our LPO remained calm, stayed focused, and ensured a proper head count of every single person exiting the building.

Within moments, he let me know: "We're up," said the LPO. Everyone was out of the building, which included the operator who had fallen to the street. It was welcome news.

In less than a minute, the SEAL breacher broke through the

locked gate. Now, we had a way down to our wounded man and we could all get the hell off the exposed rooftop. If we got shot at here, with no cover, we would take substantial casualties.

"Let's move," I urged, as the voice of our chief joined in to assist in this effort, directing shooters to fall back to the stairwell down and keeping shooters with guns up to cover other SEALs as they descended to the street. SEAL shooters rushed down to the street below and set security there with weapons pointed up and down the street. Then others moved to recover the down man. With that, our entire element followed suit down the stairway and out onto the street. Once down, we moved out quickly to a safe distance from the impending IED blast. There, we halted briefly to double-check our head count to ensure no one was left behind. Fire team leaders reported to squad leaders, who reported to our LPO, who reported to me: "We're up." In only minutes from the time we exited the building, our SEAL platoon, EOD, and Iraqi soldiers moved out on foot to safety with a full head count.

BOOOOOOOOMMMMM!!!!! The deep concussion of the massive blast and huge fireball lit up the night and rained frag down for a full city block in all directions.

It was our EOD technician's explosive charge that set off the IED, right on time with their stopwatch. The terrific concussion shattered the stillness of the night. IEDs were devastating—and deadly. But no American or Iraqi troops would be wounded or killed by that particular one, thank God. Luckily, the SEAL operator who had fallen through the roof had landed on his rucksack, which helped break his fall. He was shaken up, with a nasty laceration on his elbow, but was otherwise OK. Upon our return to base, the docs sewed him up, and he was soon out with us again on the next operation.

PRINCIPLE

On the battlefield, countless problems compound in a snowball effect, every challenge complex in its own right, each demanding attention. But a leader must remain calm and make the best decisions possible. To do this, SEAL combat leaders utilize Prioritize and Execute. We verbalize this principle with this direction: "Relax, look around, make a call."

Even the most competent of leaders can be overwhelmed if they try to tackle multiple problems or a number of tasks simultaneously. The team will likely fail at each of those tasks. Instead, leaders must determine the highest priority task and execute. When overwhelmed, fall back upon this principle: Prioritize and Execute.

Multiple problems and high-pressure, high-stakes environments are not exclusive to combat. They occur in many facets of life and particularly in business. Business decisions may lack the immediacy of life and death, but the pressures on business leaders are still intense. The success or failure of the team, the department, the company, the financial capital of investors, careers, and livelihoods are at stake. These pressures produce stress and demand decisions that often require rapid execution. Such decision making for leaders can be overwhelming.

A particularly effective means to help Prioritize and Execute under pressure is to stay at least a step or two ahead of real-time problems. Through careful contingency planning, a leader can anticipate likely challenges that could arise during execution and map out an effective response to those challenges before they happen. That leader and his or her team are far more likely to win. Staying ahead of the curve prevents a leader from being overwhelmed when pressure is applied and enables greater decisiveness. If the team has been briefed and understands what actions to take through such likely contingencies, the team can then rapidly execute when those problems arise, even without specific direction from leaders. This is a critical characteristic of any high-performance, winning team in any business or industry. It also enables effective Decentralized Command (chapter 8).

When confronted with the enormity of operational plans and the intricate microterrain within those plans, it becomes easy to get lost in the details, to become sidetracked or lose focus on the bigger effort. It is crucial, particularly for leaders at the top of the organization, to "pull themselves off the firing line," step back, and maintain the strategic picture. This is essential to help correctly prioritize for the team. With this perspective, it becomes far easier to determine the highest priority effort and focus all energies toward its execution. Then senior leaders must help subordinate team leaders within their team prioritize their efforts.

Just as in combat, priorities can rapidly shift and change. When this happens, communication of that shift to the rest of the team, both up and down the chain of command, is critical. Teams must be careful to avoid target fixation on a single issue. They cannot fail to recognize when the highest priority task shifts to something else. The team must maintain the ability to quickly reprioritize efforts and rapidly adapt to a constantly changing battlefield.

To implement Prioritize and Execute in any business, team, or organization, a leader must:

- evaluate the highest priority problem.
- lay out in simple, clear, and concise terms the highest priority effort for your team.
- develop and determine a solution, seek input from key leaders and from the team where possible.
- direct the execution of that solution, focusing all efforts and resources toward this priority task.

- move on to the next highest priority problem. Repeat.
- when priorities shift within the team, pass situational awareness both up and down the chain.
- don't let the focus on one priority cause target fixation. Maintain the ability to see other problems developing and rapidly shift as needed.

APPLICATION TO BUSINESS
Jocko Willink

There was only one major problem: the company was losing money. Through years as a profitable player in the pharmaceutical industry, the company experienced several phases of expansion. All seemed well, but recently revenues had taken a slight downward trend. At first, that trend could be blamed on "market conditions" or "seasonal discrepancies," but when the downward trend continued, it was clear that the lower revenues had metastasized from temporary setback to the new reality.

The CEO of this pharmaceutical company brought me in for leadership training and consultation. The CEO and his executives prepared a "State of the Company" brief that detailed the company's strategic vision in order to improve performance. The brief included multiple sections, each with a number of tasks and projects embedded within.

He sat me down and ran through the brief so I could get a feel for what they were doing. It contained a plethora of new initiatives, each with its own set of challenges. First, the CEO planned to launch several lines of new product, each with its own marketing plan. With the aim of expansion, the CEO hoped to establish distribution centers in a dozen new markets in the next eighteen to twenty-four months. Additionally, he planned to break into the laboratory-equipment market, which he hoped to sell through their access to doctors and hospitals. The CEO also discussed a new training program designed to educate managers and improve their effectiveness as leaders. Additionally, the company planned a complete Web site overhaul to update their antiquated site and improve customer experience and branding. Finally, with the aim to improve sales, the CEO also planned to restructure the company's sales force and compensation plan. This entailed an activity-management system that would more efficiently focus the sales force on income-producing activities and reduce wasted time and effort. The CEO went into great detail through a multitude of very impressive sounding plans. He was clearly passionate about the company and excited to implement this array of new initiatives to get the company back on track. At the end of the brief, the CEO asked if I had any questions.

"Have you ever heard the military term 'decisively engaged'?" I asked.

"No, I haven't. I was never in the military," the CEO replied with a smile.

"Decisively engaged," I continued, "is a term used to describe a battle in which a unit locked in a tough combat situation cannot maneuver or extricate themselves. In other words, they cannot retreat. They *must* win. With all your new initiatives, I would say you have a hell of a lot of battles going on," I observed.

"Absolutely. We are spread pretty thin," the CEO acknowledged, wondering where this was going.

"Of all the initiatives, which one do you feel is *the most important*?" I asked. "Which one is your *highest priority*?"

"That's easy," the CEO quickly answered. "The activity management of our sales force is the highest priority. We have to make sure our sales people are engaged in the right activities. If they aren't getting in front of customers and selling our products, we will no longer be in business," said the CEO.

"With all that you have planned, do you think your team is clear that this is your highest priority?" I asked.

"Probably not," the CEO admitted.

"On the battlefield, if the guys on the front line face-to-face with the enemy aren't doing their jobs, nothing else matters. Defeat is inevitable," I replied. "With all your other efforts—all your other focuses—how much actual attention is being given to ensuring your frontline salespeople are doing the best job possible? How much of a difference would it make if you and the entire company gave them one hundred percent of your attention for the next few weeks or months?"

"It would probably make a huge difference," the CEO admitted.

"As a SEAL, I often saw this with junior leaders on the battlefield," I continued. "With so much going on in the chaos and mayhem, they would try to take on too many tasks at once. It never worked. I taught them to Prioritize and Execute. Prioritize your problems and take care of them one at a time, the highest priority first. Don't try to do everything at once or you won't be successful." I explained how a leader who tries to take on too many problems simultaneously will likely fail at them all.

"What about all the other initiatives?" the CEO asked. "They will help us as well."

"I'm not saying to throw them away," I replied. "They sound like great initiatives that are definitely important. But you won't move the needle on them when you are spread so thin. My suggestion is to focus on one and when that one is completed, or at least has some real momentum, then you move on to the next one and focus on it. When that one is done, then move on to the next, and so on down the line until you have knocked them all out."

"Makes sense," the CEO replied. "I'll give it a try." He was eager to turn the company's performance around.

For the next several months the CEO focused the efforts of the entire company on supporting the frontline sales force, making it clear that this was the company's highest priority. The labs set up tours for customers. The marketing designers helped create new, informative pamphlets for products. Sales managers set minimum marks for the number of introductory meetings with doctors and medical administrators that the sales force had to achieve each week. The company's marketing team created online videos interviewing their top salespeople on the most successful techniques so that others could watch and learn. It was a full focus of effort on the highest priority initiative to increasing the company's business.

This focus on a singular initiative unified the efforts of the entire company. Progress was seen quickly and gained momentum. The CEO recognized the traction, and the effectiveness of the method: Prioritize and Execute.

Sunrise over South-Central Ramadi. An M2 Bradley Fighting Vehicle provides cover for American and Iraqi troops on the ground and a SEAL sniper overwatch out beyond the forward line of advance. The morning call to prayer signaled daybreak in Ramadi, soon followed by vicious enemy attacks that continued throughout the day.

(Photo courtesy of the authors)

CHAPTER 8
Decentralized Command

Jocko Willink

SOUTH-CENTRAL RAMADI, IRAQ: A RECKONING

"We've got armed enemy fighters on top of a building. Appear to be snipers," the radio blared. The concern and excitement in the American Soldier's voice relaying the information was evident.

This report was alarming and immediately struck a cord with everyone on the radio net. Enemy snipers were deadly. While they could never compare to the level of skill, training, and equipment that our own U.S. military snipers possessed, the enemy certainly had some skilled marksmen who inflicted substantial damage, regularly killing or wounding American and Iraqi soldiers with accurate rifle shots.

Two different elements of our Task Unit Bruiser SEALs were out there in enemy territory among a hostile insurgent force with friendly U.S. Army troops moving into the area. My job was command and control of thirty plus SEALs and their partner force of Iraqi soldiers, but I could only manage this effectively through Decentralized Command. It was the only way to operate.

•   •   •

On the battlefield, I expected my subordinate leaders to do just that: *lead*. I had groomed and trained them—Leif and his fellow SEAL officers, their platoon chiefs, and senior petty officers—to make decisions. I trusted that their assessment of the situations they were in and their decisions would be aggressive in pursuit of mission accomplishment, well thought out, tactically sound, and would ultimately further our strategic mission. They confirmed that trust over and over again throughout our months in Ramadi. Leif and my other leaders were put in some of the worst situations imaginable: enemy fire, confusion and chaos, friendly fire, and worst of all, the pain and emotion of our brother SEALs wounded or killed. In each of those situations, they led with authority and courage, making rapid, sequential, life and death decisions in harrowing situations with limited information. I trusted them.

They had earned that trust through many months of training, of getting it wrong and learning from their mistakes as I watched them closely and coached them in the leadership principles I had learned through fifteen years in the SEAL Teams. Both of my platoon commanders were relatively new to the Teams, but luckily, they were both eager to learn, eager to lead, and most important, humble yet confident to command.

But once we were in Ramadi, I could no longer be with them to look over their shoulders and guide them. I had to empower them to lead. After seeing them evolve during our training cycle into bold, confident leaders, I knew Leif in Charlie Platoon and his fellow platoon commander in Delta Platoon would make the right decisions. And I knew they would ensure that their subordinate leaders within each of their platoons would make the right decisions. I unleashed them on the battlefield to execute with full confidence in their leadership.

Pushing the decision making down to the subordinate, frontline leaders within the task unit was critical to our success. This

Decentralized Command structure allowed me, as the commander, to maintain focus on the bigger picture: coordinate friendly assets and monitor enemy activity. Were I to get embroiled in the details of a tactical problem, there would be no one else to fill my role and manage the strategic mission.

The proper understanding and utilization of Decentralized Command takes time and effort to perfect. For any leader, placing full faith and trust in junior leaders with less experience and allowing them to manage their teams is a difficult thing to embrace. It requires tremendous trust and confidence in those frontline leaders, who must very clearly understand the strategic mission and ensure that their immediate tactical decisions ultimately contribute to accomplishing the overarching goals. Frontline leaders must also have trust and confidence in their senior leaders to know that they are empowered to make decisions and that their senior leaders will back them up.

This skill of Decentralized Command had not been magically bestowed upon Task Unit Bruiser. It had come only through difficult preparation and training, driven home during the months of effort before we deployed to Iraq. We learned our greatest lessons in this during MOUT (military operations, urban terrain) training at Fort Knox, Kentucky. There, under intense pressure and extremely challenging scenarios, we learned how to employ this tenet effectively in even the most chaotic scenarios.

The MOUT facility was a multiblock mock city of concrete structures, ranging from simulated one-room houses to large and complex multistory buildings built to prepare military units for the challenges of urban combat—exactly the environment in which U.S. forces were then heavily engaged in Iraq. The SEAL training detachment, or TRADET (which I would later command), was tasked with preparing SEAL platoons and task units for deployments to Iraq and Afghanistan, and we knew they would put us through the ringer. The TRADET instructor cadre constructed training scenarios to confuse, disorient, physically and mentally stress and overwhelm the participating SEAL units, particularly the leaders. The instructor cadre would "mud-suck"* us at every turn. Their role players acting as "enemy forces" in the training scenarios often wouldn't follow the rules of play. Some SEALs scoffed at this, thinking the training was unrealistically challenging, and accused TRADET of cheating.

I disagreed. The enemy we would face in Iraq had no rules. They didn't care about collateral damage. They didn't care about fratricide or friendly fire. Iraqi insurgents were experts at analyzing and exploiting our weaknesses. They were brutal savages, and their method of operation was to think of the most horrific, cowardly, and *effective* ways to kill us. So we actually *needed* TRADET to do the same thing to us.

During the first few days of Task Unit Bruiser's MOUT training, my SEAL leaders tried to control everything and everyone themselves. They tried to direct every maneuver, control every position, and personally attempted to manage each one of their men—up to thirty-five individuals in Task Unit Bruiser. It did not work. In a striking realization that military units throughout history have come to understand by experience, it became clear that no person had the cognitive capacity, the physical presence, or the knowledge of everything happening across a complex battlefield to effectively lead in such a manner. Instead, my leaders learned they must rely on their subordinate leaders to take charge of their smaller teams within the team and allow them to execute based on a good understanding of the broader mission (known as Commander's Intent), and standard operating procedures. That was effective Decentralized Command.

So, we divided into small teams of four to six SEALs, a man-

---

* a SEAL term for a serious cheap shot or sucker punch

ageable size for a leader to control. Each platoon commander didn't worry about controlling all sixteen SEAL operators assigned, only three: his squad leaders and his platoon chief. Each platoon chief and leading petty officer only had to control their fire team leaders, who each controlled four SEAL shooters. And I only had to control two people— my two platoon commanders.

Each leader was trusted to lead and guide his team in support of the overall mission. Those junior leaders learned that they were expected to make decisions. They couldn't ask, "What do I do?" Instead, they had to state: "This is what I am *going to do*." Since I made sure everyone understood the overall intent of the mission, every leader worked and *led* separately, but in a unified way that contributed to the overall mission, making even the most chaotic scenarios much easier to handle.

When Task Unit Bruiser deployed to Ramadi, Iraq, Decentralized Command played a crucial role in our success. We supported many large-scale operations and participated in virtually every big push into Ramadi, as coalition forces established footholds in enemy territory.

A few months into our deployment, we conducted our largest operation yet. It included two different U.S. Army battalions, each with hundreds of Soldiers, a U.S. Marine battalion, nearly one hundred armored vehicles on the ground, and American aircraft in the skies overhead. Many of these units operated on different communications networks, which greatly added to the complexity and compounded the risk.

Our SEAL sniper teams would lead the way into the area of operations. By occupying the high ground with the best visibility over the battlefield, Task Unit Bruiser SEALs would gain substantial tactical advantage over the enemy and protect other U.S. forces on the ground. But all this movement could create chaos. My job was to provide command and control to coordinate between my SEAL sniper overwatch teams from Charlie and Delta Platoons and the U.S. Army and Marine Corps units.

This operation centered around a major north–south road that was sandwiched between two notoriously violent neighborhoods— the Mala'ab District, a war-torn neighborhood to the east, and to the west, the J-Block: an American designation for an equally violent section of Central Ramadi. In the Mala'ab, Task Unit Bruiser suffered our first casualty during the initial weeks of our deployment. A young SEAL operator sustained a gunshot wound from an enemy armor-piercing machine gun round, which shattered his femur and ripped a massive hole in his leg. SEAL machine gunner Mike Monsoor laid down suppressive fire and helped drag him out of the street to safety. Luckily, the wounded SEAL survived and returned to the States for a long road to recovery. The SEALs in Corregidor were in firefights on an almost daily basis in the Mala'ab.

Leif and the SEALs of Charlie Platoon had been likewise heavily engaged in constant gun battles with enemy fighters. In the J-Block, only a couple of weeks prior, Ryan Job was shot in the face by an enemy sniper and left blind. Later, on the same day Ryan was wounded, Marc Lee was shot and killed just down the street in the J-Block from where Ryan had been wounded. Marc was the first member of Task Unit Bruiser killed in action and the first Navy SEAL killed in Iraq.

We were still reeling from those losses suffered during what was one of the most furious battles that had taken place in Ramadi. Leif had also been wounded, hit in the back with a round during the battle. Although injured, it had not stopped him from continuing to lead during that operation. Nor had it dulled his desire to hunt down the enemy and kill them.

It was no coincidence that our largest operation would take place in this area. It was a reckoning.

The operation began as our SEALs, under cover of darkness,

patrolled on foot into position—Charlie Platoon from COP Falcon to the west, and Delta Platoon from COP Eagle's Nest to the east. They passed their positions over the radio periodically so that I, staged with our Army counterparts at COP Falcon, and other friendly forces could track their movement.

Both Charlie and Delta Platoons had preselected locations for their sniper overwatch positions based on careful map studies of the area. With the greater strategic picture to coordinate, I had left this entirely up to them. They also had full authority to shift locations if those preselected positions weren't adequate once they were on the ground. As they had been trained, the senior leader of each SEAL sniper overwatch element made their decisions based on the underlying commander's guidance that drove our overwatch operations:

1. Cover as many possible enemy ingress and egress routes as possible.
2. Set up positions that mutually support each other.
3. Pick solid fighting positions that could be defended against heavy enemy attack for an extended period of time if necessary.

With their lives and the lives of their men at risk, my platoon commanders understood this guidance as well—perhaps even better than I. Therefore, I did not need to spell it out for each operation; it was embedded in their thoughts. With it, my frontline leaders were empowered to make the tactical decisions during the operation. They were the ones who were on scene to make the call while I was located over a kilometer away at COP Falcon, tracking the mission alongside the U.S. Army commanders.

Sometimes, despite detailed map studies and planning, my frontline leaders discovered that their preplanned locations were not viable. On numerous occasions, our overwatch elements arrived at a building they had planned to utilize only to realize that the building was set farther back from the road than it appeared on the map or did not have optimal angles to cover enemy routes and protect friendly positions. Other times, the building was surrounded by "dead-space"—areas that would be difficult to see and difficult to defend. Then it was up to the platoon leadership to select another building that could best accomplish the mission.

Here, Decentralized Command was a necessity. In such situations, the leaders did not call me and ask me what they should do. Instead, they told me what they were going to do. I trusted them to make adjustments and adapt the plan to unforeseen circumstances while staying within the parameters of the guidance I had given them and our standard operating procedures. I trusted them to *lead*. My ego took no offense to my subordinate leaders on the frontlines calling the shots. In fact, I was proud to follow their lead and support them. With my leaders running their teams and handling the tactical decisions, it made my job much easier by enabling me to focus on the bigger picture.

On this particular operation, Charlie Platoon's preplanned position worked well. But Delta Platoon realized that they could not utilize the building they had planned to use. Delta's platoon commander and his senior platoon leadership scouted out another building that could work. The commander radioed and told me his platoon would move across the street to the other building, building 94.

I responded to him over the radio, "This is Jocko; I copy you want to move to building 94. Do it." Delta Platoon then immediately pushed this information to the rest of the friendly forces, including the U.S. Army battalion staff and company leadership with which I was co-located at COP Falcon. I sat back and watched as their plan was relayed and ensured the information was clear at higher headquarters. Once all friendly forces had been notified, and Delta Platoon confirmed that, they initiated movement into the newly selected building.

Building 94 proved to be a very good vantage point. One of the tallest buildings in the area, at four stories in height, it had a clear view of the major north–south road and of the location where the Army would soon construct COP Grant, the new combat outpost. Building 94 was easily defensible, and offered good firing positions that covered many potential enemy routes in and out of the area.

Once Delta Platoon was in position, their radioman reported, "Building 94 secure. Overwatch positions set in the fourth story and on rooftop."

"Copy," I acknowledged.

The radioman then relayed that information to other units in the area, and I confirmed that the other units understood the location of Delta's new position.

With Charlie and Delta Platoons now secured in their positions, American troops flooded into the area. This stage of the mission left U.S. forces highly vulnerable. With no permanent security yet in place, brave Army engineers began building the COP, a construction project in a hostile combat zone. Tensions rose in the streets and among the command-and-control element I was with back at COP Falcon. As friendly forces moved in, reports of possible enemy movement came in over the radio nets: lights came on in buildings, while in others, lights went out; vehicles started up, departed driveways, and moved through the streets; a military-age male maneuvered through the alleyways observing friendly troop movements. A report described a possible enemy force of two to four military-age males exiting a building and dispersing. Other men were seen talking on radios.

This was the most nerve-racking time—before the shooting started, waiting with anxious anticipation for a fight to happen. Our SEALs and the hundreds of U.S. troops in this operation had fought fierce battles with the enemy in the bordering neighborhoods for the past several months. Much American blood had been spilled, including the blood of our SEAL brothers. Now it was only a matter of time before the enemy attacked, which we expected would be ferocious.

Then, from a Bradley Fighting Vehicle equipped with thermal sight for nighttime operations, the report came over the radio: "We've got armed enemy fighters on top of a building. Appear to be snipers."

A single enemy bullet had struck Ryan Job, severely wounding him, leaving him blind, and eventually leading to his death. A young Marine from 2nd ANGLICO, whom we frequently worked with, had been shot and killed by a single rifle shot just a few weeks before. Many others had been wounded or killed by a single round. Just as our snipers struck fear into the hearts of our enemy, an enemy sniper was a nightmare scenario for us: shooting accurately from unseen positions, inflicting casualties, and fading away. So now this report across the net that enemy snipers had been spotted caused everyone's defenses to spike and escalated the tensions in their trigger fingers.

Charlie and Delta Platoons, in their separate overwatch positions, heard the report on their radios and were also amped up by the call. Perhaps one or more of these enemy snipers were the culprits responsible for shooting Ryan and our Marine comrade. Any one of our SEALs would gladly eliminate the enemy snipers with lethal force. But despite the romantic vision of a sniper-versus-sniper stalking and shooting match, our preferred contest was a much more lopsided affair: enemy sniper versus the massive firepower of a U.S. M1A2 Abrams Main Battle Tank. An enemy sniper might barricade himself in a room behind sandbags and concrete. While this made for a difficult rifle shot, it was no match for the tanks' electronically enhanced optics and giant 120mm smoothbore cannon fired from behind the safety of heavy armor. We all hoped for a quick engagement by the Bradley that had spotted the enemy sniper.

Of course, I wanted as much as anyone to see an enemy sniper or, even better, multiple snipers eliminated. But this was a complex battlefield, which could confuse and confound even the most experienced Soldiers and SEALs. The fog of war in a chaotic urban environment grows thick rapidly and could muddle even the most seemingly obvious situations.

The company commander (a U.S. Army captain) in charge of the Bradley Fighting Vehicle that reported the enemy snipers was an exceptional warrior and leader, whom our SEALs had come to deeply respect and admire. He and his Soldiers were an outstanding group. We had formed a tremendous bond with them through dozens of operations working together. Our SEAL snipers supported their operations, and they in turn responded continuously to our calls for help by rolling out in their tanks down extremely dangerous, uncleared roads to bring firepower to bear and provide evacuation of our SEAL casualties. Every time we called for help, the company commander fearlessly placed himself and his men at great risk. He personally saddled up and drove out in his tank to bring the thunder on our behalf and beat back enemy attacks on SEAL positions. Now, the company commander heard the report of enemy snipers. He responded over his radio, "Give a description of the target."

The Bradley's vehicle commander answered: "Several military-age males on a rooftop. They appear to have some heavy weapons, and some have what appear to be sniper weapons with scopes."

Monitoring the radio calls, I stood next to the company commander in the makeshift TOC inside COP Falcon. Knowing I had SEAL snipers on the rooftop near where the enemy was spotted, I quickly asked, "Find out what building number they see the enemy in." The company commander radioed his Bradley commander for an exact position.

"Building 79," replied the Bradley vehicle commander.

"Your guys aren't in building 79, are they?" the company commander asked me, just to be sure.

I looked at my battle map to coordinate the numbers I was hearing over the net. I located building 79, just down the street from where Delta Platoon was located, in building 94.

"Negative," I replied to the captain. "I've got SEALs in building 94; not in 79."

"Alright. Let's engage!" said the captain, fired up to take out some enemy snipers. Every one of us was eager to hammer enemy fighters and protect the U.S. troops on the ground in harm's way. But we had to be sure.

"Stand by," I said. "Let's confirm what we have here."

I keyed up my radio to talk to my SEALs on the less formal net that only we utilized. I spoke directly to Delta's platoon commander: "We have some enemy activity in your vicinity, possible snipers; want to engage with a Bradley main gun.* I need you to confirm your position—one hundred percent."

"Roger," he replied, "I have already triple-checked. Building direct to our south is 91. South of that is the road. The roof of our building has an L-shaped room on the roof. You can see it on the battle map. I'm sitting in it. It is confirmed: we are in building 94. One hundred percent. Over."

I acknowledged the Delta Platoon commander's transmission. Then, to the company commander next to me, I said, "It's confirmed, my guys are in building 94."

"Alright then, lets hammer these guys," the company commander replied.

"Hold on," I said, checking one more time. "Let's confirm what your guys are seeing."

"We have confirmed: enemy snipers on the rooftop of building 79," responded the company commander. "There are no

---

* 25mm chain gun with high-explosive rounds

other friendlies in that building. We need to engage while we can." He didn't want to miss a critical chance to take out enemy snipers.

I didn't like the idea of delaying an opportunity to eliminate enemy snipers any more than he did. But knowing the confusing chaos of the urban battlefield and how easily mistakes can happen, I had to be certain.

"Do me a favor," I asked the company commander. "Just to confirm, have your Bradley vehicle commander count the number of buildings he sees from the major intersection [where he was positioned] up to the building where he has eyes on the enemy snipers."

The company commander looked at me with a little frustration. If these were indeed enemy snipers, they might target U.S. forces at any moment. Allowing them to live even for a few more minutes meant they might very well kill Americans.

"I just want to be sure," I added. The company commander didn't work for me. I couldn't order him to delay. But through multiple combat operations together with our SEALs in this difficult environment, we had developed a strong professional working relationship. He loved our SEALs and appreciated the damage we inflicted on the enemy. He now trusted me enough to comply with my request.

"OK," he said. The company commander keyed up his radio and instructed his Bradley vehicle commander: "For final confirmation, count the number of buildings from the intersection where you're located to the building where you see the enemy snipers."

The Bradley vehicle commander paused at this, likely wondering why he was being asked to do this while enemy snipers waited to attack. But he did as directed, replying on the radio, "Roger that. Stand by."

It should have taken no more than fifteen seconds to count

the buildings up the block to the target building, but the silence over the radio was longer—too long.

Finally, the radio silence broke: "Correction: The suspected enemy position is Building 94. I say again, 94. I counted the buildings up the block. We misjudged the distance. Over."

"Hold your fire!" the company commander quickly said with authority over his battalion net, recognizing that the "enemy" reported in building 94 were really friendlies. "All stations: Hold your fire. Personnel in building 94 are friendly. I say again, building 94 is a friendly position. We have SEAL snipers on the roof of that building."

"Roger," said the Bradley vehicle commander in a solemn tone, recognizing his mistake had almost caused fratricide.

"Roger," answered the captain. Alarmed at how easily such a mistake could happen and acknowledging how deadly and devastating it could have been, the company commander looked at me and said heavily, "That was a close one."

Without formal street signs or numbers—with confusing intersections and alleyways—such a mix-up was something that could easily happen. But had they engaged, it would have been horrific. The 25mm heavy gun from the Bradley fired high explosive rounds that would have ripped through the rooftop, likely killing or wounding multiple SEALs in that position.

Thankfully, our troop operated under Decentralized Command. My platoon commanders didn't just tell me what the situation was, but what they were going to do to fix it. That sort of Extreme Ownership and leadership from my subordinate leaders not only allowed them to lead confidently, but also allowed me to focus on the bigger picture—in this case, monitoring the actions of coordinating units in this dynamic environment. Had I been engulfed in trying to lead and direct Charlie and Delta Platoons' tactical decisions from my distant position, I may very well have missed the other events unfolding. This could have had catastrophic results.

Instead, Decentralized Command worked and enabled us, as a team, to effectively manage risk, prevent disaster, and accomplish our mission. Soon, the real enemy fighters struck with violent attacks to protect "their" territory along the central north–south street. But our enemy's enthusiasm was extinguished quickly when SEAL snipers and machine gunners killed them in the very streets they aimed to defend. Decentralized Command enabled us to operate effectively on a challenging battlefield and support our U.S. Army comrades to construct the new combat outpost and ensure more Soldiers came home safely. Ultimately, this furthered the strategic mission to stabilize Ramadi and secure the populace, which would prove highly successful over the coming months.

PRINCIPLE

Human beings are generally not capable of managing more than six to ten people, particularly when things go sideways and inevitable contingencies arise. No one senior leader can be expected to manage dozens of individuals, much less hundreds. Teams must be broken down into manageable elements of four to five operators, with a clearly designated leader. Those leaders must understand the overall mission, and the ultimate goal of that mission—the Commander's Intent. Junior leaders must be empowered to make decisions on key tasks necessary to accomplish that mission in the most effective and efficient manner possible. Teams within teams are organized for maximum effectiveness for a particular mission, with leaders who have clearly delineated responsibilities. Every tactical-level team leader must understand *not just what to do but why they are doing it*. If frontline leaders do not understand why, they must ask their boss to clarify the why. This ties in very closely with Believe (chapter 3).

Decentralized Command does not mean junior leaders or team members operate on their own program; that results in chaos. Instead, junior leaders must fully understand what is within their decision-making authority—the "left and right limits" of their responsibility. Additionally, they must communicate with senior leaders to recommend decisions outside their authority and pass critical information up the chain so the senior leadership can make informed strategic decisions. SEAL leaders on the battlefield are expected to figure out what needs to be done and do it—to tell higher authority what they plan to do, rather than ask, "What do you want me to do?" Junior leaders must be proactive rather than reactive.

To be effectively empowered to make decisions, it is imperative that frontline leaders execute with confidence. Tactical leaders must be confident that they clearly understand the strategic mission and Commander's Intent. They must have implicit trust that their senior leaders will back their decisions. Without this trust, junior leaders cannot confidently execute, which means they cannot exercise effective Decentralized Command. To ensure this is the case, senior leaders must constantly communicate and push information—what we call in the military "situational awareness"—to their subordinate leaders. Likewise, junior leaders must push situational awareness up the chain to their senior leaders to keep them informed, particularly of crucial information that affects strategic decision making.

With SEAL Teams—just as with any team in the business world—there are leaders who try to take on too much themselves. When this occurs, operations can quickly dissolve into chaos. The fix is to empower frontline leaders through Decentralized Command and ensure they are running their teams to support the overall mission, without micromanagement from the top.

There are, likewise, other senior leaders who are so far removed from the troops executing on the frontline that they become ineffective. These leaders might give the appearance of control, but they actually have no idea what their troops are doing and cannot effectively direct their teams. We call this trait "battlefield aloofness." This attitude creates a significant disconnect between leadership and the troops, and such a leader's team will struggle to effectively accomplish their mission.

Determining how much leaders should be involved and where leaders can best position themselves to command and control the team is key. When SEAL task units train in assaults—in what we call close-quarters battle, or CQB—we practice this in a "kill house." A kill house is a multiroom facility with ballistic walls, which SEALs, other military, and police units use to rehearse their CQB skills. For young SEAL officers learning the ropes of leadership, running through the kill house with the platoon provides a great training opportunity to determine how much they should be involved and where to position themselves. Sometimes, the officer gets so far forward that he gets sucked into every room clearance, meaning he is continually entering rooms and engaging targets. When that happens, he gets focused on the minutia of what's going on in the immediate room and loses situational awareness of what is happening with the rest of the team and can no longer provide effective command and control. Other times, the officer gets stuck in the back of the train, on cleanup duty. When that happens, he is too far in the rear to know what is happening up front and can't direct his assault force. I advised many officers that the right amount of involvement—the proper position for them—was somewhere in the middle, generally with the bulk of their force: not so far forward that they get sucked into every room clearance, but not so far back that they don't know what is going on up front. Contrary to a common misconception, leaders are not stuck in any particular position. Leaders must be free to move to where they are most needed, which changes throughout the course of an operation. Understanding proper positioning as a leader is a key component of effective Decentralized Command, not just on the battlefield. In any team, business, or organization, the same rule applies.

The effectiveness of Decentralized Command is critical to the success of any team in any industry. In chaotic, dynamic, and rapidly changing environments, leaders at all levels must be empowered to make decisions. Decentralized Command is a key component to victory.

APPLICATION TO BUSINESS

"Can I take a look at your org chart?" I asked the regional president of an investment advisor group. The "org chart" depicted his team's organizational structure and chain of command. Responsible for dozens of branches and over a thousand employees, the president was smart and driven. He didn't have a great deal of leadership confidence, though he seemed eager to learn.

"We don't really have one that is current," the president responded. "I like to hold that information close. If it gets out and people see it, they might get upset that they actually report to someone they see as one of their peers. I've had to deal with this before."

"So how do they know who is in charge?" I asked. "Without a clear chain of command—people knowing who is in charge of what—you cannot have empowered leadership. And that is critical to the success of any team, including the SEAL Teams or your company here."

"Let me pull up what we have," said the president.

He opened a document on his computer and swung an organizational chart onto the large plasma screen on the wall of the conference room.

I stood up and took a look. The team for which he was responsible was a region of substantial size and breadth. There were branches spread across a huge geographic area of the United States.

But there was something that stood out to me. The org chart lacked uniformity and seemed disorganized.

"What's this here?" I asked, as I pointed to a location that listed twenty-two people who worked there.

"That's a branch," the president answered.

"And who leads all those people?" I asked.

"The branch manager," he responded.

"He leads all twenty-one of those people? They all report to him?" I inquired.

"Yes, he is in charge of them all," said the president.

I looked at another area on the org chart. I tapped another office location, this one with three people in it. "And what is this here?" I asked.

"That is also a branch," the president replied.

"Who leads these people?" I asked again.

"The branch manager," he said.

"He leads two people?" I asked.

"That's right," said the president.

"So one branch manager leads twenty-one people, and the other branch manager leads two people?" I clarified.

"Yeah . . . a little strange, but it makes sense on the ground," the president offered.

"How?" I asked. If it wasn't clear to me looking at the org chart, I knew it was highly likely that it didn't make sense to the frontline troops that were out there executing the company's mission.

"Well, the bigger branches have more people because they are more successful, and they generally have a stronger manager. Because he or she is effective, the branch grows and requires more employees, which increases the number of direct reports. Over time some branches can get pretty big," the president explained.

"What happens to the efficiency of the branch when they grow?" I asked.

"You know, honestly, once a branch reaches a certain size, rapid growth slows," he admitted. "The branch manager usually just focuses on the best performers, and the rest kind of get lost in the shuffle of day-to-day business. Over time, most of these branch managers seem to lose track of the bigger picture of what we are trying to do and where we are strategically trying to grow."

"And what about the smaller branches?" I asked. "Why do they not grow?"

"Surprisingly, it is for a similar reason," he replied. "When a branch only has a couple people in it, there isn't enough revenue for the branch manager to really make money. So those managers are forced to personally generate business themselves. When they are in the field selling, they generally don't have time to focus on leadership and management of their teams and they lose track of the bigger picture—building and growing."

"So what would you say the ideal size would be for a team or branch in your company?" I asked.

"Probably five or six, four or five financial advisors and support people," answered the president.

"That makes perfect sense," I said. "The SEAL Teams and the U.S. military, much like militaries throughout history, are based around building blocks of four-to-six-man teams with a leader. We call them 'fire teams.' That is the ideal number for a leader to lead. Beyond that, any leader can lose control as soon as even minimal pressure is applied to the team when inevitable challenges arise."

"So how do you lead larger teams on the battlefield?" asked the president with genuine curiosity.

"Sometimes for our units, we can operate with as many as one hundred fifty personnel on a particular operation," I answered. "While we might only have fifteen or twenty SEALs, when you tack on Iraqi soldiers and mutually supporting troops from the

U.S. Army or Marine Corps, our ranks could easily grow to over a hundred or a hundred and fifty," I explained. "But the truth is, even with all those men out there, I could only truly lead, manage, and coordinate with about four to six, max."

I could see this had sparked some interest with the president. "That is why we had to utilize Decentralized Command," I explained. "I couldn't talk to every shooter in every platoon, squad, and fire team. I would talk to the platoon commander. He would take my guidance and pass it down to his squad leaders. His squad leaders would pass it on to their fire team leaders. And they would execute. If there was an Army company supporting us, I would talk to the company commander, or perhaps one of the platoon commanders, and again, they would pass my guidance down to their subordinate leadership."

"Couldn't things get confused? Like in the old game of telephone, where you whisper a word around a circle of people and it comes back different from how it started?" asked the president.

"That is why simplicity is so important," I answered. "Proper Decentralized Command requires simple, clear, concise orders that can be understood easily by everyone in the chain of command. I spelled out my Commander's Intent directly to the troops so they would know exactly what the ultimate goal of the mission was. That way they would have the ability to execute on the battlefield in a manner that supported the overarching goal, without having to ask for permission. Junior leaders must be empowered to make decisions and take initiative to accomplish the mission. That was critical to our success on the battlefield. And it will greatly help you here."

"But can't you end up with a bunch of little individual elements just doing whatever they want—helter-skelter?" asked the president with skepticism.

"You could end up with that *if* you, as a leader, failed to give clear guidance and set distinct boundaries," I explained. "With clear guidance and established boundaries for decision making that your subordinate leaders understand, they can then act independently toward your unified goal."

"I get it," said the president—"a mission statement."

"That's part of it," I replied, "but there is more. A mission statement tells your troops what you are doing. But they have got to understand *why* they are doing it. When the subordinate leaders and the frontline troops fully understand the purpose of the mission, how it ties into strategic goals, and what impact it has, they can then lead, even in the absence of explicit orders."

"That makes sense," he acknowledged.

"The teams have to be small enough that one person can truly lead them," I continued. " 'Span of control' is the commonly used business term. How many people can a leader effectively lead? In combat, depending on the experience and quality of the leader, the skill level and experience of the troops, and the levels of violence and potential mayhem in an area; those numbers vary. You need to find out the optimal size for your teams. And if it is five or six, with a leader at the top, then that is the way you should set them up."

From a leadership perspective, I explained to the president, there is truly nothing more important than an understanding of the dynamics of Decentralized Command. This is proper command and control in a nutshell. It is one of the most complex strategies to pull off correctly. As a leader, it takes strength to let go. It takes faith and trust in subordinate, frontline leaders and their abilities. Most of all, it requires trust up and down the chain of command: trust that subordinates will do the right thing; trust that superiors will support subordinates if they are acting in accordance with the mission statement and Commander's Intent.

Trust is not blindly given. It must be built over time. Situations will sometimes require that the boss walk away from a problem and let junior leaders solve it, even if the boss knows he might solve it more efficiently. It is more important that the junior leaders are allowed to make decisions—and backed up even if they don't make them correctly. Open conversations build trust. Overcoming stress and challenging environments builds trust. Working through emergencies and seeing how people react builds trust.

"Junior leaders must know that the boss will back them up even if they make a decision that may not result in the best outcome, as long as the decision was made in an effort to achieve the strategic objective," I explained, "That complete faith in what others will do, how they will react, and what decisions they will make is the key ingredient in the success of Decentralized Command. And this is integral to the success of any high-performance winning team."

"Understood," the president replied. "I will make it happen."

PART III

SUSTAINING VICTORY

SEAL Team Three, Task Unit Bruiser, Charlie Platoon Mission Planning Space at Camp Marc Lee. Ordnance table with ammunition at the ready, including loaded rifle magazines, machine gun rounds, hand grenades, signal flares, 40mm grenades, and 84mm rockets. The photos on the wall commemorate fallen SEAL brothers Mike Monsoor (left), Marc Lee (center), and Ryan Job (right) who later died after a surgery to repair wounds received in combat.

(Photo courtesy of the authors)

CHAPTER 9

Plan

Leif Babin

RAMADI, IRAQ: HOSTAGE RESCUE

"They have IEDs buried in the yard and bunkered machine gun positions in the house," said our intelligence officer with a grave look of concern.

It was a hostage rescue mission, the ultimate high-stakes operation: not only bad guys to kill, but an innocent victim to save. We had trained for missions like this, but they were rare. Now Task Unit Bruiser had the opportunity to execute such an operation for real.

A young Iraqi teenager, the nephew of an Iraqi police colonel, had been kidnapped by an al Qaeda–linked terrorist group. They demanded his family pay a $50,000 ransom and threatened to behead the young man otherwise. Kidnappings and beheadings were common occurrences in Ramadi and Anbar Province in those days. Often the hostages were tortured or killed, even if the family paid the ransom. These terrorist kidnappers were evil people, plain and simple, and could be counted on to carry out their gruesome threat. For Task Unit Bruiser, there was no time to waste. We needed to put together a plan in a hurry, brief that plan to our troops, and launch as soon as possible.

Our intelligence indicated the hostage location was a house on the outskirts of a Ramadi suburb. The roads into the area were heavily IED'ed, and the threat extremely high. It was a dangerous, enemy-controlled neighborhood. But that's where the hostage and the bad guys who held him were believed to be, and we had to figure out the best way into and out of the area. Our plan had to maximize the chance of mission success while minimizing the risk to our assault force of SEALs, EOD bomb technicians, and our partner force of Iraqi soldiers.

Task Unit Bruiser had an intelligence department of a dozen SEAL and non-SEAL support personnel. At the head of Bruiser's intel shop was a young ensign (the most junior officer rank in the Navy) recently graduated from the U.S. Naval Academy. He wasn't a SEAL. His specialty was intelligence. He was new and inexperienced, but he was smart, hardworking, and highly motivated. In deference to the character from Comedy Central's *South Park* cartoon series, we nicknamed this young intelligence officer "Butters." Butters and his team of intelligence specialists data-mined hundreds of reports and gathered as much information as they could to help facilitate our planning. Meanwhile, we—the Task Unit Bruiser SEALs—set about putting together the plan.

As Charlie Platoon commander, I would serve as assault force commander for more than a dozen SEALs, an EOD technician, and fifteen Iraqi soldiers who would enter and clear the house. Jocko, as Task Unit Bruiser commander, would be the ground force commander with responsibility for command and control of all assets—the assault force, our vehicles, aircraft, and any other supporting elements—involved in the operation.

With the clock ticking, we analyzed the mission, laid out what intelligence we had, and detailed the supporting assets that were available: our own armored Humvees and two U.S. Navy HH-60

Jocko Willink (left) and Leif Babin (right) at Camp Marc Lee in 2006 just prior to the launch of a combat mission in Ramadi, Iraq, with Task Unit Bruiser. (Courtesy of the authors)

Frogmen on the high ground: Task Unit Bruiser SEALs take the rooftop during a heavy firefight (or "Big Mix-It-Up") with insurgents in the Mala'ab District of eastern Ramadi. Marc Lee at left. (Courtesy of Todd Pitman)

Jocko's office: Task Unit Bruiser's Tactical Operations Center, the main building on Camp Marc Lee, once belonged to Saddam Hussein's regime. The stairs, at left, are those described in the opening of chapter 4 as SEALs raced to the rooftop under fire and engaged enemy fighters shooting at them from across the nearby Euphrates River. (Courtesy of the authors)

Camp Marc Lee. Task Unit Bruiser's Navy combat engineers, known as "Sea Bees," constructed this sign at the entrance of what was previously known as "Sharkbase," on the outskirts of the larger U.S. base of Camp Ramadi. We named the camp in recognition of the heroism and sacrifice of Marc after he was killed in action on August 2, 2006. The tents in the background (at left) are where Charlie Platoon and Task Unit Bruiser SEALs slept. The tactical operations center building, Jocko's office, is at right in the distance. (Courtesy of the authors)

Improvised explosive devices (IEDs) were the enemy's most devastating weapon in Iraq, accounting for the vast majority of American casualties. Here, what remains of a large mine-resistant ambush protected (MRAP) vehicle from Task Force Dagger, the IED clearance team, is towed into Combat Outpost Falcon in July 2006. The vehicle sustained catastrophic damage from an IED at a major intersection in South-Central Ramadi. Charlie Platoon snapped this photograph prior to stepping off on a foot patrol to set up a sniper overwatch on this intersection in the building described in the events of chapter 7. (Courtesy of the authors)

Just back from a nighttime combat operation, SEALs and explosive ordnance disposal operators from Charlie Platoon, Task Unit Bruiser, congregate on Camp Ramadi in the pre-dawn haze as they wait for transport of prisoners and intelligence gathered on the operation. Then, it was off to "Big Chow" at the Camp Ramadi chow hall. (Courtesy of the authors)

Jocko Willink (left) and Leif Babin (right) prior to a joint keynote presentation for DrivingSales Executive Summit in the Bellagio Grand Ballroom, Las Vegas, Nevada, in October 2015, the week *Extreme Ownership* was published. (Courtesy of the authors)

Jocko Willink presents leadership lessons learned in combat during a keynote presentation for Echelon Front. (Courtesy of the authors)

Leif Babin discusses the leadership lessons learned from the Battle of Ramadi during a keynote presentation for Echelon Front. (Courtesy of Echelon Front)

Cover and Move: Jocko Willink (left) and Leif Babin (right) debrief with a team of business leaders following a simulated combat field training exercise. (Courtesy of Echelon Front)

Jocko Willink delivers a speech on Extreme Ownership for TEDx at the University of Nevada in 2016. (Courtesy of Chris Holloman, TEDx)

Jocko Willink (left) and Leif Babin (right) engage the audience in a question and answer session at the first-ever Extreme Ownership Muster (Muster 001) in San Diego, California, on October 21, 2016, with over three hundred highly engaged leaders and aspiring leaders in attendance. Ten years earlier to the day, Jocko and Leif departed Ramadi, Iraq, together with the last of Task Unit Bruiser's personnel for the return home. (Courtesy of Echelon Front)

The Echelon Front team at Extreme Ownership Muster 002 in New York City on May 4, 2017: from left to right, Leif Babin, J. P. Dinnell, Dave Berke, Echo Charles, and Jocko Willink. (Courtesy of Echelon Front)

Discipline Equals Freedom: Participants at Extreme Ownership Muster 001 in San Diego push themselves during the 0445 Club (4:45 a.m.) workout as Jocko and Leif provide encouragement to GET AFTER IT. (Courtesy of Echelon Front)

"Own everything in your world." An engaged audience of leaders capture combat lessons learned for application to their lives at Extreme Ownership Muster. (Courtesy of Echelon Front)

Stand by to get some: Nearly three hundred participants gather in Times Square for the 0445 Club (4:45 a.m.) workout at Muster 002 in New York City, May 4, 2017. (Courtesy of Echelon Front)

Muster: to gather together a group of people for the preparation of battle or war; a formal gathering of troops for inspection; a call to formation for the purpose of careful examination; to bring into being or action. (Courtesy of Echelon Front)

Seahawk helicopters. We put together a solid plan. A small team of SEAL snipers would clandestinely move into position some distance away to maintain eyes on the target and cover our assault force as we approached the target building. Our assault force would then enter the house, clear all rooms, eliminate threats, and (with any luck) recover the hostage. Jocko would remain with the vehicles and coordinate supporting assets until the target building was clear. We would all then return to base and get the hostage to medical care.

Moving with a purpose, I drove across Camp Ramadi, the large U.S. base on the outskirts of the city where the bulk of American forces lived and worked, for a quick meeting with the U.S. Army company commander in charge of the area where the target building was located. The major and his company had been deployed to Ramadi more than a year. They had fought fierce battles against a deadly enemy all through this particular section of the city, had lost several brave Soldiers, and suffered many more wounded. He knew the neighborhood like the back of his hand. His tanks and troopers would support us on the operation in the event we got in a bind. The major and his company were U.S. Army National Guardsmen, which meant that at home they were part-time Soldiers. Back in the world, he was a schoolteacher. But here in Ramadi, he and his men were full-time warriors, and damn good ones. He was an outstanding combat leader and professional officer. We had tremendous respect for the major and his company and valued his expertise in the area. I went over our plan with him, and he gave me some pointers as to how we could best get into the area undetected, and how his Abrams tanks and Bradley Fighting Vehicles might best support us. I listened carefully.

Back at our SEAL camp, known as "Sharkbase,"* we finalized

---

* We later changed the name to Camp Marc Lee in honor of Marc, the first SEAL killed in action in Iraq.

an innovative plan designed to catch the terrorists by surprise and reduce risk to our force while giving us the greatest chance of success. We then gathered all the SEAL operators into the mission planning space to brief the plan. In addition to the SEALs, EOD bomb technicians, and interpreters who would accompany us on the operation (we would link up later and brief the Iraqi troops), we pulled in the key support personnel from our task unit, who would remain behind and man the TOC. It was critical that we all understood the plan, how and when to communicate and what to do if and when things went wrong. Time was of the essence if we were to succeed in this hostage rescue. Quickly, we powered through the brief.

I gave my closing comments as assault force commander. Our shooters had just been fed a lot of information. My final remarks were a way to prioritize that information—the three most important things I wanted the assault force to remember and keep first and foremost in their minds:

1) Maintain the element of surprise; stealth is more important than speed as we approach this target.
2) After the breach, once we make entry, speed is most important. Let's get this target cleared and secured in a hurry.
3) Good PID (positive identification) of any potential threats. Be wary not to injure the hostage. And be ready to render medical assistance.

As ground force commander in charge of the operation, Jocko gave his closing comments, simplifying the complex legalese of our rules of engagement into a clear, concise statement that everyone understood: "If you have to pull the trigger, make sure the people you kill are bad."

With that, the brief concluded and SEALs streamed out of the building. Everyone jocked up in their op gear, loaded vehicles, and conducted final equipment checks in a hurry. Jocko and I were the only ones left in the mission planning space talking through final big-picture details of our plan.

Suddenly, Butters burst into the room. "We just got some new intel," he said, in a concerned and excited voice. "They have IEDs buried in the yard and bunkered machine gun positions in the house." It meant the terrorists holding this hostage were ready for a fight, and the risk to our force was high. Butters stared at us with a grave look of concern.

Jocko looked at me. "I guess you guys are gonna get some," he said with a confident smile and a nod. He fully understood the risks. But he also knew our plan was sound and our assault force and supporting assets were well prepared to meet the enemy threat.

"I guess so," I said, smiling back at Jocko and nodding in agreement, adding a phrase we used when facing anything particularly challenging or miserable: "Good times."

We walked out to the vehicles, where our SEAL assaulters and vehicle crews were standing by, ready to depart.

"Here's the latest intel update," I passed to the troops. I told them about the reported IEDs in the yard and bunkered machine gun positions.

"Roger that," came the response from several SEALs. "Let's get some."

They were fired up. That was the Task Unit Bruiser way.

It wasn't cockiness or overconfidence. On the contrary, each man knew this was a dangerous operation and that he might very well come home in a body bag. But despite the new intelligence, we were confident in our plan. Our goal was to maintain the element of surprise and hit the bad guys before they even realized we were there. This would give us the greatest chance to rescue the hostage alive and protect SEAL assaulters from enemy threats. After the brief, each individual operator understood the overall plan, his specific role, and what to do if things went wrong. Then we quickly walked through the operation in rehearsal with full gear. As a result, we were confident we could execute with proficiency. We had addressed and mitigated every risk that we could through planning. But *every* risk could not be controlled. This mission was inherently dangerous. Whether or not we could rescue the hostage alive would remain to be seen.

We loaded up our vehicles and launched on the operation, driving out the gate and into the darknesss.

As we staged our vehicles some distance away, the assault force dismounted and lined up in patrol formation. I listened for updates from our sniper overwatch on my radio.

"No movement on target," they reported. "All looks quiet." Of course that didn't mean all was truly quiet, but only that they couldn't see any movement.

The night was dark as the assault force stepped off and swiftly but silently made our way up to the target building. As the assault force commander, I served as a double-check to my point man's navigation to ensure that we were in the right place. I kept my head on a swivel, constantly looking around to keep an eye on the target building and on the rest of the assault force.

As we crept closer, you could feel the tension rising. Once at the target, EOD led the way scanning for IED threats. Our SEAL breach team moved to the entry door and placed a big explosive breaching charge on the door.

BOOM!

It's on, I thought to myself.

With an Iraqi hostage to rescue, we had planned to let the Iraqi soldiers lead the way. But typical for our partner force, they choked with fear and balked at stepping over the shattered and twisted metal of the door and into the smoke-filled room beyond. From here, every nanosecond counted. Our SEAL combat advisors, ready for this contingency, grabbed the Iraqi soldiers and unceremoniously flung them through the door and into the house. This was no time to delay.

Our SEAL assault force followed right on the Iraqi soldiers' heels, and when the Iraqis again failed to enter the next room, our SEALs quickly took the lead and rapidly cleared the house. Within a minute, every room had been cleared and all prisoners were under our control.

"Target secure," I called. No shots had been fired. Now we had to figure out who we had captured.

A bewildered young Iraqi teen was among those we had detained. We pulled him aside and, after some questioning through the interpreter, confirmed he was indeed the hostage who had been kidnapped. Marc Lee, part of the SEAL assault force, was never one to miss an opportunity to insert humor into any situation. Marc boldly strolled up to the Iraqi kid and, in his best impersonation of Lieutenant James Curran played by the actor Michael Biehn in the 1990 movie *Navy SEALs*, said: "We're a SEAL Team, we're here to get you out. There's no reason to thank us because we don't exist. You never saw us. This never happened." We got a good laugh at that as the Iraqi kid, who didn't speak a word of English, was nonetheless thankful and clearly relieved to have been rescued from his captors.

The plan had been perfectly executed. The first clue the bad guys had that SEALs were there was when their door blew in. We caught them completely by surprise in a manner they had not expected. I made my way to the rooftop of the target building, keyed up my radio, and called Jocko, who was now with the blocking force outside: "Jocko, this is Leif. Target secure." I passed our proword for "we have the hostage."

We had rescued the hostage alive and in one piece. We gave our Iraqi soldiers all the credit. The positive strategic impact of our Iraqi partner force successfully rescuing an Iraqi hostage was substantial. It served as a big win for the fledging Iraqi security forces in liberating the local populace from the brutality of the insurgency.

Best of all, none of our guys were hurt. We found no IEDs buried in the yard or bunkered machine gun positions in the house, though certainly the kidnappers had access to such weapons. We were lucky. But we had also made our luck. We had maintained the element of surprise. Our plan had worked like a charm, a testament to the solid mission planning skills we had developed in Task Unit Bruiser. Having the humility to lean on the expertise of the good U.S. Army major and his Soldiers who lived and fought in this area for a full year had helped us greatly in this success.

Back in San Diego a year later, I served as a leadership instructor at our SEAL basic training command. I used this very scenario for a leadership decision-making exercise. To a classroom filled with newly promoted SEAL platoon commanders and platoon chiefs, I set up the scenario: Iraqi kid held hostage, known location, hostage rescue mission planned and ready to go. "Just before launch," I told them, "the intelligence officer informs you there are IEDs buried in the yard and bunkered machine gun positions in the house. What do you do?"

There were varying degrees of combat experience among the participants in the room.

"Don't go," said one SEAL officer. "It's not worth the risk." Some in the room agreed.

A platoon chief said, "Replan the mission." Several others agreed with him.

I paused for a few moments to let them consider the options.

"Let me ask you a question," I said to the class. "On what capture/kill direct-action raid can you be certain there are no IEDs buried in the yard or bunkered machine gun positions in the house?"

Heads shook around the room. The answer was obvious: none. You could never assume that such hazards weren't waiting for you on a target. You had to assume they were, and you had to plan for them on *every* operation and mitigate the risk of those threats as much as possible. To assume otherwise was a failure of leadership. That was what mission planning was all about: never taking anything for granted, preparing for likely contingencies, and maximizing the chance of mission success while minimizing the risk to the troops executing the operation.

In Task Unit Bruiser, we were able to launch that hostage rescue operation, despite the new intel of deadly threats, because we had already taken those things into account and planned accordingly. We had implemented specific steps to mitigate the risk of potential IEDs in and around the target building. We had carefully planned our operation to maintain the element of surprise, so that even if the bad guys were manning bunkered machine gun positions, they wouldn't know we were coming until it was too late. Therefore, we didn't need to replan the operation. We were ready. And as a result of good planning and solid execution of that plan—combined with a little luck—we were successful.

Understanding how SEALs plan a combat mission provides techniques that apply across the spectrum. For any team in any business or industry, it is essential to develop a standardized planning process.

PRINCIPLE

What's the mission? Planning begins with mission analysis. Leaders must identify clear directives for the team. Once they themselves understand the mission, they can impart this knowledge to their key leaders and frontline troops tasked with executing the mission. A broad and ambiguous mission results in lack of focus, ineffective execution, and mission creep. To prevent this, the mission must be carefully refined and simplified so that it is explicitly clear and specifically focused to achieve the greater strategic vision for which that mission is a part.

The mission must explain the overall purpose and desired result, or "end state," of the operation. The frontline troops tasked with executing the mission must understand the deeper purpose behind the mission. While a simple statement, the Commander's Intent is actually the most important part of the brief. When understood by everyone involved in the execution of the plan, it guides each decision and action on the ground.

Different courses of action must be explored on how best to accomplish the mission—with the manpower, resources, and supporting assets available. Once a course of action is determined, further planning requires detailed information gathering in order to facilitate the development of a thorough plan. It is critical to utilize all assets and lean on the expertise of those in the best position to provide the most accurate and up-to-date information.

Leaders must delegate the planning process down the chain as much as possible to key subordinate leaders. Team leaders within the greater team and frontline, tactical-level leaders must have ownership of their tasks within the overall plan and mission. Team participation—even from the most junior personnel—is critical in developing bold, innovative solutions to problem sets. Giving the frontline troops ownership of even a small piece of the plan gives them buy-in, helps them understand the reasons behind the plan, and better enables them to believe in the mission, which translates to far more effective implementation and execution on the ground.

While the senior leader supervises the entire planning process by team members, he or she must be careful not to get bogged down in the details. By maintaining a perspective above the microterrain of the plan, the senior leader can better ensure compliance with strategic objectives. Doing so enables senior leaders to "stand back and be the tactical genius"—to identify weaknesses or holes in the plan that those immersed in the details might have missed. This enables leaders to fill in those gaps before execution.

Once the detailed plan has been developed, it must then be briefed to the entire team and all participants and supporting elements. Leaders must carefully prioritize the information to be presented in as simple, clear, and concise a format as possible so that participants do not experience information overload. The planning process and briefing must be a forum that encourages discussion, questions, and clarification from even the most junior personnel. If frontline troops are unclear about the plan and yet are too intimidated to ask questions, the team's ability to effectively execute the plan radically decreases. Thus, leaders must ask questions of their troops, encourage interaction, and ensure their teams understand the plan.

Following a successful brief, all members participating in an operation will understand the strategic mission, the Commander's Intent, the specific mission of the team, and their individual roles within that mission. They will understand contingencies—likely challenges that might arise and how to respond. *The test for a successful brief is simple: Do the team and the supporting elements understand it?*

The plan must mitigate identified risks where possible. SEALs are known for taking significant risk, but in reality SEALs calculate risk very carefully. A good plan must enable the highest chance of mission success while mitigating as much risk as possible. There are some risks that simply cannot be mitigated, and leaders must instead focus on those risks that actually can be controlled. Detailed contingency plans help manage risk because everyone involved in the direct execution (or in support) of the operation understands what to do when obstacles arise or things go wrong. But whether on the battlefield or in the business world, leaders must be comfortable accepting some level of risk. As the U.S. Naval hero of the American Revolution and Father of the U.S. Navy, John Paul Jones, said: "Those who will not risk cannot win."*

The best teams employ constant analysis of their tactics and measure their effectiveness so that they can adapt their methods and implement lessons learned for future missions. Often business teams claim there isn't time for such analysis. But one must make time. The best SEAL units, after each combat operation, conduct what we called a "post-operational debrief." No matter how exhausted from an operation or how busy planning for the next mission, time is made for this debrief because lives and future mission success depend on it. A post-operational debrief examines all phases of an operation from planning through execution, in a concise format. It addresses the following for the combat mission just completed: What went right? What went wrong? How can we adapt our tactics to make us even more effective and increase our advantage over the enemy? Such self-examination allows SEAL units to reevaluate, enhance, and refine what worked and what didn't so that they can constantly improve. It is critical for the success of any team in any business to do the same and implement those changes into their future plans so that they don't repeat the same mistakes.

---

* Quote from U.S. Naval Academy Web site, Public Affairs Office, John Paul Jones quotes, www.usna.edu/PAO/faq-pages/JPJones.php.

While businesses can have their own planning process, it must be standardized so that other departments within the company and supporting assets outside the company (such as service contractors or subsidiary companies) can understand and use the same format and terminology. It must be repeatable and guide users with a checklist of all the important things they need to think about. The plan must be briefed to the participants, geared toward the frontline troops charged with execution so they clearly understand it. Implementing such a planning process will ensure the highest level of performance and give the team the greatest chance to accomplish the mission and win.

A leader's checklist for planning should include the following:

- Analyze the mission.
  - Understand higher headquarters' mission, Commander's Intent, and endstate (the goal).
  - Identify and state your own Commander's Intent and endstate for the specific mission.
- Identify personnel, assets, resources, and time available.
- Decentralize the planning process.
  - Empower key leaders within the team to analyze possible courses of action.
- Determine a specific course of action.
  - Lean toward selecting the simplest course of action.
  - Focus efforts on the best course of action.
- Empower key leaders to develop the plan for the selected course of action.
- Plan for likely contingencies through each phase of the operation.
- Mitigate risks that can be controlled as much as possible.
- Delegate portions of the plan and brief to key junior leaders.
  - Stand back and be the tactical genius.

- Continually check and question the plan against emerging information to ensure it still fits the situation.
- Brief the plan to all participants and supporting assets.
—Emphasize Commander's Intent.
—Ask questions and engage in discussion and interaction with the team to ensure they understand.
- Conduct post-operational debrief after execution.
—Analyze lessons learned and implement them in future planning.

APPLICATION TO BUSINESS

"We've got to establish a planning process," said the company's vice president of emerging markets. "Our success has stemmed from sending our experienced people into new areas. They figure things out, put a plan in action, and as a result, we win. But as our company grows—as we enter new markets—we need a standardized process for planning, a repeatable checklist others with less experience can follow."

The emerging-markets VP was an impressive leader and a key driver of the company's overall success. Like a good SEAL combat leader, he was aggressive and exercised Extreme Ownership to solve challenges and accomplish his mission. While he didn't have much patience for the company's bureaucracy, his drive made him highly successful, and he pushed his team to the highest standards of performance. His leadership and personal efforts had directly contributed to the company's rapid expansion and growth, with hundreds of new retail stores and hundreds of millions of dollars in revenue. His team was highly effective, establishing strong footholds in areas that had traditionally been dominated almost exclusively by their competitors. They were making bold moves and, as a result, huge gains.

I had just delivered an Echelon Front presentation on SEAL

leadership concepts to his emerging markets team, and in the discussion afterward, the VP had turned to planning.

"I constantly harp on my team about planning," said the VP. He asked one of his key leaders, a regional manager, "How many times have you heard me harp on planning?"

"Constantly," the regional manager responded. I could tell the regional manager respected her boss, but her body language indicated she didn't share his concerns about the importance of establishing a planning process. No doubt she was thinking: *We're doing well. Why do I need to take on the additional pain and paperwork requirement of writing down a planning process and teaching it to my key leaders?*

But she was wrong. And her boss—the emerging markets VP—had great strategic vision in understanding the importance of planning for the company's long-term success.

"Early in my career as a SEAL officer, there was a time when I felt that military mission planning was needless and burdensome," I told them. "But I was wrong. Establishing an effective and repeatable planning process is critical to the success of any team."

I told them how I had learned proper mission planning and briefing through years of trial and error and many, many mistakes and iterations of doing it wrong. It started back in my earliest days of SEAL training.

The PLO is for the boys. It was a statement often repeated in SEAL platoons and task units when I first joined the SEAL Teams. That statement implied that the brief for a combat mission should be designed and developed for the SEAL operators that would execute the operation. PLO stood for "platoon leader's order," a term used by SEALs since the Vietnam era. The rest of the U.S. military called it an operations order (OPORD). After 9/11, joint operations in close coordination with U.S. Army, Marines, and

Air Force, through the wars in Afghanistan and Iraq, caused SEALs to adopt the OPORD term. But by whatever name, it meant the same thing: a mission brief. This brief laid out the specific details of who, what, when, where, why, and how a combat operation would be conducted. The OPORD was prepared for and given to the SEAL operators and supporting assets who were to participate in an operation. It was supposed to allow every member of a SEAL element and other U.S. (or foreign allied) forces involved to understand the overall plan, their role in the plan, what to do when things went wrong, and how to contact help if the worst-case scenario took place. A good plan was critical to mission accomplishment, and briefing that plan to the troops enabled effective execution of the plan. Without successful execution, the best-laid plans were worthless.

The trouble was, as a new SEAL officer in training, *The PLO is for the boys* concept simply hadn't held true. In training scenarios I had encountered, the PLO or OPORD brief had, in reality, always seemed to be about impressing the instructors or the senior officer in the room with our PowerPoint prowess. Through more than a year and a half of training in the SEAL pipeline, there were always SEAL instructors and/or SEAL officers sitting in on the brief to evaluate. Without fail, the instructor staff would tear apart our plan and, in particular, our brief, hitting every detail. Their criticism focused mostly on the presentation slides themselves, with one clear message: there needed to be more—more slides, more graphs, more timelines, more charts, more phase diagrams, more imagery, more everything. It was humbling but also overwhelming.

As a junior officer in a SEAL platoon, my job was to oversee the plan and put together the OPORD brief to best capture the tactical plan developed by our SEAL chief, a number of key players within the platoon, and me. I would compile all the information together into a Microsoft PowerPoint presentation and along with those key players deliver it to the operators in the SEAL platoon and troop that would execute the mission. While the junior SEAL operators were preparing gear and the SEAL chiefs and leading petty officers were debating tactics and figuring out who was in charge of what portion of the mission, the officers worked on PowerPoint slides to assemble all this information into a brief.

Military mission planning seemed daunting. There were so many moving pieces and parts to every combat operation; so many variables. The OPORD briefing format we were given was developed for a 96-hour planning cycle: it assumed we would have at least four days to prepare for a combat mission. The format consisted of more than seventy PowerPoint slides. In actual practice, we had only a few hours to plan for our training exercises, so the long and detailed format invariably left us far too little time. We wasted most of our efforts building slides and neglected important pieces of the plan.

On my first deployment as a SEAL officer, we deployed to Baghdad, Iraq. The war in Iraq at that time thrust many U.S. military units into heavy combat. But I didn't get to experience the flood of combat operations as I had hoped. We spent most of our time providing security for one of the top officials of the interim Iraqi government. And I spent most of my time in the tactical operations center sitting at a desk making phone calls, monitoring our team via radio, and building PowerPoint slides. As SEAL officers, we were so inundated with PowerPoint that some officers had patches made for their uniforms to jokingly designate themselves "PowerPoint Rangers, 3,000 hours." It was typical SEAL humor to laugh at the misery.

Luckily, my executive officer saw the importance of getting his young leaders into combat, and he tasked me to lead a small element of SEALs in a series of sniper missions supporting a battalion of the historic "Big Red One"—the U.S. Army's 1st Infantry

Division—in the city of Samarra. We were able to make a difference and lower the number of attacks on U.S. Army Soldiers. But after three weeks, we only had one confirmed kill on an enemy fighter and a couple more probable kills. We coordinated with the Army units but didn't really conduct any detailed planning or briefing. If anything, I learned some bad habits when it came to planning.

When I joined Task Unit Bruiser at SEAL Team Three and became platoon commander for Charlie Platoon, I began working for Jocko. He expected me (and my key leaders in Charlie Platoon) to utilize the standard planning process used by small units in the rest of the military. He expected us to own it—Extreme Ownership.

Through a six-month-long training workup, Task Unit Bruiser learned to work together as a team across the full spectrum of SEAL operations in a host of different environments. At the end of every block of training, the final phase culminated in a series of field training exercises (FTXs). These were full-scale training missions that required us to put together a plan, brief that plan to our troops, and then execute. Our performance in training would dictate where we would be sent on deployment.

Of the three SEAL task units at our team, not everyone would deploy to the fight in Iraq. Our team had to allocate one task unit for what would be a largely noncombat deployment to the Philippines. Task Unit Bruiser, like the other task units, wanted to fight, to put our skills to use where we could make a difference. It was a competition: to excel in training so that we would be chosen by the command to deploy to Iraq.

By the time we were in our final block of training, a decision of who would go where was imminent. Our SEAL Team commanding officer (CO) and operations master chief informed us that they would visit us in Task Unit Bruiser to observe our brief for the final FTX. We knew that in order for us to be chosen, we had to knock this one out of the park.

"No pressure," said Jocko to the other SEAL platoon commander and me with a sarcastic smile. "Whether or not we get the chance of a lifetime to deploy to the war in Iraq all depends on whether you two can pull off a good brief."

Frantically, we put each of our platoon's key leaders to work developing a plan for the FTX mission and we began building the brief. But as we pieced it together, it was clear our brief was lacking in many areas. It was heavy on PowerPoint slides, overly complex, and not explicitly clear on the different pieces and parts of the execution. We were running out of time.

"We are going to fail," insisted the other platoon commander to Jocko and me. Frankly, I wasn't a whole lot more confident.

"Listen," said Jocko. "Here is what I want you to do: forget about all this crazy PowerPoint. I want this plan to be clear to everyone that is actually *in* your platoon. I'm not worried about the CO or the master chief. Brief it to your guys: the troops who will be executing the mission."

"The true test for a good brief," Jocko continued, "is not whether the senior officers are impressed. It's whether or not the troops that are going to execute the operation actually understand it. Everything else is bullshit. Does any of that complex crap help one of your SEAL machine gunners understand what he needs to do and the overall plan for what will happen on this operation?"

"No," I responded.

"Far from it!" Jocko continued. "In fact, it's confusing to them. You need to brief so that the most junior man can fully understand the operation—the lowest common denominator. That's what a brief *is*. And that is what I want you to do. If there is some flak over this from the CO, don't worry. I will take it."

With this guidance, we revamped our OPORD presentations. We simplified and cut down the number of PowerPoint slides and focused on the most important pieces of the plan, which would give our troops a chance to ask questions to clarify anything that wasn't understood. We hung maps on the walls—the same ones that we would carry in the field—and referenced them so that everyone was familiar. We incorporated hand sketches and manning lists on dry-erase boards. We had the troops brief the parts they were planning or leading and asked them questions during the process to ensure their piece of the plan was clear and that they understood it fully. That was something we never had time for when we were bogged down creating massive PowerPoint briefs with a hundred slides.

Most importantly, Jocko explained to us that, as leaders, we must not get dragged into the details but instead remain focused on the bigger picture.

"The most important part of the brief," said Jocko, "is to explain your Commander's Intent." When everyone participating in an operation knows and understands the purpose and end state of the mission, they can theoretically act without further guidance. This was a completely different mind-set for us, and we ran with it.

While Jocko pushed us to focus on Commander's Intent and the broader plan, he encouraged us to let the junior leaders in the platoon sort out and plan the details. "As a leader, if you are down in the weeds planning the details with your guys," said Jocko, "you will have the same perspective as them, which adds little value. But if you let them plan the details, it allows them to own their piece of the plan. And it allows you to stand back and see everything with a different perspective, which adds tremendous value. You can then see the plan from a greater distance, a higher altitude, and you will see more. As a result, you will catch mistakes and discover aspects of the plan that need to be tightened up, which enables you to look like a tactical genius, just because you have a broader view."

I realized this was exactly what Jocko did to us all the time.

It was a race against time, but just before the CO and master chief arrived, our platoons finished their portions of the plan and we talked through them. As Jocko had predicted, we noticed things they didn't see. With some minor adjustments, we filled in the holes. We ran through the plan with Jocko one last time, rehearsed the presentations, tightened up a few things, and made final adjustments. Already, our confidence had grown because we were briefing what we truly knew and understood and what we knew our platoon members also completely understood. Finally, our briefs were ready.

When the CO and master chief arrived, they sat in the back of the room as we presented our OPORD brief to the platoons. The other platoon commander and I gave an overview of the mission and then our key leaders got up and briefed the details. We pulled everyone out of their seats and gathered them around the map to walk through where we were going. We talked through each phase of the mission in plain English so that everyone understood. We stopped at key points and asked questions of the troops to ensure they were absorbing the information. We even had individual platoon members brief back portions of the plan to us to verify they had a clear understanding and could run the mission themselves if needed. When something wasn't completely clear, our SEAL operators asked for clarification, which enabled us to feel confident they understood and were taking ownership of their role. When the brief concluded, this time—much to our surprise—the CO and master chief gave us credit for a solid brief and delivery. The CO said that of all the mission briefings he had listened to during the workup, these were the ones he understood most clearly. We still had work to do to further enhance and refine our mission planning skills, but we had turned the corner by understanding what mission planning and briefing was all about.

Shortly thereafter, we received word that Task Unit Bruiser

had been chosen to deploy to Iraq. It was the news we had been waiting for. That set us on a path that led a few months later to the city of Ar Ramadi and through some of the toughest sustained urban combat in the history of the SEAL Teams. In that challenging environment, detailed mission planning and briefing played a critical role in our success. We planned and briefed hundreds of combat operations in Task Unit Bruiser and executed them with precision. We participated in the mission plans and OPORD briefs with U.S. Army and Marines for dozens of large-scale battalion and brigade-size operations, some involving as many as a thousand U.S. Soldiers and Marines on the ground and nearly one hundred tanks and armored vehicles.

We owned our planning process. After each combat operation, we pulled our platoon together and talked through the details in a post-operational debrief. In a concise and to-the-point format, we analyzed what had worked and what hadn't, how we might refine our standard operating procedures, and how we could do it better. As a result, we constantly learned and grew more effective. That ensured we performed at the highest levels and enabled our success. In such a dangerous environment, it helped us maintain an edge and allowed us to effectively mitigate some risks, which meant more of our guys came home alive.

Mission planning played an integral part in our success on the battlefield. The right process mattered. Disciplined planning procedures mattered. Without them, we would have never been successful.

With that lengthy story of how I learned to properly plan as a SEAL leader, I addressed how the emerging-markets VP and his regional manager would certainly benefit from such a system.

"You could use a planning procedure like we had," I told them. "You should develop a standard process with terminology and planning method that are interchangeable and can be utilized across all elements within your team and within the company."

"That is exactly what we need," said the emerging markets VP. "We need to capture our standard operating procedures for planning. We need a process that is repeatable. Can you teach this to my team?"

"Absolutely," I said.

Over the next few weeks, I sent a workbook to the emerging-markets VP, his regional manager, and their senior staff. The workbook provided an overview of the military-mission planning process we had used with some adaptation to the business world. We scheduled several conference calls in which I explained our process and why. The VP and his leadership team adapted this planning process to the challenges of their industry. Once they had a good understanding of the planning framework, we scheduled a presentation to key leaders with the emerging markets team.

I flew out and presented the foundational knowledge of the planning process from the workbook in detail. We then gave the team a planning exercise using a realistic future operation similar to those they routinely encountered. The regional manager and I guided the team as they put together the plan.

After an hour or so, they had built the basics of their plan into a brief to present to us, just as a SEAL platoon or task unit would present an OPORD. During the presentation, the regional manager and I analyzed their plan. Afterward, we debriefed them on their plan's strengths and weaknesses, talked about where it was ambiguous and needed clarification, and brought up points that had been glossed over or neglected and why they were important. I instructed them to revise the plan with those thoughts in mind, under the tutelage of their regional manager.

A month later, I placed a phone call to the regional manager to track the team's progress. She sent me a copy of their latest detailed plan.

"I like the plan you sent," I told her. "It has improved much from the first attempt."

"Yes," the regional manager agreed. "And we just executed on that plan, and it went well. As a result of the planning, the team was able to anticipate and address some contingencies. Before, such contingencies would have cost us business and a decent loss in revenue. But now, with our planning process in place, we were prepared and the team knew how to respond. As a result, we continued to generate revenue."

"Great," I said.

"With everyone understanding my 'Commander's Intent'," said the regional manager, "the team is able to be more decisive on the front lines. They can support the mission without having to run every question up the chain of command. Our ability to plan is enabling us to better execute and win."

Command and Control from the high ground: Jocko (right) and SEAL senior enlisted advisor (left) overlook the battlefield with U.S. Army company commander from Charlie Company, 1/506th 101st Airborne, call sign "Gunfighter." Charlie Company's battle-hardened Soldiers took the fight to the enemy on a daily basis.

(Photo courtesy of Todd Pitman)

CHAPTER 10
Leading Up and Down the Chain of Command

Leif Babin

CAMP MARC LEE, RAMADI, IRAQ: LEADING DOWN THE CHAIN OF COMMAND

The night sky suddenly lit up like a laser light show at a rock concert. Some distance across the river, U.S. security positions in the heart of Ramadi were under attack. Almost immediately, American sentries returned fire with a massive barrage from heavy machine guns, sending their own streaks of brilliant orange-red tracers back at enemy positions. Seconds passed before the distant rattle and boom of machine gun fire mixed with intermittent explosions reached us. As any military veteran knew, tracers were generally placed every fifth round in belt-fed machine guns, which meant there was a hell of a lot of hot lead flying around in the darkness that we couldn't see. The distant firefight continued for sometime. As Jocko and I watched, flaming streaks from the engines of an unseen U.S. attack aircraft (likely a Marine F/A-18 Hornet) appeared in the sky over the distant fight. Light flashed as a missile ignited off the wing, streaked across the sky, and exploded in a brilliant burst of light. Hopefully, they had smoked the enemy without any American casualties. It was all quite a show. But here in Ramadi, it was nothing out of the ordinary.

It had been a still and clear evening until the distant firefight lit up the night. The baking temperatures of the Iraqi summertime heat had recently given way to a tolerable, cooler fall. Jocko and I sat on the dusty rooftop of the large three-story concrete building that served as our tactical operations center on the base that had been our home, Camp Marc Lee. Our SEAL task unit had been in Ramadi for nearly six months. Soon, we were scheduled to return to the States. With no combat operations pending that evening, Jocko and I had a rare moment to reflect as we looked across the peaceful, dark waters of the Euphrates River and the lights of Ramadi on the far bank and beyond. We reminisced about the combat operations our task unit had participated in and all that had happened here.

Task Unit Bruiser had conducted hundreds of operations and endured many an onslaught from enemy attacks like the one we just witnessed. We had been in dozens of firefights, had thousands of rounds shot at us, shot back thousands of our own, and frequently called in fire support from U.S. tanks or aircraft. Our SEALs had done substantial damage to the enemy. Witnessing the triumph of success, we knew we had made a difference. But we had also endured extraordinary loss. Two months earlier, in the midst of a huge battle for the heart of the city, we had lost Marc Lee, the first SEAL killed in action in the Iraq War and the man in whose honor we named the camp. Marc's death was devastating. It left a hole that could never be filled. The same day we lost Marc, another beloved Charlie Platoon SEAL, Ryan Job, had been hit in the face by an enemy sniper round. Ryan lost an eye and took substantial damage to his face. But we waited for hopeful news from the doctors that sight would return in his remaining eye. Three weeks later, as he recovered in a hospital in Germany, those hopes were dashed when we learned Ryan would never see again: he was blind. This news was absolutely crushing. Then, just as our deployment came to a close, a Task Unit Bruiser SEAL in Delta Platoon, Mike Monsoor, was out on what would likely have been his last combat operation before returning home, when an enemy hand grenade was tossed into Delta Platoon's position. Mike dove on top of that grenade, shielding his teammates around him from the bulk of the blast and sacrificing himself for them. Each of these fallen SEALs were beloved teammates, friends, and brothers. We would forever mourn their loss.

On the rooftop that night, as Jocko and I talked about all we had been a part of in Ramadi, we knew Task Unit Bruiser had fulfilled a key role in the U.S. Army Ready First Brigade's (1st Armored Division) strategy that successfully wrested control of key Ramadi neighborhoods from the insurgents. After months of effort and countless firefights, U.S. forces and their Iraqi Army partner forces now had a presence where they previously had none. They could now secure the populace from the savage insurgents who had long controlled most of the city. This, and the foresight of the Ready First Brigade's leadership, set the conditions for tribal sheiks to successfully rise up against al Qaeda in Iraq and unite with U.S. forces in what would become the Anbar Awakening.

Task Unit Bruiser was proud to have played a role in the Ready First Brigade's success. We had killed hundreds of insurgent fighters, helped to eliminate many of their safe havens, and deeply disrupted their freedom of movement. Now, with the Ready First's combat outposts in place throughout much of the city, the enemy no longer exercised complete control over many neighborhoods of Ramadi. But the distant firefight we had just witnessed from the rooftop was a reminder that the enemy was still capable, deadly, and determined to fight back for control of the city.

What lasting impact did we truly have here? I wondered.

•   •   •

Soon afterward, we turned over our operations to the next SEAL task unit that took our place. Our time in Ramadi came to an end as the last of us from Task Unit Bruiser boarded a big U.S. Air Force C-17 cargo aircraft for the flight home.

Once back stateside, it was quite a transition from the intense violence in the bloody streets of Ramadi to the peace and tranquility of San Diego, California. For many of us it was an emotional return. After all the blood, sweat, and tears that Task Unit Bruiser—and our brothers- and sisters-in-arms in the U.S. Army and Marine Corps—had spilled there, I felt torn. We had lost the first SEALs killed in action in the Iraq War. As a leader, nothing had prepared me for that monumental burden I must forever carry for not bringing all my guys home to their families. If only I could trade places with them. When Ryan got shot and Marc was killed, they were doing exactly what I had asked of them. I was in charge; I was responsible. My fellow platoon commander felt the same way about Mike Monsoor. I knew Jocko felt that burden for each man.

Hearing American pundits in the media talking about all the "blood and treasure" spent in Iraq, I reacted with fury. To them, the casualty figures were just statistics—numbers on a page. To us, they were teammates and friends—brothers. Their families suffered the greatest hardship. These men were deeply missed and painfully mourned. Others had been seriously wounded and some would never fully recover. Their lives, and those of their families and friends would likewise never be the same. The true sacrifices endured by the troops who fought this war were far beyond anything that most Americans could comprehend.

Within our own beloved SEAL community, we heard the mutterings of criticism about our operations from the armchair quarterbacks in the rear echelon, far from the battlefield. They clearly didn't understand what we had done and why. They didn't witness the impact of our operations or the difference we had made.

With angry emotion, I wrestled with how best to professionally respond to those critics, particularly from senior officers with no real combat experience. Part of me wanted to punch them in the mouth. But a bigger part of me just wanted them to understand what we had accomplished and why. I knew that anyone who truly comprehended what Task Unit Bruiser had done and who understood the incredible victory the U.S. Army Ready First Brigade had achieved in Ramadi would respect not only the bravery and dedication of the troops but also the strategic success—securing Ramadi and Anbar Province from the brink of disaster. It had been a monumental triumph for U.S. forces on one of the toughest battlefields anywhere, when many doubted we could win. The doubters had been proved wrong.

Some within the SEAL community said we took too much risk, that our sniper operations were just playing "whac-a-mole." Used to a paradigm of traditional Special Operations, they could not comprehend the adaptations we had made or the risk those adaptations held. Nor did they understand the nature of counterinsurgency and the spectacular reversal toward peace and security that had been achieved.

Some of the politicians and most senior military brass in Washington felt that killing bad guys only created more enemies. But they didn't have a clue. Our lethal operations were crucial to securing the populace. Each enemy fighter killed meant more U.S. Soldiers and Marines came home alive; it meant more Iraqi soldiers and police lived to fight another day; and it meant more of Ramadi's civilian populace could live in a little less fear. No longer could the enemy ruthlessly torture, rape, and murder innocent civilians. Once the local people no longer feared the insurgents, they were willing to join with U.S. and Iraqi forces to defeat them.

Shortly after Task Unit Bruiser's return to the United States in late October of 2006, Jocko was asked to build a presentation for the chief of naval operations—the most senior admiral in the Navy, a member of the U.S. joint chiefs of staff, and a direct advisor to the president. Jocko took a map of Ramadi and built an overlay that depicted the geographic areas that had been completely under enemy control—al Qaeda battlespace—when we first arrived. These were areas that, when I arrived in Ramadi, the SEAL platoon commander who had spent the previous six months there pointed to and said to me: "Don't go in there. You will all get killed and no one [U.S. forces] will even be able to reach you to get you out."

From this map of Ramadi, Jocko built a PowerPoint slide that depicted how the Ready First Combat Team's Seize, Clear, Hold, Build strategy systematically, through months of effort, established a permanent presence in the enemy-held neighborhoods and pushed out the enemy fighters. U.S. forces and the Iraqi forces with them demonstrated to the people of Ramadi that we were now the strongest side. As a result, the local populace joined us and turned against the insurgents who had terrorized them. The slide depicted how Task Unit Bruiser SEALs had been the lead element for virtually every major operation to build a combat outpost in enemy territory and take those neighborhoods back.

When Jocko showed me the slide he had built, it all came together for me for the first time. Though I had been directly involved in the planning of almost all of these missions, had been on the ground leading a team of operators, coordinated with the other elements on the battlefield, and had written detailed reports of what had happened after each mission, I still had not linked them all together nor considered the strategic impact they had had. But now, Jocko's brief captured in simple terms all that had been accomplished in the Battle of Ramadi.

This was a striking realization: I was Charlie Platoon commander, second in seniority only to Jocko in Task Unit Bruiser. And yet, immersed in the details of the tactical operations, I had not fully appreciated or understood how those operations so directly contributed to the strategic mission with spectacular results beyond anyone's wildest dreams.

"Damn," I said to Jocko. "I never really put it all together like that before." This one slide made it immediately clear why we had done what we had done. While this knowledge could never ease the pain endured by the loss of incredible SEAL friends and teammates, it certainly helped to put in perspective why we had taken such risk and what had been accomplished.

As platoon commander, I had detailed insight into the planning and coordination with the Army and Marine battalions and companies that was far beyond most of the SEAL operators in my platoon. Yet, if I didn't fully comprehend or appreciate the strategic impact of what we had done, how could I expect my frontline troops—my junior SEAL operators not in a leadership role—to get it? The answer: I couldn't. For a young SEAL shooter with a very limited role in the planning process who was out working on his weapons and gear, conducting maintenance on our vehicles, or building demolition charges for the breacher, he walked into our mission briefs wondering: *What are we doing next?* He had no context for why we were doing the operation or how the next tactical mission fit into the bigger picture of stabilizing and securing Ramadi.

I realized now that, as their leader, I had failed to explain it to them. Clearly, there was some level of strategic perspective and comprehension that would only come with time and reflection. But I could have done a far better job as a leader to understand for myself the strategic impact of our operations and passed this insight to my troops.

When Jocko saw my reaction to the slide and the presentation he had built, he too realized that he should have more fully detailed the strategic impact of what we were doing and why. It was a realization for him that even when a leader thinks his troops understand the bigger picture, they very often have difficulty connecting the dots between the tactical mission they are immersed in with the greater overarching goal.

Looking back on Task Unit Bruiser's deployment to Ramadi, I realized that the SEALs in Charlie Platoon who suffered the worst combat fatigue, whose attitudes grew progressively more negative as the months of heavy combat wore on, who most questioned the level of risk we were taking on operations—they all had the least ownership of the planning for each operation. Conversely, the SEAL operators who remained focused and positive, who believed in what we were doing, and who were eager to continue and would have stayed on beyond our six-month deployment if they could— they all had some ownership of the planning process in each operation. Even if they only controlled a small piece of the plan— the route into or out of a target, the breach scene on an entry door, coordination with supporting aircraft, managing an assault force of Iraqi soldiers—those SEAL operators still better understood the mission, the detailed steps taken to mitigate those risks we could control, the Commander's Intent behind why we were conducting that specific operation. The SEALs with little or no ownership were somewhat in the dark. As a result, they had a harder time understanding why we were taking the risks we were taking and what specific impact we had in the campaign to liberate Ramadi.

Looking back, one of the greatest lessons learned for me was that I could have done a far better job of leading down the chain of command. I should have given greater ownership of plans to the troops—especially those who were negative and weren't fully committed to the mission. I should have taken the time to better understand how what we were doing contributed to the strategic mission. I should have asked those questions to Jocko and on up my chain of command. I should have put together a routine strategic overview brief and regularly delivered this to Charlie Platoon's operators so that they could understand what we had accomplished and how our missions furthered the strategic goals of stabilizing Ramadi and securing the populace. With the physical hardship of operating in Iraqi summertime heat reaching 117 degrees Fahrenheit, carrying heavy loads of gear, and routinely engaging in fierce firefights with enemy forces, the SEAL operators in Charlie Platoon needed greater context to understand why that was necessary. Seeing the Ramadi overview slide that Jocko had built, I now understood what we had done and, more important, understood what leading down the chain of command was all about. It was a hard lesson to learn but one I will never forget.

PRINCIPLE: LEADING DOWN THE CHAIN

Any good leader is immersed in the planning and execution of tasks, projects, and operations to move the team toward a strategic goal. Such leaders possess insight into the bigger picture and why specific tasks need to be accomplished. This information does not automatically translate to subordinate leaders and the frontline troops. Junior members of the team—the tactical level operators—are rightly focused on their specific jobs. They must be in order to accomplish the tactical mission. They do not need the full knowledge and insight of their senior leaders, nor do the senior leaders need the intricate understanding of the tactical level operators' jobs. Still, it is critical that each have an understanding of the other's role. And it is paramount that senior leaders explain to their junior leaders and troops executing the mission how their role contributes to big picture success.

This is not intuitive and never as obvious to the rank-and-file employees as leaders might assume. Leaders must routinely communicate with their team members to help them understand their role in the overall mission. Frontline leaders and troops can then connect the dots between what they do every day—the day-to-day operations—and how that impacts the company's strategic goals. This understanding helps the team members prioritize their efforts in a rapidly changing, dynamic environment. That is leading down the chain of command. It requires regularly stepping out of the office and personally engaging in face-to-face conversations with direct reports and observing the frontline troops in action to understand their particular challenges and read them into the Commander's Intent. This enables the team to understand why they are doing what they are doing, which facilitates Decentralized Command (as detailed in chapter 8).

As a leader employing Extreme Ownership, if your team isn't doing what you need them to do, you first have to look at yourself. Rather than blame them for not seeing the strategic picture, you must figure out a way to better communicate it to them in terms that are simple, clear, and concise, so that they understand. This is what leading down the chain of command is all about.

CAMP MARC LEE, RAMADI, IRAQ: LEADING UP THE CHAIN OF COMMAND

"You gotta be kidding me!" I shouted as I burst into Jocko's office inside the TOC. I was fuming. "Are they *serious*?"

Our TOC was located in a large three-story building on the bank of the Euphrates River, which previously housed some of Saddam Hussein's senior military brass before the 2003 U.S. invasion of Iraq. Now the once elaborate building was battered and worse for wear. It was the centerpiece of our SEAL camp, just beyond the large U.S. forward operating base of Camp Ramadi at the edge of the war-torn city. Invading armies had camped along this very riverbank for millennia: Babylonians, Assyrians, Persians, Greeks, Arabs, Ottoman Turks, and British troops. Now American forces, including Navy SEALs and support personnel of Task Unit Bruiser, were here for a time.

I was furious and venting my frustration at Jocko. "Unbelievable. How do they expect us to actually plan our operations when they are bombarding us with ludicrous questions?" I asked.

Jocko had just forwarded me an e-mail from our higher headquarters staff, led by our SEAL Team's commanding officer (CO). The e-mail in question asked for clarification on an upcoming operation that Charlie Platoon planned to execute in the next few hours.

As one of two platoon commanders in Task Unit Bruiser, I was Jocko's direct report, his immediate subordinate. Jocko reported directly to the CO, often through the CO's staff, who had sent the e-mail. While Task Unit Bruiser was located in Ramadi, the CO and his staff were some thirty miles to the east in Fallujah, a city that had been cleaned up by the massive U.S. Marine offensive in 2004. Now, two years later, Fallujah remained fairly stable. It was a far different environment than the constant violence of Ramadi. Our operational plans required the CO's approval and on up the chain of command to the next level. The CO and his staff also provided many of the resources and support we needed to execute our missions in Ramadi.

"What's the issue?" Jocko asked me, seeing that I was fired up. "The e-mail?" He too was frustrated with the frequent questions and scrutiny.

"Yes, the e-mail," I replied. "Every little thing we do, *they* don't get!" The oft blamed "they," in this case, was anyone outside of my immediate group of Charlie Platoon and Task Unit Bruiser.

Jocko laughed. "I know you're frustrated. . . ." he said. "I'm frustrated too—"

I cut him off. "It's actually insane. We are busting our butts, risking our lives and kicking some serious ass on the toughest battlefield in Iraq. And I have to answer idiotic questions like whether we have a QRF lined up?"

The QRF, or quick reaction force, consisted of U.S. Soldiers or Marines who would respond with armored vehicles, a couple of dozen troops, and heavy firepower when our SEALs got into a serious bind and were pinned down by enemy forces. Many of us in Task Unit Bruiser had been to Iraq previously, and a few had seen some decent combat. On those previous deployments, activating the QRF was virtually unheard of. But here in Ramadi, it was a common occurrence. On any operation at any time, we knew we could be attacked by an overwhelming number of enemy fighters and our position overrun. In just the first few months on the ground here, we (Charlie Platoon and our brethren in Delta Platoon) activated our QRF more times than I could count.

The e-mail Jocko had just forwarded to me from our higher headquarters asked a series of questions that our CO wanted to know prior to approving our pending operation. One of the questions read, "Did you coordinate an appropriate QRF?"

I found this question almost an insult. "Do they really think we would do any type of operation whatsoever here without a significant QRF package fully coordinated and on standby?" I asked. "We even set up QRFs for our administrative convoys. This is Ramadi. Going out there without a QRF would be suicide."

Jocko smiled. Over the previous weeks, he had vented similar frustration to me, probably more so than he should have. We would privately laugh at some of the questions that flowed from our higher headquarters. On one recent operation Charlie Platoon had planned, we were asked whether mortars were a danger for us. Mortars—with up to twenty pounds of high-explosive cased in half-inch-thick steel—fell from the sky and exploded with a tremendous concussion that threw lethal shrapnel in all directions. Often, enemy fighters fired mortars with impressive accuracy. Mortars were a danger for us on *every* operation, even while sitting on base. We selected buildings with thicker concrete walls that could provide some protection, and we tried never to be predictable so the enemy could not anticipate our next move. Besides that, mortars were a risk largely beyond our control. We had to focus our planning efforts on the risks we could control.

Jocko had been every bit as frustrated with some of the questions and shared that with me. But since that time, he had come to the realization that the frustrations we had with our superiors were misguided. The CO and his staff weren't bad guys out to make our lives harder and stifle our operations. They were good people trying to do their jobs the best they could and give us what we needed to accomplish our mission. But they weren't on the battlefield with us. They didn't fully understand the threats we dealt with on a daily basis and how hard we were working to mitigate every risk we possibly could. Still, this was combat and there were inherent risks. In Ramadi, U.S. troops were killed or wounded almost every day.

"We waste our time answering question after question," I said. "It takes effort away from our planning and preparation for the actual op itself. It's actually dangerous!"

Jocko knew I had a point. But he needed me to see beyond the immediate front-sight focus of my team—Charlie Platoon— and understand the bigger picture. Jocko tried to calm me down and help me see our combat operations through the CO's eyes; from the perspective of his staff in the special operations task force. "The CO has to approve every mission. If we want to operate, we need to put him in his comfort zone so that he approves them and we can execute," Jocko said.

"The more we give them, the more they ask for," I fired back.

"They want an updated seating chart for our vehicles five minutes before the launch of every op, even though we have to make last-minute changes. They want the names of every individual Iraqi soldier working with us, even though I won't know that until just prior to launch."

Jocko just nodded, realizing that I needed to vent. He knew I was a capable and already proven leader. He had trained and mentored me for the past year to prepare me for the rigors of combat operations and then unleashed me to lead Charlie Platoon on the battlefield. But he also knew I needed to see the importance of pushing information up the chain, beyond my platoon and task unit. I needed to understand how to lead up the chain of command and why it was important.

The amount of information we had to gather and the required paperwork we were forced to submit just to get approval for each combat mission was staggering. It wasn't what people saw in war movies or television shows. Never in my boyhood dreams of battlefield glory had I envisioned such things would be required. But it was the reality.

"We know our combat operations are making an impact on the battlefield here. They are important," said Jocko. I nodded in agreement.

Jocko continued: "But all of these operations need the CO's approval. He has to be comfortable with what we are doing. And we need his support to get additional approvals from higher up the chain. So we can complain about this all day and do nothing, or we can push the necessary information up the chain so that the CO is comfortable and gives us approval."

Jocko had a point. The CO and his staff were not here with us in Ramadi. They couldn't fully understand or appreciate the efforts we had made at risk mitigation and the excellent working relationships we had built with the U.S. Army and Marine battalions and companies that supported us with QRFs.

"We can't expect them to be mind readers," Jocko said. "The only way they are going to get this information is from what we pass to them, the reports we write and the phone calls we make. And we obviously aren't doing a good enough job if they still have major questions."

"Well, they should come out here then," I responded.

"They should," Jocko answered. "But have we told them they should or scheduled a convoy to pick them up? I know I haven't," Jocko admitted.

This contradicted popular thinking. Typically, the frontline troops wanted senior leaders as far away as possible to avoid questions or scrutiny on the smallest of things like grooming standards and whether or not our camp was squared away.

"We are here. We are on the ground. We need to push situational awareness up the chain," Jocko said. "If they have questions, it is our fault for not properly communicating the information they need. We have to lead them."

"They are in charge of us," I questioned. "How can we lead them?"

This epiphany had come to Jocko in examining his own frustrations up the chain. "Leadership doesn't just flow down the chain of command, but up as well," he said. "We have to own everything in our world. That's what Extreme Ownership is all about."

I nodded, coming around to his logic. Jocko's guidance had not yet steered me wrong in the year we had worked together. He had taught me to be the combat leader I needed to be. But this was a whole new attitude, a completely different mind-set from anything I had seen or been taught. Instead of blaming others, instead of complaining about the boss's questions, I had to take ownership of the problem and lead. This included the leaders *above* me in our chain of command.

"We need to look at ourselves and see what we can do better,"

Jocko continued. "We have to write more-detailed reports that help them understand what we are doing and why we are making the decisions we are making. We have to communicate more openly in calls, and when they have questions, we need to immediately get them whatever information they need so that they understand what is happening out here."

I now understood. Far from simply trying to overburden us with questions, our CO and his staff were working hard to get the information they needed so that they could approve our plans, forward them up the chain for further approval and enable us to launch on combat missions to get after the enemy. I needed to check my negative attitude, which was corrosive and ultimately only hampered our ability to operate.

I now accepted Jocko's challenge full on. "You're right," I said. "I can bitch about their questions and scrutiny all I want, but at the end of the day, it gets us no closer to getting our operations approved. If I get them the information they need and put the CO in his comfort zone with what we are doing, we are going to be much more effective getting ops approved, which will enable us to inflict greater damage on the bad guys and win."

"Exactly," Jocko said.

From that day forward, we began a campaign of leading up the chain of command. We provided extremely detailed mission-planning documents and post-operational reports.

We pushed the understanding of this to our team leaders within the platoon. We invited the CO, our command master chief, and other staff to visit us in Ramadi and offered to take them along on combat operations. Our command master chief accompanied us on several missions. The more information we passed, the more our CO and staff understood what we were trying to accomplish. He better appreciated our detailed planning efforts, how we coordinated our quick reaction forces, and the substantial lengths to which we went to mitigate the risks. The CO grew more comfortable with our combat operations. He and his staff developed trust in us. As a result, all the combat missions we submitted received approval, which allowed Charlie Platoon and Task Unit Bruiser to deliver huge impact on the battlefield.

PRINCIPLE: LEADING UP THE CHAIN

If your boss isn't making a decision in a timely manner or providing necessary support for you and your team, don't blame the boss. First, blame yourself. Examine what you can do to better convey the critical information for decisions to be made and support allocated.

Leading up the chain of command requires tactful engagement with the immediate boss (or in military terms, higher headquarters) to obtain the decisions and support necessary to enable your team to accomplish its mission and ultimately win. To do this, a leader must push situational awareness up the chain of command.

Leading up the chain takes much more savvy and skill than leading down the chain. Leading up, the leader cannot fall back on his or her positional authority. Instead, the subordinate leader must use influence, experience, knowledge, communication, and maintain the highest professionalism.

While pushing to make your superior understand what you need, you must also realize that your boss must allocate limited assets and make decisions with the bigger picture in mind. You and your team may not represent the priority effort at that particular time. Or perhaps the senior leadership has chosen a different direction. Have the humility to understand and accept this.

One of the most important jobs of any leader is to support your own boss—your immediate leadership. In any chain of command, the leadership must always present a united front to the troops. A public display of discontent or disagreement with the chain of command undermines the authority of leaders at all levels. This is catastrophic to the performance of any organization.

As a leader, if you don't understand why decisions are being made, requests denied, or support allocated elsewhere, you must ask those questions up the chain. Then, once understood, you can pass that understanding down to your team. Leaders in any chain of command will not always agree. But at the end of the day, once the debate on a particular course of action is over and the boss has made a decision—even if that decision is one you argued against—you must execute the plan *as if it were your own*.

When leading up the chain of command, use caution and respect. But remember, if your leader is not giving the support you need, don't blame him or her. Instead, reexamine what you can do to better clarify, educate, influence, or convince that person to give you what you need in order to win.

The major factors to be aware of when leading up and down the chain of command are these:

- Take responsibility for leading everyone in your world, subordinates and superiors alike.
- If someone isn't doing what you want or need them to do, look in the mirror first and determine what you can do to better enable this.
- Don't ask your leader what you should do, tell them what you are going to do.

APPLICATION TO BUSINESS

"Corporate doesn't understand what's going on out here," said the field manager. "Whatever experience those guys had in the field from years ago, they have long forgotten. They just don't get what we are dealing with, and their questions and second-guessing prevents me and my team from getting the job done."

The infamous *they.*

I was on a visit to a client company's field leadership team, the frontline troops that executed the company's mission. This was where the rubber met the road: all the corporate capital initiatives, strategic planning sessions, and allocated resources were geared to support this team here on the ground. How the frontline troops executed the mission would ultimately mean success or failure for the entire company.

The field manager's team was geographically separated from their corporate headquarters located hundreds of miles away. He was clearly frustrated. The field manager had a job to do, and he was angry at the questions and scrutiny from afar. For every task his team undertook he was required to submit substantial paperwork. In his mind, it made for a lot more work than necessary and detracted from his team's focus and ability to execute.

I listened and allowed him to vent for several minutes.

"I've been in your shoes," I said. "I used to get frustrated as hell at my chain of command when we were in Iraq. They would scrutinize our plans, ask questions that seemed stupid, and load on a massive paperwork requirement that I had to submit both prior to and after every operation."

"You had to deal with that as a Navy SEAL at war?" asked the field manager, surprised. "I wouldn't have guessed that."

"I absolutely did," I said. "Before every combat mission, we had to get approval up the chain of command at least two levels from a faraway boss who didn't fully understand what we were up against. That required me putting the intricate details of the operation in a multitude of PowerPoint slides and then an additional Word document of several typed pages, just to get approval. Once approved and we launched, then I had to generate even more paperwork when we got back: a multislide storyboard brief with photographs, and a detailed multipage operational summary. If we killed any bad guys on a combat mission—which in Ramadi was virtually every operation—we had to provide sworn statements describing precisely what happened and how our actions complied with the rules of engagement for each enemy fighter killed. And that doesn't even include the pages of required intelligence paperwork we had to compile."

"I didn't figure you guys would have to deal with such stuff," said the field manager.

"No matter how big or bureaucratic your company seems," I said, "it pales in comparison to the gargantuan U.S. military bureaucracy. And imagine how much more emotional and frustrating it was for us when our lives were on the line everyday. I often worked myself into a rage over some very similar issues to yours here.

"But we had two choices," I said. "Throw our hands up in frustration and do nothing, or figure out how to most effectively operate within the constraints required of us. We chose the latter.

"Let me ask you a question," I continued. "Do you think the company senior executives at corporate headquarters want you to fail?"

The field manager looked puzzled. He had clearly never considered the question.

"Could they be scheming about how to make your job more difficult, how they can keep you and your team flustered with questions, scrutiny, and paperwork or how they might totally sabotage your mission?" I asked.

Of course, this wasn't the case. Having worked with the company's executive team, I knew they were a smart bunch of driven, eager overachievers who wanted their frontline troops to not only accomplish the mission but to eclipse all competitors and set the standard for the industry.

"No, they don't want me to fail," admitted the field manager.

"Alright," I said. "Then if they are asking questions, criticizing your plan, and requiring paperwork, it means they are in need of some critical information. When Jocko was my task unit commander, he had this same talk with me in Ramadi. That's what changed my mind-set about this and allowed us to become far more effective."

"What changed your mind?" the field manager asked.

"I realized that if my chain of command had questions about my plans or needed additional information or more detailed paperwork, it was not their fault," I said. "It was *my* fault. I knew we were making the right decisions and being careful to mitigate every risk we could control. I knew our combat operations were critical to achieving strategic victory in Ramadi. So if my boss wasn't comfortable with what I was doing, it was only because I had not clearly communicated it to him."

The field manager looked at me, beginning to understand.

"So if they have questions, it's my fault that they didn't get the information they need?" asked the field manager. This completely contradicted his way of thinking and everything he had experienced in his leadership upbringing. That "us versus them" mentality was common to just about every level of every chain of command, whether military unit or civilian corporation. But breaking that mentality was the key to properly lead up the chain of command and radically improve the team's performance.

"Listen: the senior leadership at corporate headquarters wants you to succeed," I said. "That's a given. It's up to you to inform them and help them understand some of the challenges you are dealing with here on the ground. If you have questions about why a specific plan or required paperwork is coming down the pipe, don't just throw up your hands in frustration. Ask those questions up the chain to clarify, so that you can understand it. Provide them with constructive feedback so they can appreciate the impact those plans or requirements have on your operations. That is what Extreme Ownership is all about."

"I guess I never really thought about it like that," said the field manager.

"That's 'leading up the chain of command,'" I explained.

The field manager came around to this realization. He accepted that he needed to do better in pushing situational awareness, information, and communication up the chain.

"If you think they don't fully understand the challenges you are facing here, invite your senior executives out to the field to see your team in action," I said.

Over the following weeks and months, the field manager took a different tack with his senior leadership at corporate headquarters. He took the initiative to understand what specific information they needed and went overboard pushing that information to them.

He also hosted the senior executives in a field visit to their frontline troops. It built camaraderie between the corporate leadership team and the field manager's operations team on the ground. The face-to-face interaction helped the senior executives understand some of the field manager's challenges. And the field manager's time with the senior executives made him realize all the more that his leaders were smart folks who wanted him to succeed. It went a long way toward breaking down the barriers that had built up between his field team and corporate headquarters. He was now ready to lead up the chain.

Charlie Platoon sniper overwatch: Leif (right) reports enemy activity and
coordinates friendly movement via radio as SEAL snipers, including Chris Kyle
(left), engage enemy fighters maneuvering to attack coalition forces.

(Photo courtesy of the authors)

CHAPTER 11
Decisiveness amid Uncertainty

Leif Babin

SNIPER OVERWATCH, RAMADI, IRAQ: TAKE THE SHOT

"I've got a guy with a scoped weapon in the second-story window of building 127," said Chris.

This was a bit out of the ordinary. Chris Kyle* was Charlie Platoon's point man and lead sniper—the most experienced sniper in the platoon and one of the best in the SEAL Teams. He had been nicknamed "The Legend" in jest on a previous deployment to Iraq. But as a driver of our sniper operations in Ramadi, he was racking up confirmed kills on enemy fighters at a rate that promised to surpass the most successful snipers in U.S. military history.

What made Chris Kyle such a great sniper was not that he was the most exceptional marksman. His secret was that he practiced Extreme Ownership of his craft. Intimately involved in planning and scouting potential sniper overwatch positions, he put himself in the right place at the right time to maximize his

---
* Chris Kyle, author of *The New York Times* bestseller *American Sniper*, and the inspiration for the movie *American Sniper*.

effectiveness. While others might get bored and lose focus after an hour of two of staring through the reticle of their sniper scope, Chris maintained discipline and stayed vigilant. He was lucky, but more often than not he made his luck.

If Chris or any of our SEAL shooters could PID—positively identify—a bad guy with a weapon committing a hostile act or determine reasonable certainty of hostile intent, they were cleared to engage. They didn't need my permission. If they asked for it, that meant reasonable certainty of hostile intent was in question.

"Can you PID?" I asked.

"Just saw a dark shape of a man with a scoped weapon for a split second," replied Chris. "Then he stepped back from the window and disappeared behind a curtain."

"Roger that," I said. "What building again?" I checked the battle map that labeled each building or structure in the sector with a number. All of us in this U.S. Army brigade task force operation, including a half dozen different U.S. Army and Marine Corps battalions and thousands of Soldiers and Marines on the ground, were operating on the same battle map, which was crucial. But matching the numbers and street names on the map to what we were seeing in front of us on the ground could be quite a challenge. Here there were no streets signs or address numbers. This was Ramadi. Amid the urban sprawl of trash-covered streets and alleyways were huge bomb craters and walls pockmarked by bullets and spray-painted with Arabic jihadist graffiti, which our interpreters translated for us, such as: "We will fight until we reach either of the two heavens: victory or martyrdom." We were here to ensure it was the latter.

Ahead of a huge Army force of U.S. Soldiers on foot, M1A2 Abrams Main Battle Tanks and M2 Bradley Fighting Vehicles, our SEAL platoon had foot-patrolled into the area in the early morning darkness. We set up our sniper overwatch position in a two-story building a few hundred meters down the street from where a U.S. Army battalion would establish their newest combat outpost. Once again we were deep in the heart of enemy territory. We covered the Soldiers as they moved into the area on foot, accompanied by tanks and Bradleys.

Now the sun had risen and hundreds of U.S. Soldiers had arrived, clearing through the surrounding buildings. Chris and other SEAL snipers had already killed several enemy fighters maneuvering to attack—just another day in South-Central Ramadi. After every engagement, I relayed situational reports (or SITREPs) to the U.S. Army company in charge of the new combat outpost— Team Warrior of the 1st Battalion, 36th Infantry Regiment, assigned to Task Force Bandit.

The snipers did the bulk of the shooting. As an officer, my job wasn't to pull the trigger but to provide command and control and coordinate with the friendly units in the area.

However, the report from Chris of a guy with a scoped weapon in a second-story window raised some questions. U.S. Soldiers were clearing buildings just beyond the direction he was looking, and we needed to be absolutely clear as to what we were seeing. I crouched next to Chris and kept fairly low to try and prevent my head getting shot off. He held his sniper rifle steady and, through his high-power scope, carefully observed the window where he had last seen the dark silhouette of the man with a weapon.

"You still have eyes on?" I asked Chris, meaning did he still have a visual on the potential target.

"Negative," Chris responded without taking his eye from his riflescope.

Looking down the street he was observing, I could see a few hundred meters in that direction. The streets and alleyways were narrow and confusing. The maze of one-and two-story buildings blended together. Our view was partially obstructed by low-hanging power lines and the occasional palm tree or parked car.

In recent weeks, enemy snipers had wreaked havoc in this area, killing a young Marine and an Army Soldier and critically wounding more. Ryan Job had been shot only a couple of blocks down the street from our position. Marc Lee had been killed just a few houses down from the building we now occupied. Their loss was devastating and this fight was extremely personal to us. We did our utmost to eliminate every enemy fighter to ensure more of our teammates and our U.S. Army and Marine Corps brothers-in-arms came home alive.

Killing an enemy sniper, who had likely killed our own, would exact some measure of vengeance and protect American lives. But there were friendlies—U.S. Soldiers—throughout this area so we had to be sure.

I got on the radio—the company communications net—and requested Team Warrior's company commander. He was a respected leader and an outstanding Soldier I had come to admire in the months we had worked together.

"Warrior, this is Red Bull,* I said, when he came up on the net. "We saw a man with a scoped weapon in the second story of building 127. Can you confirm you don't have any personnel in that building?" I listened as he contacted his platoon commander, responsible for the buildings in that area, on the company net. The platoon commander soon answered that they did not.

"Negative," the company commander replied (via radio) to my inquiry. "We don't have anyone in that building." His Soldiers had cleared through that area an hour or so before.

"Request you engage," said the company commander. His platoon commander had confirmed that none of his guys were in building 127. Therefore, the man Chris had seen must be an in-

---

* Our call sign at the time in that particular battlespace.

surgent sniper. And because the threat of enemy snipers was significant, the company commander (like me) wanted our SEAL snipers to take out any enemy snipers before they could kill Warrior's troops.

But Chris obviously didn't feel good about the situation, and I certainly didn't either. There were a lot of friendlies in the vicinity—Warrior's Soldiers—just a block beyond where Chris had seen the individual. Chris maintained eyes on the window in question through his sniper scope and waited patiently. He knew what he was doing and needed no direction from me.

"Just saw him again," said Chris. He described how, for a brief moment, the dark silhouette of an individual peered out from behind the window's curtain. Chris couldn't make out anything but the shape of a man and the faint lines of a weapon with a scope. Then, like a ghost, the man faded back into the darkness of the room and the curtain was pulled across the window, blocking any view into the room. We couldn't PID the individual.

I again called Warrior's company commander on the radio.

"We just saw the individual with the scoped weapon again, same location," I told him.

"Roger," the company commander responded. "Take that guy out," he insisted in an exasperated tone. It was clear he was wondering, *What the hell are these SEALs waiting for? An enemy sniper is a threat to my men: kill him before he kills us!*

We certainly did not want any of Warrior's Soldiers to get killed or wounded. We were here to prevent such attacks, and I felt the pressure to comply. Was it a bad guy or wasn't it? I couldn't say with any certitude. But I had to make a decision.

What if we don't take that shot, I thought to myself, *and Warrior Soldiers get killed because we failed to act?* That would be horrible. It would be a heavy burden to bear.

On the other hand, I thought, *what if we take this shot and it turns out to be a good guy—a U.S. Soldier—in that window?* That outcome would be worst of all. I knew I could never live with myself if that happened. Despite the forceful pressure to comply, I had to take a step back and see the bigger picture. I remembered from my boyhood days in Texas a basic rule of firearms safety my father taught me: know your target and what is beyond it. That made the decision all too clear. We couldn't chance taking this shot. Regardless of the pressure, I couldn't risk it.

"Negative," I responded to Warrior's company commander. "Too many friendlies in the area, and we can't PID. I recommend you send some Soldiers to reclear that building."

I didn't work for the company commander and he didn't work for me. He couldn't order me to take the shot, and I couldn't order him to clear the building. But we had worked together before. I knew and respected him as a leader and I knew he probably felt the same for me. He would have to trust in my judgment.

I listened on the net as Warrior's company commander again called up his platoon commander to discuss my recommendation. From the tone in their voices, they were clearly not happy. What I was asking them to do—an assault on an enemy-occupied building—put their Soldiers at great risk. It could very well get some of them killed.

"Shoot him," came the response yet again from the company commander. "Take that guy out," he said, this time more forcefully.

"Negative," I said, sternly. "Don't feel comfortable with that." I wasn't backing down, no matter the pressure to comply.

The company commander's patience had worn thin. He had a hell of a lot on his plate managing more than 100 Soldiers, multiple tanks, and Bradleys as his men cleared through dozens of buildings. Responsible for the establishment of this new combat outpost deep in enemy territory, he also had to coordinate Warrior's movement with his battalion and the supporting companies. Now all he knew was that we had reported a potential bad guy with a scoped weapon, possibly an enemy sniper. And we were asking his Soldiers to leave the relative safety of the buildings they were in, run across a hostile street in broad daylight, and risk their lives because we didn't feel comfortable taking the shot.

I couldn't blame the company commander for his frustration. I empathized. But Chris was one of the best snipers anywhere. He had already single-handedly accounted for dozens of enemy killed and certainly didn't need any urging from me to pull the trigger on bad guys he could PID. His level of caution signaled that I, as his SEAL platoon commander, needed to make the tough decision—the best decision I could—based on the information I had. As the situation developed, if information suddenly changed, we would still have the opportunity to engage and could do so with a clearer picture of what was actually happening. Jocko had always encouraged us to be aggressive in decision-making. But part of being decisive was knowing and understanding that some decisions, while immediately impactful, can be quickly reversed or altered; other decisions, like shooting another human being, cannot be undone. If we waited to take this shot we could later change course, while a decision to pull the trigger and engage this shadowy target would be final.

With that in mind, I held my ground. "We cannot engage." I told the company commander over the radio. "I recommend you clear that building."

The radio was quiet for a few moments. I'm sure the company commander bit his tongue in frustration. Then, reluctantly, he directed his platoon commander to reclear the building. From his voice over the radio, I could tell the platoon commander was furious. But he knew he had to address the threat. He directed a squad of his Soldiers to break out of the building they were in, reclear building 127, and search for the mysterious "guy with the scoped weapon."

"We will cover your movement," I told the company commander.

"If he so much as moves while our guys are in the open," he replied, "shoot that son of a bitch."

"Roger," I responded. If the individual gave us even an inkling that he was hostile, Chris would take the shot.

Standing next to Chris with his sniper rifle trained on the window, I had my radio headset on, ready to coordinate with Warrior's Soldiers.

Suddenly, ten Soldiers from Warrior Company burst out of the door of a building and dashed across the street.

Immediately, all became clear!

"Halt the clearance team and return to COP," I directed Warrior's company commander over the net.

Instantly, I recognized our error. Chris and I had been looking one block farther than we had realized. Instead of looking at the building we thought was building 127 on our battle map, we were looking at one of the buildings where U.S. Soldiers from Warrior were gathered. Though it was a mistake easily made in this urban environment (and one that happened more often than any U.S. commanders wished to admit), it could have had deadly and devastating consequences. The guy with a scoped weapon Chris had seen in the window was not an enemy sniper. It was a U.S. Soldier standing back from the window with a Trijicon ACOG scope on his U.S. military issued M16 rifle.

Thank God, I thought, literally thanking God. I was grateful for Chris's initial judgment—an exceptional call not to take a shot he couldn't clearly identify. He had done exactly as he should have and notified me to ask for guidance. Others with less experience might have rushed decisions and pulled that trigger. I was thankful I had held my ground and ultimately made the right decision.

Even still, it scared the hell out of me, to think just how close we had come to shooting a U.S. Soldier. Had we succumbed to the pressure, Chris would have put a large caliber round into an American soldier, almost certainly killing him. As the leader in charge, regardless of who pulled the trigger, the responsibility would have been mine. Living with such a thing on my conscience would have been hell. For me, the war would have been over. There would be no choice but to turn in my Trident (our SEAL warfare insignia) and hang up my combat boots. For Charlie Platoon and Task Unit Bruiser, it would have undone all the great work we accomplished, the many U.S. Soldiers and Marines we had saved. All that would be meaningless had I given the order and Chris pulled the trigger.

I keyed up my radio on Warrior's company net and explained what had happened to the company commander. He too understood how easily a building misidentification could happen. It happened all the time. He too breathed a huge sigh of relief that we hadn't engaged.

"I'm glad you didn't listen to me," he admitted.

In the uncertainty and chaos of the battlefield, despite the pressure to take the shot, I had to act decisively, in this case holding back my lead sniper from taking a shot on a target because we didn't have clear, positive identification. It was one of any number of combat examples from our time in Ramadi that demonstrated how critical it was for leadership to be decisive amid uncertainty.

In combat as in life, the outcome is never certain, the picture never clear. There are no guarantees of success. But in order to succeed, leaders must be comfortable under pressure, and act on logic, not emotion. This is a critical component to victory.

PRINCIPLE

Books, movies, and television shows can never truly capture or articulate the pressure from uncertainty, chaos, and the element of unknown with which real combat leaders must contend. The combat leader almost never has the full picture or a clear and certain understanding of the enemy's actions or reactions, nor even the knowledge of the immediate consequences for momentary decisions. On the battlefield, for those immersed in the action, the first recognition of an attack might be the wicked snap and violent impact of incoming rounds, flying shards of concrete and debris, or the screams of pain from wounded comrades. Urgent questions arise: Where are they shooting from? How many are there? Are any of my men wounded? If so, how badly? Where are other friendly forces? Is it possible they are friendly forces mistakenly shooting at us? The answers are almost never immediately obvious. In some cases, the answers to who attacked and how will never be known. Regardless, leaders cannot be paralyzed by fear. That results in inaction. It is critical for leaders to act decisively amid uncertainty; to make the best decisions they can based on only the immediate information available.

This realization is one of the biggest lessons learned for our generation of combat leaders—both in the SEAL Teams and throughout other U.S. military branches—through the years of combat in Iraq and Afghanistan. There is no 100 percent right solution. The picture is never complete. Leaders must be comfortable with this and be able to make decisions promptly, then be ready to adjust those decisions quickly based on evolving situations and new information. Intelligence gathering and research are important, but they must be employed with realistic expectations and must not impede swift decision making that is often the difference between victory and defeat. Waiting for the 100 percent right and certain solution leads to delay, indecision, and an inability to execute. Leaders must be prepared to make an educated guess based on previous experience, knowledge of how the enemy operates, likely outcomes, and whatever intelligence is available in the immediate moment.

This "incomplete picture" principle is not unique to combat. It applies to virtually every aspect of our individual lives, such as personal health-care decisions or whether or not to evacuate from the predicted path of a major storm. It particularly applies to leadership and decision making in business. While business leaders may not generally face life or death situations, they are certainly under intense pressure. With capital at risk, markets in flux, and competitors actively working to outmaneuver opponents, professional careers and paychecks are at stake. Outcomes are never certain; success never guaranteed. Even so, business leaders must be comfortable in the chaos and act decisively amid such uncertainty.

APPLICATION TO BUSINESS

"Which one do you believe?" Jocko asked. It was time to make a decision. But the executives didn't have an answer. There was much at stake for the company and the outcome was far from certain. They weren't sure what to do.

Jocko and I sat in a meeting room with the CEO of a successful software company and the CEO of one of the company's subsidiaries, an engineering company. Not yet five years from the software company's launch, the company had experienced rapid growth and exponentially increasing revenues.

Much of the company's leadership and that of their engineering company were young, talented individuals driven to succeed. Jocko and I were brought in to give them the tools to lead their teams, aggressively expand their reach, and dominate the competition.

The engineering company, led by a talented CEO, had already produced great results for the parent company. They had landed several lucrative contracts and rapidly established a good reputation for quality and service.

Jim, the CEO of the parent company, and Darla, the CEO of the subsidiary company, were proud of the effective teams and processes they had developed. They each had recruited substantial talent from their previous companies to join their current teams. Darla had five promising senior engineers, who each ran teams of half a dozen personnel or more. It had been an impressive year for Darla and her engineering company.

But like any organization, there were challenges. Constant pressure from competitors' recruiting efforts, trying to lure away their most talented people, presented the most substantial impediment to the company's long-term success. The five senior engineers were primary targets. Companies knew that if they could convince a good senior engineer to join their firm, the engineer's team—his or her most talented players—might follow.

The senior engineers were highly competitive. Rather than collaborate and support one another as the company expanded, some tried to outdo each other, hoping to position themselves for promotion ahead of their peers.

Two senior engineers, Eduardo and Nigel, had built up particular animosity for each other and had become quite cutthroat. The two engineers constantly bickered and butted heads. They blamed each other when their own projects hit delays or ran over budget. Each criticized the other's work and passed that criticism to their CEO, Darla, to try to undermine each other.

For months Darla had done her best to quell their issues and animosity. She held conference calls and face-to-face meetings with them. Darla had even taken Eduardo and Nigel to dinner several times to help them try to bury the hatchet. But nothing seemed to work. Now their relationship had deteriorated to a point that it had become dysfunctional and destructive to the rest of the team.

Jocko and I joined an off-site meeting with the senior executives from the parent company and the subsidiary companies to deliver a presentation on leadership and teamwork. During the off-site, Darla's two senior engineers' head butting reached crisis mode. She received an e-mail from Eduardo that stated he could no longer work with Nigel and insisted that Nigel be fired. Eduardo also mentioned a rumor that Nigel had met with a recruiter from another company and was considering leaving. Shortly thereafter, Darla received an e-mail from Nigel saying that he had caught wind that Eduardo had discussed a possible move to another company with some of his team. Not to be outdone, Nigel insisted that he could no longer work with Eduardo and that Eduardo must be fired.

Darla showed the e-mails to Jim, the parent company CEO, during a break in the off-site schedule. The two CEOs, Jim and Darla, asked Jocko and me for our thoughts on the dilemma with the two engineers. Darla was frustrated and nervous as to how the situation might play out. Concerned about a potential mass exodus, much of the technical knowledge on current projects could be lost. That would mean missed deadlines and degradation in quality and services. It might cost Darla's company future contracts.

When Jocko asked, "Which one do you believe?" Jim just listened quietly, waiting for Darla's input.

"I'm not sure which one, or if I believe either," Darla finally responded, "but this could get bad very quickly. Losing either one of them and some of their key folks would be painful for us. Losing both of them—and key members of their teams—could be devastating."

"Not exactly a position of strength to negotiate from," Jim added.

"Does anything in their contract prevent them from leaving and taking people with them?" Jocko asked.

"Nothing that will hold up," said Jim. "As hot as this industry is right now, people won't sign non-competes. No one likes to be locked down."

"How good are their teams?" I asked.

"Surprisingly good, despite all this drama," Darla replied.

"And how loyal are the teams to Eduardo and Nigel?" Jocko asked.

"Hard to tell," said Darla, "but there are no real die-hard fans in either group, from what I have seen."

The break was over and the off-site agenda started again. Strategic discussions took place but Darla wasn't engaged. She was clearly frustrated by the drama within her team, and with so much at stake, she seemed uncertain and unclear on what to do about it.

When the next break in the leadership off-site came, again, Jim, Darla, Jocko, and I assembled in a meeting room to discuss options.

"I think I better just let this play its course," Darla stated. She had decided not to decide.

"What makes you say that?" I asked. In the SEAL Teams, we taught our leaders to act decisively amid chaos. Jocko had taught me that, as a leader, my default setting should be aggressive— proactive rather than reactive. This was critical to the success of any team. Instead of letting the situation dictate our decisions, we must dictate the situation. But for many leaders, this mind-set was not intuitive. Many operated with a "wait and see" approach. But experience had taught me that the picture could never be complete. There was always some element of risk. There was no 100-percent right solution.

"Well, I'm really not sure what is going on," Darla responded.

"Eduardo and Nigel could both be lying, or they could both be telling the truth. There is no way to know. And there isn't enough information for me to act, so I think I just have to let it play out."

"How do you think this will most likely play out?" I asked.

"Time will tell. But they don't like working with each other," Darla responded. "When they realize I'm keeping them both, one will leave. If they choose to leave, they will have offers from our competitors very quickly. They will likely take some key players from the team with them."

"Are there any other options?" Jocko inquired.

"Well, I could fire one of them. But which one?" Darla asked. "What if I fire the wrong one? I just don't think I know enough to make a decision."

"I think you might," Jocko said. Darla knew enough to determine how the scenario was likely to play out, and thus she knew enough to make a decision. "There is another option," said Jocko.

"What's that?" Darla said incredulously.

"You could fire them both," said Jocko. Darla and Jim looked at each other, puzzled. "When Leif and I were in Task Unit Bruiser together," Jocko continued, "another task unit at our SEAL Team had a major issue between the task unit commander and one of the platoon commanders. Both were key leaders in positions critical to the task unit's performance. But these guys just couldn't get along. They hated each other. Each bad-mouthed the other to our SEAL Team's commanding officer and his staff. Finally, our commanding officer—our CEO—declared he had had enough. He gave them the weekend to figure out a way they could work together. On Monday morning, they both still insisted they could not work together and each demanded that the other be fired.

Instead, and to their surprise, the commanding officer fired them both."

It took a moment to sink in. Darla was surprised. She had not considered this option.

"I don't want to lose either of them, much less both of them!" Darla replied.

"Let me ask you this," I asked Darla. "Are either one of them stellar leaders?"

"Not exactly," Darla admitted.

Jocko responded, "They haven't found a way to work together. They are both possibly interviewing at other companies. And now, they are plotting against each other. All this has detrimental impact to your company's performance. *Not exactly* the kind of leaders I would want working for me."

"But, if I do that, what happens to their teams?" Darla asked. She was concerned about the immediate consequence that the loss in technical knowledge and expertise would mean to the company and how their teams might react.

"You said that you didn't think there are any die-hard fans of either within the team," said Jocko. "Even if there are one or two loyalists, do you really want people loyal to these types of leaders working at your company? Let me ask you this: Are there any high-potential frontline personnel that could take their jobs? It may be time for a battlefield promotion. It's likely the real in-depth knowledge on the various projects is with the frontline troops, not with Eduardo and Nigel."

"That's probably true," Darla said.

"Absolutely true," Jim added, who had been quietly listening to the conversation.

"How do you want to be perceived?" I asked Darla. "Do you want to be seen as someone who can be held hostage by the demands—the threats—they are making? Do you want to be seen as indecisive?"

"No," Darla said, flatly.

"As a leader, you want to be seen—you *need* to be seen—as decisive, and willing to make tough choices. The outcome may be uncertain, but you have enough understanding and information to make a decision," I said.

"This is one of those moments," said Jocko. "The people on the front lines, they understand these dynamics. They know what is going on. They will respect this, and their loyalty to you and your company will increase."

"That makes sense," Darla admitted.

"I'll tell you something else," I added. "These guys are cancers. Their destructive attitudes will metastasize within the team and spread to others. The quicker you cut them out, the less damage they will do, the less negativity they will spread, and, most important, the fewer people they will pull away with them."

"What do you think, Jim?" Darla asked.

"I think it makes sense," Jim replied. "Jocko and Leif have been hammering us to be aggressive and maneuver to get the best advantage over the enemy; to be decisive amid uncertainty. I think now is the perfect time to do just that," Jim replied. "Execute."

Darla was excused from the off-site meetings for an hour to come up with a plan. She called her lead developer and discussed her intent. He loved it and quickly offered up two candidates from each team who were ready and eager to step up. The two candidates had worked together in the past and already had a good professional relationship. The lead developer pulled each of the two individuals aside and met with them to check their willingness. He quickly reported back to Darla that they each were ready and excited to make the step up, adding that they both had a deep knowledge of the most critical ongoing projects.

Darla debriefed Jim on the plan specifics. Then Darla decisively executed the plan. She had the company's Human Resources

(HR) department draft a letter to both Eduardo and Nigel. HR served them each their respective letter of termination, and security escorted them from the building. The Information Technology department turned off their e-mail, their phone service, and their access to the internal intranet. For Nigel and Eduardo, it was game over. For Darla and her new leaders, it was game on.

Bruiser SEALs patrol into enemy territory. Ramadi's urban combat environment presented immense challenges: every piece of trash a potential IED, every window, door, balcony, and rooftop a potential enemy firing position.

(Photo courtesy of Todd Pitman)

CHAPTER 12

Discipline Equals Freedom—The Dichotomy of Leadership

Jocko Willink

BAGHDAD, IRAQ: THE DISCIPLINE TRANSFORMATION

"Target secure," came the call over our SEAL platoon's intersquad radio. We had just blown in the front door of the target building with a large explosive charge, and our SEAL assaulters systematically cleared through every room, eliminating threats and making sure we were in total control of the entire structure. Now it was time to determine who we had killed or captured and gather intelligence.

I was a SEAL platoon commander on my first deployment to Iraq. The bulk of our operations consisted of what we called direct-action "capture/kill" missions or targeted raids. For these operations, we operated almost exclusively at night.

The missions usually unfolded in a similar, somewhat predictable manner. Based on intelligence either from our higher headquarters or garnered from previous operations, we determined the location of a terrorist (or terrorists). Our SEAL platoon would then plan and execute an assault on the target building—a home, place of work, or safe house—in order to capture the terrorists and gather intelligence. Entering a target building, our SEALs quickly secured all the rooms and controlled the people found inside. We would then conduct quick battlefield questioning on military-age males, identify suspected terrorists or insurgents and detain them, then turn them over to a detention facility for further questioning or confinement. Before leaving the target, we searched the building for intelligence and evidence that might help convict in the Iraqi court system the captured persons. Such evidence might be bomb-making material, weapons, or anything else that could either lead us to other insurgents or help build a case against the suspects we detained.

We had trained extensively to patrol through cities, breach doors, clear buildings, and capture or kill bad guys. But we weren't police. We had very little training on how to search buildings for intelligence and properly collect evidence. But how hard could it be? On our platoon's first few operations we did what any rowdy group of highly trained, armed young men would do: we ransacked the place. While the terrorists proved highly adept at hiding weapons and evidence, SEALs showed particular skill at breaking things to find what had been hidden. We flipped over furniture, emptied desks and dresser drawers onto the floor, ripped down curtains and pictures from the walls. We smashed anything that looked like it might have some kind of hiding space in it, including televisions, cabinets, or radios. Often, we found evidence where you might least expect it. But we created such a mess in the process that we had to go through everything again to double-check what had actually been searched. This meant moving everything that had been dumped onto the floor to check under carpets for trapdoors, where contraband might be hidden. While we often found the evidence or intelligence we were looking for, on several occasions critical intelligence and evidence was missed or left behind because no specific person had been designated as responsible for its collection. The whole search process took substantial time, generally around forty-five minutes to complete. Remaining in a target building for that long, after the noise of an explosive breach and the assault team clearing the building alerted everyone in the neighborhood to our presence, made us vulnerable to counterattack from insurgents in the area.

After we had conducted a number of missions like this, a new Iraqi court system (composed of Iraqi judges and American advisors) imposed stricter requirements for collected evidence, including a documented chain of custody and the required paperwork for each item and a written explanation of where *exactly* the evidence had come from—right down to which room in which building. That way, in the new court system, the evidence could be used with a higher degree of confidence.

Suddenly, our SEAL platoon's rudimentary and highly undisciplined method of searching—the ransack—became even more problematic. So I tasked my assistant platoon commander (known as the assistant officer in charge or AOIC) with creating a more efficient search procedure for evidence to ensure our compliance with the new Iraqi court requirements. A young, enthusiastic, and aggressive SEAL, my AOIC was fired up to operate and lead. He took the assignment seriously and dove in.

A couple of days later he presented me with his plan. At first look it appeared complex, a possible violation of the Simple principle. But as he broke it down for me, it became clear that each person was assigned a simple task to execute while other members of the assault force conducted other tasks concurrently. It was a simple plan and a systematic method to enhance our effectiveness at searching for evidence. The plan designated a search team with specific individuals responsible for specific tasks: one would draw a sketch of the house and room layout, another would label each room with a number, another would video and photograph evidence where it was found. Each room would have a single SEAL operator who was designated the "room owner," responsible for everything in the room. Searches would happen systematically in an organized manner, starting from the floor up, so that we no longer had to search beneath what had been dumped on the floor.

The room owner would collect any contraband or possible evidence found and place it into a plastic bag that he carried. He would label that bag so that everyone would know who had found the evidence and in what room. For each room, when the search was completed, the room owner put an "X" through the labeled room number so that everyone knew the room had been searched. Finally, the room owner would maintain possession of the bags he collected on target until we were back on base and he could personally hand them over to the intelligence exploitation team in an organized manner, following the chain of custody procedures. Once back at camp, the sketcher and the labeler would lay out tape on the floor with the room numbers on them. The assault force would then file through and put their bag of evidence in the appropriate spot. When the exploitation team started to analyze the information, they would already know what building and what room it was found in. They also knew who had collected the intelligence, in case there were any questions.

While the plan at first sounded complex, when broken down into individual roles, it was actually fairly simple. In addition, I figured if each one of these jobs took perhaps ten minutes to accomplish, and they were all being executed simultaneously, this disciplined procedure would enable us to complete the task with far greater efficiency and speed than our undisciplined ransack method.

My AOIC had developed an excellent plan that promised to greatly enhance our evidence collection. Now we had to brief that plan to our SEAL platoon. I had the AOIC put together some PowerPoint slides that laid out the new process. It was a relatively simple brief explaining the roles, responsibilities, and sequence of the method. We called in the platoon and ran through the plan.

Since human beings tend to resist change, we met instant dissent. "This will take too long," one SEAL complained.

"Why are we changing the way we do this? If it ain't broke, don't fix it!" another added.

"I'm not going to sit on target waiting to get shot while we do all this!" a senior SEAL exclaimed. "This is going to get somebody killed." According to him, implementing this plan would spell our imminent doom.

Virtually our entire SEAL platoon was vehemently against the new plan.

So I had to explain *why*. "Listen," I started: "Who here has searched a room that had already been searched?" The platoon admitted just about everyone had. "Who here has looked into a messy bedroom on a target and wondered whether or not it has been searched?" Again, most everyone had done so. I continued, "Who searched the upstairs bathroom on our last target?" They looked at me with blank stares. I knew the answer and told them: "No one." Upon our return, we had determined that the bathroom hadn't been searched at all; we had missed it. "The fact is we are not doing the best job. Evidentiary standards are increasing. We have to do better. This method gives us a good standard operating procedure to utilize. With discipline and training, we will be much more effective in our search procedures than we have been. So we are going to try this method. Let's give it some test runs and see how it works."

There was grumbling, but the SEAL platoon reluctantly complied. We jocked up in our op gear and headed out to some abandoned buildings on base that we used for walk-through rehearsals prior to missions. Once there, we talked through the plan one more time and then we ran through it—a full-scale dress rehearsal. The first run took us half an hour, a substantial amount of time, but still less than the forty-five minutes it had taken before. We shifted to another building and ran through it again. Now people knew their jobs and better understood the flow. The second run took about twenty minutes. We moved to another building. This time, it took ten minutes. The guys were now believers. Implementing a disciplined search method drastically improved our effectiveness and efficiency. It meant we were less likely to miss key evidence and intelligence. It also improved our speed, which meant we could spend less time on target, which decreased the risk of enemy counterattack.

That night we put the new method into practice for the first time on an actual combat mission in downtown Baghdad. Like clockwork, we cleared, secured, and searched the target building—all in less than twenty minutes. When we returned to our compound, all of the evidence we gathered was placed into neat piles organized by room. Going forward, we made minor adjustments to our new procedures for even greater efficiency, like creating ziplock bags that were hung around prisoners' necks to hold the personal belongings and evidence found on their person. With a baseline of solid, disciplined search procedures, it was easy to make minor adjustments to enhance our team's efficiency and effectiveness.

Not only were we faster with the new method, the quality of our evidence collection vastly improved. Using the previous ransack method, time constraints and the inability to keep track of sloppily stored evidence limited us from hitting multiple targets per night. But with our new, disciplined method, we could execute raids and complete our searches so quickly that we could now hit two and sometimes even three targets in a single night, all while keeping evidence separate and organized. Our freedom to operate and maneuver had increased substantially through disciplined procedures. Discipline equals freedom.

●   ●   ●

Discipline starts every day when the first alarm clock goes off in the morning. I say "first alarm clock" because I have three, as I was taught by one of the most feared and respected instructors in SEAL training: one electric, one battery powered, one windup. That way, there is no excuse for not getting out of bed, especially with all that rests on that *decisive moment*. The moment the alarm goes off is the first test; it sets the tone for the rest of the day. The test is not a complex one: when the alarm goes off, do you get up out of bed, or do you lie there in comfort and fall back to sleep? If you have the *discipline* to get out of bed, you win—you pass the test. If you are mentally weak for that moment and you let that weakness keep you in bed, you fail. Though it seems small, that weakness translates to more significant decisions. But if you exercise discipline, that too translates to more substantial elements of your life.

I learned in SEAL training that if I wanted any extra time to study the academic material we were given, prepare our room and my uniforms for an inspection, or just stretch out aching muscles, I had to *make* that time because it did not exist on the written schedule. When I checked into my first SEAL Team, that practice continued. If I wanted extra time to work on my gear, clean my weapons, study tactics or new technology, I needed to *make* that time. The only way you could *make* time, was to get up early. That took discipline.

Waking up early was the first example I noticed in the SEAL Teams in which discipline was really the difference between being good and being exceptional. I saw it with some of the older, experienced SEALs. Those who were at work before everyone else were the ones who were considered the best "operators." That meant they had the best field craft, the most squared away gear, they were the best shots, and they were the most respected. It all tied into discipline. By discipline, I mean an intrinsic self-discipline—a matter of personal will. The best SEALs I worked with were invariably the most disciplined. They woke up early. They worked out every day. They studied tactics and technology. They practiced their craft. Some of them even went out on the town, drank, and stayed out until the early hours of the morning. But they still woke up early and maintained discipline at every level.

When SEALs launch combat operations, discipline is paramount. SEAL operators might have to carry loads of fifty to a hundred pounds of gear. Temperatures can be either extremely hot or freezing cold. When on a patrol and it comes time to rest, SEAL operators can't just flop down and take a load off. They must move tactically—slowly and quietly. When they want to eat or drink, they can't just drop everything and dig into their gear. Instead, SEAL operators have to wait until they are in a secure position. Though they might be exhausted from lack of sleep, when they get a chance to rest, SEAL operators must remain vigilant and aware so that the enemy does not surprise them. Nothing is easy. The temptation to take the easy road is always there. It is as easy as staying in bed in the morning and sleeping in. But discipline is paramount to ultimate success and victory for any leader and any team.

Although discipline demands control and asceticism, it actually results in freedom. When you have the discipline to get up early, you are rewarded with more free time. When you have the discipline to keep your helmet and body armor on in the field, you become accustomed to it and can move freely in it. The more discipline you have to work out, train your body physically and become stronger, the lighter your gear feels and the easier you can move around in it.

As I advanced into leadership positions, I strived to constantly improve my personal discipline. I realized very quickly that discipline was not only the most important quality for an individual but also for a team. The more disciplined standard operating procedures (SOPs) a team employs, the more freedom they have to practice Decentralized Command (chapter 8) and thus they can execute faster, sharper, and more efficiently. Just as an individual excels when he or she exercises self-discipline, a unit that has tighter and more-disciplined procedures and processes will excel and win.

I carried the idea of disciplined standard operating procedures into Task Unit Bruiser. While there were all kinds of preexisting SOPs that SEAL platoons and task units followed—how we react to enemy contact in predetermined maneuvers called "immediate action drills," the way we patrol as a standard method that varies little from platoon to platoon—in Bruiser, we took them even further. We standardized the way we loaded vehicles. We standardized the way we mustered in a building on a target. We standardized the way we "broke out" (or exited) from buildings. We standardized the way we got head counts to ensure we had all of our troops. We even standardized our radio voice procedures so that the most important information could be communicated quickly and clearly to the whole troop without confusion. There was a disciplined methodology to just about everything we did.

But there was, and is, a dichotomy in the strict discipline we followed. Instead of making us more rigid and unable to improvise, this discipline actually made us more flexible, more adaptable, and more efficient. It allowed us to be creative. When we wanted to change plans midstream on an operation, we didn't have to recreate an entire plan. We had the freedom to work within the framework of our disciplined procedures. All we had to do was link them together and explain whatever small portion of the plan had changed. When we wanted to mix and match fire teams, squads, and even platoons, we could do so with ease since each element operated with the same fundamental procedures. Last, and perhaps most important, when things went wrong and the fog of war set in, we fell back on our disciplined procedures to carry us through the toughest challenges on the battlefield.

While increased discipline most often results in more freedom, there are some teams that become so restricted by imposed discipline that they inhibit their leaders' and teams' ability to make decisions and think freely. If frontline leaders and troops executing the mission lack the ability to adapt, this becomes detrimental to the team's performance. So the balance between discipline and freedom must be found and carefully maintained. In that, lies the dichotomy: discipline—strict order, regimen, and control—might appear to be the opposite of total freedom—the power to act, speak, or think without any restrictions. But, in fact, discipline is the *pathway* to freedom.

PRINCIPLE

Every leader must walk a fine line. That's what makes leadership so challenging. Just as discipline and freedom are opposing forces that must be balanced, leadership requires finding the equilibrium in the dichotomy of many seemingly contradictory qualities, between one extreme and another. The simple recognition of this is one of the most powerful tools a leader has. With this in mind, a leader can more easily balance the opposing forces and lead with maximum effectiveness.

A leader must lead but also be ready to follow. Sometimes, another member of the team—perhaps a subordinate or direct report—might be in a better position to develop a plan, make a decision, or lead through a specific situation. Perhaps the junior person has greater expertise in a particular area or more experience. Perhaps he or she simply thought of a better way to accomplish the mission. Good leaders must welcome this, putting aside ego and personal agendas to ensure that the team has the greatest chance of accomplishing its strategic goals. A true leader is not intimidated when others step up and take charge. Leaders that lack confidence in themselves fear being outshined by someone else. If the team is successful, then recognition will come for those in charge, but a leader should not seek that recognition. A leader must be confident enough to follow someone else when the situation calls for it.

A leader must be aggressive but not overbearing. SEALs are known for their eagerness to take on tough challenges and accomplish some of the most difficult missions. Some may even accuse me of hyperaggression. But I did my utmost to ensure that everyone below me in the chain of command felt comfortable approaching me with concerns, ideas, thoughts, and even disagreements. If they felt something was wrong or thought there was a better way to execute, I encouraged them, regardless of rank, to come to me with questions and present an opposing view. I listened to them, discussed new options, and came to a conclusion with them, often adapting some part or perhaps even all of their idea if it made sense. If it didn't make sense, we discussed why and we each walked away with a better understanding of what we were trying to do. That being said, my subordinates also knew that if they wanted to complain about the hard work and relentless push to accomplish the mission I expected of them, they best take those thoughts elsewhere.

A leader must be calm but not robotic. It is normal—and necessary—to show emotion. The team must understand that their leader cares about them and their well-being. But, a leader must control his or her emotions. If not, how can they expect to control anything else? Leaders who lose their temper also lose respect. But, at the same time, to never show any sense of anger, sadness, or frustration would make that leader appear void of any emotion at all—a robot. People do not follow robots.

Of course, a leader must be confident but never cocky. Confidence is contagious, a great attribute for a leader and a team. But when it goes too far, overconfidence causes complacency and arrogance, which ultimately set the team up for failure.

A leader must be brave but not foolhardy. He or she must be willing to accept risk and act courageously, but must never be reckless. It is a leader's job to always mitigate as much as possible those risks that can be controlled to accomplish the mission without sacrificing the team or excessively expending critical resources.

Leaders must have a competitive spirit but also be gracious losers. They must drive competition and push themselves and their teams to perform at the highest level. But they must never put their own drive for personal success ahead of overall mission success for the greater team. Leaders must act with professionalism and recognize others for their contributions.

A leader must be attentive to details but not obsessed by them. A good leader does not get bogged down in the minutia of a tactical problem at the expense of strategic success. He or she must monitor and check the team's progress in the most critical tasks. But that leader cannot get sucked into the details and lose track of the bigger picture.

A leader must be strong but likewise have endurance, not only physically but mentally. He or she must maintain the ability to perform at the highest level and sustain that level for the long term. Leaders must recognize limitations and know to pace themselves and their teams so that they can maintain a solid performance indefinitely.

Leaders must be humble but not passive; quiet but not silent. They must possess humility and the ability to control their ego and listen to others. They must admit mistakes and failures, take ownership of them, and figure out a way to prevent them from happening again. But a leader must be able to speak up when it matters. They must be able to stand up for the team and respectfully push back against a decision, order, or direction that could negatively impact overall mission success.

A leader must be close with subordinates but not too close. The best leaders understand the motivations of their team members and know their people—their lives and their families. But a leader must never grow so close to subordinates that one member of the team becomes more important than another, or more important than the mission itself. Leaders must never get so close that the team forgets who is in charge.

A leader must exercise Extreme Ownership. Simultaneously, that leader must employ Decentralized Command by giving control to subordinate leaders.

Finally, a leader has nothing to prove but everything to prove. By virtue of rank and position, the team understands that the leader is in charge. A good leader does not gloat or revel in his or her position. To take charge of minute details just to demonstrate and reinforce to the team a leader's authority is the mark of poor, inexperienced leadership lacking in confidence. Since the team understands that the leader is de facto in charge, in that respect, a leader has nothing to prove. But in another respect, a leader has everything to prove: every member of the team must develop the trust and confidence that their leader will exercise good judgment, remain calm, and make the right decisions when it matters most. Leaders must earn that respect and prove themselves worthy, demonstrating through action that they will take care of the team and look out for their long-term interests and well-being. In that respect, a leader has everything to prove every day.

Beyond this, there are countless other leadership dichotomies that must be carefully balanced. Generally, when a leader struggles, the root cause behind the problem is that the leader has leaned too far in one direction and steered off course. Awareness of the dichotomies in leadership allows this discovery, and thereby enables the correction.

The Dichotomy of Leadership

A good leader must be:

- confident but not cocky;
- courageous but not foolhardy;

- competitive but a gracious loser;
- attentive to details but not obsessed by them;
- strong but have endurance;
- a leader and follower;
- humble not passive;
- aggressive not overbearing;
- quiet not silent;
- calm but not robotic, logical but not devoid of emotions;
- close with the troops but not so close that one becomes more important than another or more important than the good of the team; not so close that they forget who is in charge.
- able to execute Extreme Ownership, while exercising Decentralized Command.

A good leader has nothing to prove, but everything to prove.

APPLICATION TO BUSINESS

The chief financial officer (CFO) finally caught me alone, in between meetings, and made the point clear: the whole electrical division was losing money. The CFO could not believe that Andy, the company's CEO, kept the division running. Perhaps at some future point, the division might turn things around and become profitable. But that future was likely more than five years away— five very long years in the construction industry, where market conditions, weather, competition, contracts, and costs of labor could radically change forecasts.

"The only way we can make the electrical division profitable is if we pay them thirty to forty percent above the market rate for electrical work. And if we do that, sure, they might make money, but we will lose big."

"Why do you think Andy is keeping it open and running?"

I asked with curiosity. "He is a smart guy. He must see what's happening."

The CFO looked down to the ground and then over each shoulder. "It's Mike," he said solemnly.

"Mike, the CEO of the electrical division?" I asked.

"Yeah. He's an old friend of Andy's," answered the CFO, "and a very good friend that has stuck with him through thick and thin."

"OK," I replied, understanding what was being implied. Andy was taking care of his friend.

"What are the consequences of keeping the electrical division open?" I asked.

"If we keep it open, we will continue to bleed capital. That by itself won't kill us," answered the CFO. "But if we are that tight on cash and we encounter any unexpected cost, we would be extremely vulnerable. I don't mind risk, but this simply does not make sense."

The next day I sat down with Andy. While I had worked with this company for about a year, it was mostly with the middle managers. My latest two-day workshop had been with the C-level executives. Andy had brought me in to help with the other leaders but it turned out he too could use some guidance.

Waiting for an opportunity to open the discussion, I sat with Andy to review the strengths and weaknesses of his leadership team across divisions. Eventually, we got to Mike.

"He's a great guy," said Andy. "Known him for years. He really knows the business, inside and out."

"That's great," I replied. "His division must be making a lot of money for you."

"Well you know, I saw some good opportunity on the electrical side, and wanted to get into it," Andy said, with obvious unease. "With Mike's experience, I knew he could run a good show."

"So the division is profitable?" I asked.

"Not yet," Andy answered, "but it will be."

"How many months until it is?" I asked.

Andy paused. "Honestly," he said, "it could be three to five years."

"Ouch," I said. "That sounds like a long time in this business."

"And it could be too long. It is costing us money every month to keep him operating," Andy admitted. "But they just aren't getting any contracts outside of our company right now."

"Have you thought about shutting it down?" I asked directly.

"I have . . . but . . . you know, it will be profitable in a few years," he replied slowly.

"Let me ask you this," I said. "What if some other unforeseen event comes up? Costs you didn't expect? A major incident or accident? A large contract that falls through? Could you afford this kind of drain on the company if things went sideways?"

"Probably not," Andy replied.

"Is that the best strategy for the company?" I asked.

"You know, it's not that simple. I've known Mike for a long time. Long time," Andy said. "He has always done me right. I can't just shut him down."

There it was. Andy knew this loyalty was misguided. I just needed to get him to come to terms with it and see it for what it was.

Since Andy had just sat through my brief on the Dichotomy of Leadership, I stole one of my own lines right from it: "So one of your men is more important than the mission?" I asked bluntly.

"I didn't say that," Andy insisted.

"As a leader, you have to be close to your people," I told him. "And just like I said in the brief, the balance is that you can't be so close that one person becomes more important than the mission or the good of the team. Frankly, it sounds to me like Mike is more important than the financial stability and success of your company."

It was evident that Andy knew he was leaning too far in one direction. As with many of the dichotomies of leadership, a person's biggest strength can be his greatest weakness when he doesn't know how to balance it. A leader's best quality might be her aggressiveness, but if she goes too far she becomes reckless. A leader's best quality might be his confidence, but when he becomes overconfident he doesn't listen to others. In this case, Andy was a very loyal leader. He knew his people well and took care of his leaders and employees. But here, his loyalty to Mike was jeopardizing the financial stability of the entire company. His loyalty was out of equilibrium. But beyond the company's balance sheet, Andy's other leaders throughout the company saw what was happening, and it slowly undermined Andy's leadership as their CEO.

Finally, Andy relented, "I know, I know. I should shut it down, cut my losses. But it's hard in a situation like this."

"Of course it is. Being a leader is never easy," I said. "Imagine the U.S. Navy Sailors in World War II whose ships had been severely damaged. With their ship taking on water and in danger of sinking, those sailors sometimes had to secure the hatch to a flooded compartment when men who were their friends were still in those compartments, in order to save the ship. That's an unbelievably hard decision. But they knew if they did not make that call, they risked everyone else. They needed discipline to make the toughest decision in order to save the ship and save all the other men aboard. There is a lesson in that for your situation here with Mike. You require discipline to shut this hatch, to shut down the electrical division, in order to ensure the safety of your company—and all the other employees here."

Andy got the message. Two days later, he called me and told

me he had made a decision to cut the company's losses and commenced the shutdown of Mike's division. He knew it was the right move and was now confident in the decision. To Andy's surprise, Mike had told him he fully understood and had expected this would come. It did not impact their friendship. Andy found another place in the company to incorporate Mike's substantial experience and expertise, which allowed him to add value. The cost savings from the cut allowed them some freedom to invest in other, more-profitable divisions in the company.

Jocko and "Gunfighter" company commander, from the legendary U.S. Army 1/506th 101st Airborne, coordinate and deconflict the movement of SEALs, Iraqi soldiers, and U.S. Army troops during a large clearance operation in enemy territory.

(Photo courtesy of Todd Pitman)

AFTERWORD

There is an answer to the age-old question of whether leaders are born or made. Obviously, some are born with natural leadership qualities, such as charisma, eloquence, sharp wit, a decisive mind, the willingness to accept risk when others might falter, or the ability to remain calm in chaotic, high-pressure situations. Others may not possess these qualities innately. But with a willingness to learn, with a humble attitude that seeks valid constructive criticism in order to improve, with disciplined practice and training, even those with less natural ability can develop into highly effective leaders. Others who were blessed with all the natural talent in the world will fail as leaders if they are not humble enough to own their mistakes, admit that they don't have it all figured out, seek guidance, learn, and continuously grow. With a mind-set of Extreme Ownership, any person can develop into a highly effective leader. The qualities described throughout this book can and must be enhanced through training in order to build better leaders and teams that perform at the highest levels. Training is a critical aspect that must be utilized to develop the foundations of leadership and build confidence in leaders' abilities to communicate and lead.

Leaders may not always be the ones who generate the specific strategies, tactics, or directions that lead their teams to success. But leaders who exhibit Extreme Ownership will empower key leaders within their teams to figure out a way to win. Some of the boldest, most successful plans in history have not come from the senior ranks but from frontline leaders. Senior leaders simply had the courage to accept and run with them.

Extreme Ownership is a mind-set, an attitude. If leaders exhibit Extreme Ownership and develop a culture of Extreme Ownership within their teams and organizations, the rest falls into place. Soon, a leader no longer needs to be involved in the minor details of decisions but can look up and out to focus on the strategic mission as the team handles the tactical battles. The goal of all leaders should be to work themselves out of a job. This means leaders must be heavily engaged in training and mentoring their junior leaders to prepare them to step up and assume greater responsibilities. When mentored and coached properly, the junior leader can eventually replace the senior leader, allowing the senior leader to move on to the next level of leadership.

Much of what has been covered in this book has been covered in the past. We do not consider ourselves to be creators of a new paradigm of leadership principles. Much of what we learned or relearned has existed for hundreds and in some cases thousands of years. But, although these principles are often simple to understand in theory, it can be difficult to apply them in life. Leadership is *simple, but not easy.*

Likewise, leadership is both art and science. There are no exact answers or specific formulas to follow in every case. In any situation, there exists a great deal of gray area, neither black nor white. There may be an infinite number of options for potential solutions to any one leadership challenge. Some will be wrong and only lead to further problems, while others will solve the problem and get the team back on track. Leadership decisions are inherently challenging and take practice. Not every decision will be a good one: all leaders make mistakes. No leader, no matter how competent and experienced, is immune from this. For any leader, handling those mistakes with humility is the key. Subordinates or direct reports don't expect their bosses to be perfect. When the boss makes a mistake but then owns up to that mistake, it doesn't decrease respect. Instead, it increases respect for that leader, proving he or she possesses the humility to admit and own mistakes and, most important, to learn from them.

No book can tell a leader exactly how to lead in every situation. But this book provides a sounding board for difficult decisions, a frame of reference to use for guidance when faced with tough leadership dilemmas. While the specifics of any particular situation may vary and the characters slightly differ, the principles remain the same and can be applied, either directly or indirectly, to overcome any leadership challenge that might arise.

While there is no guarantee of success in leadership, there is one thing that *is* certain: leading people is the most challenging and, therefore, the most gratifying undertaking of all human endeavors. So, with that humbling reward in the distance, embrace the burden of command and go forward onto your battlefield, in whatever arena that may be, with the disciplined resolve to take Extreme Ownership, lead, and win.

APPENDIX

Jocko Podcast Leadership Questions and Answers

Shortly after the release of *Extreme Ownership*, Jocko Willink launched *Jocko Podcast*, which is a top-rated podcast that has spent time ranked as the #1 business podcast and was selected as one of only a dozen named "Best Podcasts of 2016" by Apple iTunes. Through in-depth book reviews and conversations with guests—veterans with extensive combat experience or people from other walks of life with unique perspectives, challenges, and trials—Jocko and his cohost and producer, Echo Charles, discuss war, leadership, business, jiu-jitsu, fighting, fitness, and life. Leif Babin is a recurring guest on the *Jocko Podcast*.

Ultimately, *Jocko Podcast* is about human nature as revealed through the lens of war, conflict, and the trials of collective and personal struggles. While the podcast does explore some of humanity's darkest episodes, it also continually seeks to uncover the good in the world that can be found and created, even in the darkest of times.

On the podcast, Jocko often answers questions submitted by

listeners through email, social media, and public interaction. Echo Charles reads the questions from listeners for *Jocko Podcast,* which range widely across an array of topics, including physical fitness, personal achievement, discipline, overcoming vices, and, of course, leadership. Since many of the answers to the leadership questions contain fundamental information about leadership, we decided to include some of them as a reference to aid leaders in their implementation of the principles we wrote about this book.

The questions and answers below are based on conversational transcripts of the podcast, and while they have been left somewhat raw to maintain their original feel, they have been edited to ensure understanding and clarity. Here are some of the leadership questions submitted by *Jocko Podcast* listeners and read by Echo Charles with answers from Jocko and Leif:

From *Jocko Podcast* 1
Echo Charles: For officers entering Special Operations, or other elite leadership positions, what advice would you have for them?

Jocko Willink: This is one of those questions that comes up a lot from people that are being promoted into a leadership position for the first time. For instance, military guys that are getting promoted into leadership positions, or people in the business world that are stepping into leadership roles for the first time. I will tell both the Special Operations folks and the folks in the business world the same thing: whether it is in business or in battle, the leadership principles stay the same.

So if you're new, what do you do? How do you step up into that leadership role?

Number one: be humble. I know it's a theme that I talk about all the time, and maybe I sound like a broken record. But everybody knows and everybody has seen the cocky guy that walks in to a leadership role and thinks he's going to run everything his way. It is "his way or the highway." And a team will almost always instantly disrespect that person.

So how do you overcome that?

You come in and you are humble. You respect people. You respect people regardless of what rank you are, regardless of whether you're making a ton more money than someone else. It doesn't matter. You treat everybody with respect. You treat them with respect and they're going to respect you.

You also have to listen to them. It means so much when one of your people comes and talks to you and you sit down and say, "Okay, let me take some notes on what you're saying." That means so much to them. And sometimes people forget that. They forget how horrible it is to look up and see the boss blowing someone off or saying, "I don't have time for you right now."

You have got to listen to people. Because listening to people helps you connect with them, and that is what you are trying to do in a leadership position: build relationships. That's what business is. That's what combat leadership is. That's what life is.

That's how you lead people. You build relationships with them. Leif and I talk about this all the time. Sure, I can give you an order if you are below me in rank, and you might carry out that order some of the time. But the people that really follow you are not the people you bark orders at; the people that really follow you are the people that you have real relationships with. Those guys will do anything for you.

The guys that worked for me, the guys that were my subordinates, they would do anything for me. And I would do anything for them—I would do anything for those guys. The guys that were in my task unit, those guys were awesome and I would do anything for those guys. I would give them anything and they would do the same for me.

Why? It wasn't because I would order them to do something. That doesn't work. You have got to build relationships.

And how do you build relationships? You build relationships by respecting people. By being humble. By listening. By telling them the truth. By having integrity and telling people the truth.

You can't lie to people. And lie is a strong word, because I don't think people are generally lying to each other on a regular basis. But leaders sometimes use half-truths and they shadow things. But you can't do that because people see right through it. Even if someone doesn't know what the truth is, they definitely know when they're not getting the truth.

So I was always straight-forward with my guys. I would say, "Okay, here's what's going on. Here's the problem. Here is what we screwed up. Here's what we need to do better. Here's the pressure I'm under from higher headquarters. Here is why I am under this pressure."

I wouldn't sugar-coat it. I wouldn't try to set something up to appear different than what the reality was.

If I'm getting told to do something that I don't believe in, I'm not going to go tell my guys, "Hey, I don't believe in this and we're going to do it anyway." No. If I don't believe in it, I have to figure out why we are doing it. I have to say, "Boss, I don't understand why we are doing this. I don't see how this is going to help us win the battle. Can you please explain it to me so I can explain it to my guys?" And my boss will be able to do that.

He will be able to do that because we are all trying to win the war. My boss is trying to win the war. I'm trying to win the war. My guys are trying to win the war. So my boss isn't going to tell me to do something that doesn't make sense and isn't logical to help us win the war. So I should believe in it. And if I don't, then I should question him.

And those are the types of things that allow us to build relationships. Open conversation. Just like ownership does. Ownership helps you build relationships. You have to take ownership when there are problems—and then you have to get the problems solved. Then, when things do go right, you pass the reward and the credit on to your team. That also helps you build relationships.

So that's what I would tell a new leader in the business world or on the battlefield.

Also, work hard. I should have said that first. Work hard—that is the foundation.

And, you also have to balance. All these things as a leader have to be balanced. For instance: when being truthful, when being honest, you also have to be tactful. Being truthful and honest doesn't give you permission to be a jerk. If you're working with your subordinates and they screw something up, you don't say, "That was a horrible job. You let me down."

No. The first thing you do is you take ownership and say, "I obviously didn't give you good-enough guidance." Then you discuss what went wrong. But the point that I'm trying to make is that there are people that are blunt, honest leaders and everyone hates them because they don't have any tact. They don't maneuver. They don't use mental jiu-jitsu. They don't think. They don't assess the whole situation. You've got to be a chess player, not a checkers player. You've got to influence people.

So don't confuse being honest with being a blunt and untactful and a jerk. You have to do jiu-jitsu. And for anyone that doesn't do jiu-jitsu, jiu-jitsu is a very nuanced game, where you're constantly trying to set things up and shape the situation.

It's not like boxing. Boxing is often a war of attrition. In boxing, I'm trying to punch you; you're trying to punch me. In jiu-jitsu, you're trying to maneuver on the other person. You're trying to get in a better position than the other person. You're trying to flank them and come from a different direction that they didn't expect. That's what the art of leadership is.

Anyone could go through a list and say, "Hey, here's what you guys screwed up on the mission. You did a horrible job. Fix it." That leader is not going to be respected. Even though he's truthful and honest and blunt, it's not going to get him where he needs to be.

There's another game that needs to be played. It's dealing with egos and it's dealing with personalities. People have different personalities. A leader has to learn to be like a woodworking craftsman. He has to learn what tools to use with different types of wood. That's what being a leader is.

If leadership was as easy as saying, "Do these seven things," then I wouldn't have a leadership book and I wouldn't have a leadership consulting business because everyone would be a great leader by just telling people what to do. There is an art to leadership and leadership is a very difficult thing to do.

It's simple, not easy. But there are simple steps. Be honest. Show integrity. Take ownership. They are simple steps, but at the same time they are incredibly nuanced and that's what makes it challenging. That is what makes it so rewarding as well.

This same question gets asked over and over again in many forms: How do I lead when I'm going into an area where I don't have much experience? How do I lead people that are older than me? How do I lead people that are younger than me? How do I lead when I am stepping into a new industry? How do I lead a bunch of men as a woman? How do I lead a bunch of women as a man? How do I lead when taking over for someone that just got fired? How do I lead when I got promoted from amongst my peers?

The answer to all these questions is always the same and is fairly simple. Be humble. Listen. Respect people up and down the chain of command. Take input but be decisive. Be honest while being tactful. Stay balanced. Understand the perspective of people on the team both above you and below you. Take ownership of problems and mistakes. Give credit to the team. Finally, build relationships—good, solid, professional relationships with your team.

From *Jocko Podcast* 19

EC: How do I get over feeling like an imposter as a new manager? I am a brand-new leader and I don't know very much. I feel like I'm about to get found out. How can I be an effective leader of my team?

JW: Welcome to leadership, my friend. Here's the thing—here's what you're actually scared of: What you're scared of is them knowing and finding out that you don't know everything.

And the thing that you need to know is that that feeling is okay. It's okay not to know everything. It's perfectly normal to be new to a leadership position and not know everything in the world. You don't have to know every single thing about a particular job that you're going into. You don't need to know everything.

What you need to do is go in and ask good questions. Listen to people. Go and say, "I've never done this procedure before," or, "I've never done work with this piece of equipment before. Can you show me how to use it? Because I want to make sure I understand. I want to make sure I get it." And people will actually respect that you are asking good questions and that you want to learn.

Now, this is not an excuse to not know anything at all. Because if you're in a new leadership position, you should be studying, reading, and learning about your new role so you have some general understanding of it. Study the manuals, the regulations, and the procedures. I'm not saying to follow all those things blindly without common sense. No. That's not what I'm saying. But there is a knowledge base that you should acquire very quickly when you take on a new leadership position. So put the work in to learn, and then apply common sense.

This is the same thing that I say every time somebody asks me: How do you lead in this situation or that situation? How do you lead new people? How do you lead more senior people? It's is the same answer every time. Be humble. Listen to them. Be on time. Work hard. Treat people with respect. Weigh decisions carefully. Talk to people and then make a good decision. Empower your folks to lead. Don't micromanage them, but give them clear guidance about what the expectations are.

It's just leadership. And when you're a new leader, you don't need to know everything. You're not expected to know everything. And showing that you can admit that you don't know everything isn't going to hurt your reputation. It is actually going to help your reputation.

So go in. Be humble. Ask questions. Learn as fast as you can. And it's okay.

You know, in the 1980s and perhaps even in the early 1990s, when guys were losing their hair and going bald, they'd do a comb-over. They would try to pull their hair over their balding scalp so it didn't look like they were going bald. And what I'm telling you, as a leader, is don't do a leadership comb-over. Do what guys do now, which is just shave their head. They just say, "Hey, I'm going a little thin up top. All good. I'm just going to shave it off."

And it's the same thing as a leader. Just say, "I'm your new leader. I don't know everything. Here's where I'm weak. Can you give me a hand?"

It's no big deal. Don't pretend. Don't hide. Don't do the leadership comb-over. No. Don't be the person that takes over and says, "I'm going to run this entire thing. I know everything. No one knows as much as I do."

That person isn't going to get respect. Stay humble and don't think you need to know everything.

From *Jocko Podcast* 34 with Leif Babin

EC: Is there a way to practice the hard conversations? I'm not known for my delicate finesse.

LB: Well, I'm glad you're not known for your delicate finesse, because neither am I. I'm a pretty direct guy and a default aggressive leader by nature. But that's something that I learned from Jocko. He often uses jiu-jitsu as an analogy and explains how, oftentimes, the direct approach doesn't really work. Particularly as a white-belt wonder in jiu-jitsu, you're going to go for one of the three moves that you know. So, people know what move is coming and it's very easy to defend against that move.

But if you can set up a move by trying to do one thing, and then suddenly go for something else, you are more likely to get it to work. In other words, using the indirect approach is generally more successful. And it's the same thing with leadership. So often, the direct approach of saying, "Do it my way," just doesn't get the job done.

Back to the question: Is there a way to practice the hard conversations? Yes, there absolutely is. That way is rehearsals. So many people think they are above doing rehearsals. Rehearsals are absolutely critical for SEAL performance on the battlefield. I don't think a lot of people realize the amount of rehearsals and walk-throughs we conduct before every operation. If we are getting ready for an operation, we might put out rocks to simulate the terrain features we will be working around or put tape on the ground to map out structures on a target site. We have everyone stand together in their sticks or squads for loading or unloading helicopters or vehicles.

The rehearsals that we do are what allow people, in the dark of night, when it's crazy and chaotic, to go to the right place and do what they are supposed to do. Things even as seemingly simple as unloading from a vehicle, we would practice. For instance, we have twenty guys sitting in the back of a big five-ton truck. It isn't just SEALs, but also Iraqi soldiers and other enablers for a particular mission. In order to get out, you have to swing open a giant, heavy, steel door. Then you've got to put a ladder out, and every-one's got to climb down that ladder, in all their gear. That can take some time.

JW: And it can turn into a *Three Stooges* scene really quick!

LB: No doubt. People can fall off. People can get injured. We've had guys fall off of trucks like that and dislocate their shoulders. But more important, if it takes the team three minutes or four minutes to do something like that—that's three or four minutes that you don't have guns pointed in every direction, at every possible threat, and that is critical. So, we had to practice that, and practice that, and practice that until we could do it in under thirty seconds. And then, if we have two assault forces, we have to make sure one assault team lined up on the left side of the road and the other assault team lined up on the right side of the road so we are organized for the assault. Those things seem really juvenile and very elementary. But even those simple things can get very complicated in dynamic situations. However, if you take the time to practice, then your performance is so much better when you get out there, in the dark of night, in the chaos of an unknown area, worrying about bad guys and where they are. Good performance comes from rehearsal.

So, for having those hard conversations, it is the same thing. You have to practice it. You have to sit down with someone who understands how the person you need to have the hard conversation with might respond. Role-play. Try different scenarios. Start with an easy scenario, a softball, then escalate to a more difficult scenario, eventually working toward worst-case scenarios.

The more you do that, the better you will be at it. And this is something that Jocko and I have done quite a bit with companies that we work with: role-play. For instance, let's say you have to counsel someone. It might seem easy to just say, "You know what, you screwed up and we're holding you accountable." But maybe this is a good guy who simply made a mistake. He messed something up and now you have to talk to him to ensure he doesn't make that mistake again. But you can't be too negative or perhaps you hurt his confidence. And with all that, you aren't 100 percent sure how he will react. It is going to be a hard conversation, and that rehearsal and role-play is critical in preparing you. It makes you better and enables you to perform better. You have to rehearse.

JW: Absolutely. And in three or four iterations with someone in a role-play scenario, they get noticeably better. You can actually watch them get better each time.

LB: Yes. Rehearse, rehearse, rehearse. And in the business world, especially with interpersonal leadership scenarios, that means role-playing. That means preparation and practice. That is how you execute with the most effectiveness and efficiency as a leader.

From *Jocko Podcast* 47

EC: What advice do you have for people who have weak, poor, or otherwise ineffective leaders? How do you manipulate that situation?

JW: When you are in a situation like this, when you have somebody that's a weak or ineffective leader, the answer is straightforward: what you do is *lead*. You lead. And I hope people that listen to this podcast regularly, I hope you all knew what I was going to say: when someone is not leading you, then you lead them. You pick up the slack for their weakness.

My leader doesn't want to come up with a plan? That's okay. I will.

My leader doesn't want to give a brief? That's fine. I will.

My leader doesn't want to mentor the younger troops? That's okay. I will do it.

My leader doesn't want to take the blame when something goes wrong? That's fine with me. I'm going to take the blame. And you have to think about that one. That one can be tricky because you think to yourself, "If I take the blame, I'm going to look bad. I'm going to look bad in front of the team and in front of the more senior boss—my weak boss's boss."

But think about it from a leader's perspective. Let's say the mission was a failure, and the boss comes in to find out what happened. Listen to the way this situation plays out: I'm the guy that was in charge of the mission and I say, "Sorry, boss, we failed. But it wasn't my fault. It was his fault," and I point the finger at someone else.

Now imagine that the guy I pointed the finger at says, "Yes. It was my fault. Here's what happened. Here are the mistakes I made. And here is what I am going to do to fix the situation next time."

Who does the senior boss respect more? The guy who blamed someone or the guy who took responsibility—the guy that took ownership? Of course, it is the guy that takes ownership of the problems. He gets the respect. And the guy that is passing the blame—the boss is looking to fire him!

So keep that in mind. Before you get intimidated about taking the blame for something because you think you are going to look bad and you're going to get fired, think about what it looks like from the senior leader's perspective. It is almost always preferable to take the blame.

Now, am I saying this as a blanket statement that is 100 percent true, all the time? No. There are some times when the boss makes an error that you should not take the blame for. Let's say some classified information got compromised and it was your boss that actually lost track of the classified material. That is not a time to take the blame. First of all, you're not telling the truth; factually, it wasn't your fault. Second, the boss made a mistake that is inexcusable. So that is not a situation where you should step up and take the blame. And if your boss is so cowardly that he tries to pin a serious incident on you, you cannot allow that.

But when you're doing an operation or a project where mistakes get made, and your boss is scared to take ownership of them—take ownership of them. You will win in the long run.

Now, here's the part that is crucial and critical—and the most challenging part of this. That is when you step up to lead, you want to make sure you aren't *stepping up* and *stepping on* your leader. You don't want to step into their spotlight. You don't want to impose yourself in their leadership limelight and glory. You don't want to do that. You can't do that. Instead, you want them to get all the credit. You don't want to have them be intimidated by you in any way and this can be difficult to do.

Because when you start taking ownership of things, it can be very intimidating for the person that's above you. They might think, "Dang. This guy is bold. He is stepping up and taking charge." And they might get intimidated by that, so you have to be careful.

So, what you have to do is some indirect maneuver warfare. Some mental jiu-jitsu. For instance, if they don't want to come up with a plan, maybe you say, "Hey, boss, what do you think of this? Would this be a good plan?" You give them the plan, but you are letting them think it is theirs by appearing to seek guidance or approval.

Maybe if your leader is not mentoring the younger guys, you say, "Hey, boss, I want spend some time with the guys after work. Do you mind if I have a little session with them and go over what we learned on our last deployment?" Here, you're asking their permission—not running out acting on your own.

You might even say, "I think it would look really good for

our team if we were doing this." If the team looks good, then the leader looks good. And you want to make your boss look good. You really do.

There are plenty of other ways you can step up and lead without stepping on your leader's toes. Because if you do step on your leader's toes, you could end up in a situation where they feel intimidated by you. That could end up with you getting put in the doghouse, or fired, or demoted, or in some other kind of trouble because they feel intimidated by you. So use caution.

There are also many leaders who aren't that aggressive, but when you start getting aggressive, they actually like it. I worked for plenty of people that loved the fact that I would step up and take care of problems. One of the reasons they liked it was because even though they weren't the most aggressive leaders, they were good, confident leaders themselves.

It is the insecure leader that you need to watch out for. The insecure leader is always worried about looking bad.

And that is another great point to make here: when you, as a leader, have somebody that is stepping up and taking charge, and you start feeling intimated by it, ask yourself, "Why am I intimidated in this situation?" It's probably your ego. You are being a weak leader—that's why you are being intimidated by your subordinates.

If your subordinate is stepping up and doing your job and doing it better than you, don't get mad. Instead, step up yourself and start figuring out how you can improve what you are doing. How can you look up and out? What other areas can you focus on since your subordinate leader has stepped up and is making things happen? Which, by the way, is exactly what you should want as a leader: for your team to step up. That is awesome. We want that. That's Decentralized Command. That's building leaders underneath you to take over your job, which should always be your goal as a leader.

Finally, every time I see someone that says, "I have a weak leader," I always say, "Lucky you!"

Take advantage of that. LEAD! Do what you want. It is such a good opportunity when you have a weak leader above you. Don't get all downtrodden because your leader doesn't motivate you. Motivate yourself! Take charge of things. Take advantage of it. Make things happen. It's awesome to have a weak leader. I love it. I get after it. It gives me so much more mobility in my job. If I have a strong leader, obviously, that's great too. But a weak leader is no factor. Step up and take advantage of it. Step up and lead.

From *Jocko Podcast* 32

EC: Does micromanaging ever work?

JW: Well, and this might surprise some people: yes. And more important, sometimes you *have to* micromanage. For instance, if you have somebody that isn't good at their job, or doesn't do a good job, or doesn't show up on time, or doesn't run things right. You know how you fix that? You've got to get in there and micromanage. Because we can't have mission failure. But then, once you've got them up to speed, you need to stop micromanaging.

Leif or the other platoon commander or assistant platoon commanders that worked for me will tell you I was a micromanaging maniac when they first started working for me. I was in their grill all the time telling them, "You've got to do this. No, move over here a little bit. No, make this adjustment." And I wouldn't give them any slack.

But then, as soon as I saw that they had a handle on their job, of course then I said, "Okay, you got this." Then I gave them all kinds of room to maneuver and let them run with it. And they crushed it.

But it started with micromanagement and morphed into De-centralized Command. So sometimes, micromanagement is an absolute necessity. But it should never be a steady state—it should never become the norm.

This also means that if you're getting micromanaged, that can be a red flag. Sure, you might have somebody that's a control freak and is a compulsive micromanager. But you also might have somebody that doesn't trust you yet. So how do you build up their trust? How do you get them to stop micromanaging you?

Is it by hiding from them? No. It's by being open. It's by saying, "Hey, boss, here is what I'm going to do and exactly how I am going to do it." You actually send them more information than they could even want. You show them how responsible you are. You show them what a good handle you have on the situation. That's how you can help overcome the micromanager—by putting them at ease.

But if someone's not doing what they're supposed to do, or they're failing, or they're letting you down, then, yes, you've got to get in their grill and micromanage them.

The other time you might need to micromanage is when you're mentoring someone. Because now I'm sitting side-by-side with you. I'm breathing down your neck a little bit. That can be viewed as micromanagement. But again, sometimes it's necessary. If you don't know the ropes yet, I've got to show you the ropes. That means I've got to sit by you and make sure you know it. If I'm teaching somebody something in a work environment, that can also be viewed as micromanagement—and it actually is. Because I'm saying, "Put this over here. Put that over there."

The person you're teaching might say, "Wait, back off. Let me do this."

You have to tell them, "No. You don't know how to do it yet. I've got to show you how to do it. I'm teaching you how to do it. Once you can do it on your own, you will be on your own."

Beyond teaching, sometimes you've got to actually show people how to do something. There was one time where a platoon commander was having some trouble leading his men. I told him, "You sit and watch. I'm going to run this squad."

So he sat down and I ran the squad, got aggressive, and told people where to go and how to move. And when I was done, the platoon commander looked at me and said, "Okay. I can do that." And he did it. As soon he saw me do it one time, he got it. He understood it.

So, sometimes micromanagement is okay. The thing is, you don't want to get stuck in the rut of micromanagement. If I mentor you, if I teach you, if I instruct you, if I show you the way, that doesn't mean stay there and keep micromanaging. Because you're not doing your job as a leader if you are micromanaging.

In reality, you shouldn't even have the capacity to micromanage everybody that works for you. If you have that much capacity, you're not doing your job. You're not looking up the chain of command. You're not looking out. You're not thinking strategically. Your troopers, your subordinate leadership, they should be stepping up and leading, and you should expect that of them.

Also, some people micromanage because of their ego. They want to do one of two things: they want to exercise their power over a person or they want to show off their knowledge. How do you handle those types of micromanagers? You work hard. You get ahead of them. You give them all the information they want, and then some. You get better at the job so they trust you and move on.

If you do have to micromanage for a short period of time, it should feel like a chore for you that you don't like doing, and it shouldn't last forever. You can get in there and you can micromanage for a certain amount of time, but then you need to say, "Okay, you got this. You know what you're doing. I'm stepping back." Then you have to step back, because no one likes to be micromanaged.

Once you get people up to speed, step back, and let them run. Let your leaders lead.

From *Jocko Podcast* 12

EC: Regarding mistakes, what are some of your own and some you've seen made by leaders you looked up to. How does a leader recover? Can a leader ever fully regain trust?

JW: This is actually pretty easy one. First part, the mistakes I've made? Read *Extreme Ownership*—most of the book is about mistakes. Mistakes that Leif and I made.

How do you recover from a mistake?

If you make a mistake, own it. The worst thing you can do if you make a mistake is try to avoid taking blame for it. That's the worst thing you can do. Think about the bosses you have had that made a mistake. If he said, "No, it wasn't my fault," you'd lose respect for him.

So you can't do that. You've got to take ownership of it.

Again, if you think about the bosses you've had that made excuses, you don't have any mercy on them. You're just ruthless on them. You pick them apart. So step number one is take ownership if you made a mistake.

That's how it's always seemed to me as I looked up the chain of command. If I saw a guy that made mistakes and he took ownership of them, then the attitude was, "Okay, the boss knows he made a mistake, and he's owning it, so we will support him." But if the boss is blaming everybody else and not taking ownership, we had a hard time with it. The level of respect went down.

As a matter of fact, we had a borderline mutiny in one of my platoons. We lower enlisted guys went to the commanding officer and said, "We won't work for our platoon commander."

So all these ideas that people have of the military, that we obey orders without question and all that, think about what we did: we went before the commanding officer and told him we didn't want to work for our boss!

Now, the commanding officer, to his credit said, "Listen, guys. You can't have a mutiny. Not at my command, not on my team. You guys suck it up and figure out a way to make it work. Go do what your told. Get in line."

EC: So the mutiny didn't work?

JW: Actually, a week later, he fired the guy. He made it perfectly clear to the officer that he had one chance, which he fell short on, and then he fired him. It was pretty crazy to see it happen. And I say this all the time, the platoon commander didn't get fired because he lacked tactical skill or wasn't physically fit. The main reason our platoon commander got fired was because he wouldn't take anyone's advice. He wouldn't listen to anyone. When he made a mistake, he constantly covered up for himself. Obviously, it didn't work out for him.

As far as regaining trust, which is the other part of the question: almost as soon as you admit that you made a mistake, you are automatically regaining trust—that's where you start regaining trust and it just goes from there. Then, you follow through with what you say. That's another way to build trust: do what you say and say what you do. That helps build the trust, which helps build the relationship. And it's a relationship that you're trying to build. Obviously, the minute you're lying to people, how do you build trust? And if you make a mistake, and you say it's not your fault, that's a lie and everyone knows it.

EC: But people have that fear that their team is going to think, "Our leader doesn't know what he is doing," or "He doesn't have a handle on the situation."

JW: That doesn't matter. That just doesn't matter. It is so much better to say, "Hey, guys, I don't know how to do this. Can you show me how?" or, "Hey, guys, I've never used this weapon before. Can you give me a familiarization on it?"

The worst thing you can do is step up to the firing line on a range with a weapon you've never used before and you don't even know how to lock and load it or clear and safe it. Then you look like a total idiot. And even worse, you look like a guy who is too arrogant and too insecure to ask for help. It's actually a sign of insecurity if you can't ask when you need help with something.

When you are too embarrassed to ask for help, that's a little knock at your door saying, "You're insecure!"

When you say to one of your people, "Hey, I'm stuck on this problem," or "I made a mistake and I need some help," people don't think you are an idiot—unless you are doing it every three seconds, because that means you haven't studied. Because you have to study. You have to know your trade; you've got to know your craft. And if you don't, you have to learn it. You have to break out the books. But once you have learned it, and there are still some things that you don't understand, well, guess what? Just ask the question.

Your frontline troopers are going to know more than you; they should know more than you. I was a radioman for eight years in the SEAL Teams, but by the time I was a lieutenant commander in a SEAL task unit, I didn't know as much as the platoon radiomen knew. So I just had to ask the questions. It's no big deal. If you're secure in your leadership, you're fine to ask some questions. It's not that big of a deal.

But you cannot lie to people. You cannot make excuses.

Back to the original question. How do you regain trust with people? Tell them the truth.

It's really a simple concept. Not always easy, but it is simple and effective.

From *Jocko Podcast* 11 with Leif Babin

EC: Aside from command, what is your favorite operator specialty? Machine gunner, breacher, corpsman, etc.?

JW: Let me tell you what I wanted my platoons to think: I wanted each guy to think that he was the most important guy. I wanted the radioman to think he was most important because he could call in fire support. I wanted the corpsman [combat medic] to think that he was most important because he was going to save everybody. I wanted the snipers to think they were most important. I wanted the machine gunners to think they were the most important because they were going to lay down the fire and get us out. I was always a big supporter of all of them. And you need them all, because it's a team.

LB: You get those people that think, "This is most important," or "My job is the best." We were just talking about Chris Kyle's portrayal in the movie *American Sniper*. You need the entire element working together. You need those machine gunners. You need the corpsmen. You have to have the radiomen passing your position and telling friendlies where you are and where the enemy is so you can get help. All that stuff is absolutely critical.

As far as a favorite specialty, I like to shoot. Combat rifle and pistol shooting has always been one of my favorite things to do. I love that about the SEAL Teams. The great training, the competition—moving and shooting against steel targets and moving targets. We go to these amazing ranges and it's super fun.

And that being said, that's not my job. That's a realization you have to come to as a leader: my job is not to shoot. There are times when I have to shoot, and I must be able to shoot accurately to eliminate a threat. I have to be able to do that like everybody else in the platoon. But as a leader, that's not my job.

I learned that in our advanced training, after BUD/S, there is another six months of what we call SEAL qualification training. Like Jocko and I always say, failure is often the best teacher. I was a squad leader, and I remember I was trying to shoot and lay down fire while my squad was "under fire" in training, and I was trying to look around at the same time. And I got a safety violation for trying to shoot live rounds downrange and attempting to look around at the same time. Guess what? You can't do both. And I deserved the safety violation. It was dangerous. You never want to pull the trigger on your weapon if you're not looking down the sights and controlling your weapon. It was exactly what should have happened.

But it was a realization to me: I can't do both. And why did I need to be shooting then? There were eight other guys in the squad laying down fire. But there was nobody else looking around. As the leader, it's my job to "high-port" my weapon, which means gun pointed to the sky, not engaging targets, and I need to be looking around. I need to take a step back off the line. Jocko often talks about "detach" and look around. A leader's job is making the calls as the command and control for the team. If you're not doing it, nobody is doing it. So, leaders have to always recognize that their role is to detach.

You also have to understand the capabilities and limitations of the different personnel, specialties, departments, and assets within your team. But, as a leader, you can't get sucked into the details. You have to stand back from the details, high-port your weapon, and be the command and control for your team to make the big, strategic decisions.

EC: What do you do when you know an order is bad but if you don't fall in line, the punishment will be terrible?

LB: Jocko, you talked about this on the podcast when you were reviewing *The Military Maxims of Napoleon*. I think the quote was: "Every general-in-chief who undertakes to execute a plan which he knows to be bad is culpable. Every general-in-chief who, in consequence of orders from his superiors, gives battle with the certainty of defeat is equally culpable." What that really means is Extreme Ownership. You own it, regardless.

You're obligated to NOT follow an illegal order. It's on you. It's your responsibility. If it's truly bad, if it's truly catastrophic, you have to be willing to take the punishment. You want to punish me for that? Okay. You want to fire me? Fine. I'm not going to execute a bad order, because I will sleep better at night knowing that I made the right decision. I'm not going to go down this path that leads to the destruction of our mission or our team. You have to be able to look yourself in the mirror, and that is most important. If you want to fire me for that, I'm okay with it.

But you have to understand that you must prioritize. Rarely are things that extreme. There are those people that have an over-the-top reaction with the doomsday predictions for a change in strategy or tactics, when it's not that big of a deal.

One example I thought of, people are shocked to hear about what it's like going to war in today's world—the massive administrative requirements. Me and the other platoon officers complained about the immense amount of paperwork we had to do all the time—and no one complained more than me! In Task Unit Bruiser, Jocko said right away that, even in the midst of arduous training for combat, when our commanding officer asked for the paperwork, we were going to do all of it. We're going to turn it in early. We're going to do it better than everybody else.

JW: Guess what I was doing? I was building myself a relationship with the commanding officer. "Oh, you want admin stuff done? No problem." We did all the little things. And then, on one of the rare times when we needed to push back on some direction from higher, we were able to make a sensible argument and get the support we needed.

LB: One of the reasons that we were able to successfully push back on the stuff that really mattered, was because all of the little things, all those paperwork requirements that other people didn't do or had complained about to the commanding officer the whole time while doing them, we had done them. Yes, it was a pain for us. I wanted to be doing other things. But we got it done. Those little things built up trust with the commanding officer and the rest of our higher headquarters. And that gave us the credibility to push back. When we prioritized the things that truly mattered, we were able to get whatever we needed approved.

JW: I talk about this often: leadership must be aligned with the frontline troops—if not there is something drastically wrong. Of course, my bosses wanted us to kill bad guys, keep our troops safe, and win the war. In business, of course the boss wants you to be profitable, keep your troops happy, deliver a good product, serve the customer, and be ethical. Those are standard things and those are aligned. So, if you send an idea up the chain of command, or you get told to do something and you don't do it because it's not going to help you be profitable, why would your boss disagree? Have the sense to know when to say, "No," and then the wherewithal and moral courage to actually say, "No."

Jocko Podcast can be found on iTunes, Google Play, Stitcher, most other podcast platforms, and on the internet at www.jockopodcast .com. Video versions can also be found on the YouTube channel, Jocko Podcast.

INDEX

From the Authors of the
#1 *New York Times* Bestseller
EXTREME OWNERSHIP

THE
DICHOTOMY
OF
LEADERSHIP

JOCKO WILLINK
AND
LEIF BABIN

TURN THE PAGE FOR
A SNEAK PEEK

St. Martin's Press

CHAPTER 8

Hold People Accountable, but Don't Hold Their Hands

Jocko Willink

BAGHDAD, IRAQ: 2003

Ba-ba-ba-ba ba-ba ba-ba-ba!

The M2 .50-caliber machine gun—which we affectionately called the Ma Deuce—was unleashing fury into the city. And it wasn't alone in its firepower. Our convoy of Humvees had taken some enemy small-arms fire from a building near the highway on which we were driving. We were in Baghdad and it was the fall of 2003, early in the Iraq War. Our Humvees were unarmored. We had completely removed the canvas vehicle doors and modified the seats to face outward so that we could scan with our weapons and engage threats. Facing outward also presented our body armor plates toward potential enemy contact to protect us from the impact of enemy bullets. The Ma Deuce .50-cal was mounted in the turret, the circular hole in the top of each Humvee, manned by a SEAL who stood with his chest and head protruding through the roof. Each Humvee carried SEAL assaulters in the back on bench seats with medium machine guns mounted on articulating swing arms so we could shoot accurately on the move.

As soon as the shooting started, a call came out over the radio.

"Contact right!"

That let everyone know that the enemy attack was to our right. Immediately, everyone who could get their weapon into position returned fire with a vengeance. Dozens of machine guns belched flames and tracer fire, along with M4 rifles. We laid down an overwhelming barrage of firepower that likely compelled whomever had engaged us to deeply regret that decision.

But just because we were shooting didn't mean we stopped the convoy or even slowed down. As we fired, the call came quickly over the radio.

"Blow through, blow through!" Which meant we would actually increase speed to get out of the ambush area. And that was exactly what we did. Within a few hundred yards, we were clear of the ambush, and the call to stop shooting came out over the radio:

"CEASE FIRE!"

We continued on, back to our base on the outskirts of Baghdad International Airport. Upon arrival, we fueled up the Humvees in preparation for the next mission and headed back to our compound for the debrief.

The debrief wasn't critical. Why would it be? We had made it through another attempted enemy ambush, and once again, we crushed them and they didn't hit any of us. In the early days of the Iraq War, we weren't yet facing the well-organized, combat-experienced, and well-funded insurgency that Task Unit Bruiser would come up against in Ramadi three years later. At this time, the enemy consisted of little more than criminals, thugs, and former Saddam Hussein regime elements running around trying to cause problems. They weren't much of a problem for us. We were well trained. We were aggressive. And we were executing missions that gave us a solid advantage over the enemy. Most of the operations we conducted were what we called "direct action" missions, with the objective of capturing or killing the suspected bad guys for planning and executing attacks against U.S. forces, Iraqi security forces, or the new interim government of Iraq.

We would gather intelligence, bounce what we knew off various other intelligence sources, trying to confirm the most important piece of information about the suspected terrorists: their location. Once we had their location, we planned our assault.

The assaults were fairly straightforward. We would stop the vehicles at a pre-designated location and patrol on foot to the target. Once at the target, we used various means to enter the outer walled compound, sometimes going over the walls, sometimes breaching the gates, sometimes both simultaneously. Within a few minutes, we had the entire target building under our control and had subdued all possible threats.

Of course, the planning for every mission was slightly different based on the specific target. We adapted our plans and the tactics, techniques, and procedures to execute operations, but at the same time, we always maintained a solid grip on the fundamental principles of combat leadership: Cover and Move, Simple, Prioritize and Execute, and Decentralized Command.

Cover and Move allowed us to maneuver safely to and from the target. We used this basic but essential tactic for every movement and it was present in every plan we developed. We kept the plans Simple. While it was sometimes tempting to utilize more complex or convoluted tactics, we always chose the most straightforward course of action so that everyone on the team knew exactly how to execute the plan. During the planning phase, we would utilize Prioritize and Execute to ensure the team concentrated our efforts on the most important facets of the target, and we would focus our resources there. Lastly, we would create our plans with Decentralized Command. The junior leaders developed supporting sections, then we would consolidate these into one comprehensive plan.

On top of the Laws of Combat, we used stealth, surprise, and violence of action to ensure we had the upper hand on the enemy whenever possible. It was never our intent to have a fair fight. It was our job to maximize our advantages over the enemy and we did everything in our power to make this happen.

Our tactics and planning usually left the enemy shaken, confused, and unable to intelligently defend themselves. Since no one in my platoon had been in combat before, the opportunity to exercise everything we had learned about planning and executing operations was gratifying—not only because we were carrying out important missions, but also because we had trained and prepared for so long.

It was awesome. It was awesome because we were getting to do real work after the long "dry years" of no combat. It was awesome because we had developed sound tactics that made us highly effective. It was awesome because we dominated the enemy; our weapons, tactics, and training were far superior. We felt like rock stars. During the few firefights we found ourselves in, they didn't stand a chance. So far, only one man had been wounded and it was relatively minor. We felt unstoppable.

That felt good.

The more missions we handled, the more confident we became. We began to try to push even harder. To complete our missions even faster. To push the envelope.

I noticed that guys started carrying less gear so they could move faster. Fewer magazines of ammunition since we hadn't been in any sustained contacts. Fewer hand grenades since we hadn't had to use them, as the enemy didn't put up much resistance. They began to carry less water since the missions were quick, and we always had the vehicles nearby with ample supplies of water in big five-gallon jugs. This was all done in the belief that if we were lighter, we could move more quickly. We could bound in and out of doors and windows and more efficiently chase down bad guys who had fled from the target buildings. We wanted to be better and more effective at our jobs, and I agreed with that.

But then arrogance started to creep in. We started to think that the enemy couldn't even touch us.

One day, before a mission, I talked with one of my guys.

"Let's go get 'em!" I joked with him, slapping him on the back. But instead of hitting the solid mass of the ballistic body armor plate we wore in both the front and back, I felt only soft web gear. I grabbed the web gear and squeezed it to confirm—he had no ballistic back plate inserted into his web gear.

"Where's your back plate?" I asked him.

"I took it out," he said.

"You took it out?" I asked, incredulous.

"Yeah. I took it out," he said, indifferent. "It's too heavy. I can move a lot quicker without it."

I was shocked. Of course, at about seven pounds each, the plates were heavy—but they stopped bullets from entering your body and killing you!

"Yeah, but what if you get shot?" I asked him.

"I'm not going to be running," he said defiantly. "The enemy isn't going to shoot me in the back. A lot of us took them out," he told me with a shrug of the shoulders, as if this idea made total sense.

"A lot of guys?" I asked him.

"Yeah. We want to be fast," he said.

Some of my guys weren't wearing body armor—a key piece of lifesaving equipment.

Idiots, I thought to myself, *what a bunch of idiots!*

Then, I quickly realized this was my fault. I was responsible for making sure my men had the right equipment every time they went in the field. That was why we held inspections—to make sure they were accountable. But our operational tempo was so fast that I didn't always have time to inspect everyone's gear. Of course, between me, my platoon chief, and our LPO (leading petty officer), gear did get inspected regularly. But we sometimes launched on missions within fifteen to twenty minutes of being tasked; there was no way we could inspect everyone's gear every single time. There had to be a better way than imposed accountability to make sure everyone was carrying all the gear they should be—including the ballistic back plate to help prevent them from taking a bullet to the back. I knew the answer. The solution to this problem wasn't accountability. The solution was the same answer to every problem in every team: leadership. I had to lead.

A few minutes later, we were standing around the magnet board for roll call in preparation for the next mission, before we loaded up the vehicles to launch. Once the LPO had gone through roll call, I said my final piece before launch.

"Remember we are trying to get off the target quickly," I said. "This is a bad area and we don't want the enemy in the neighborhood to have time to set up on us when we leave.

"And—last thing," I emphasized. "If you don't have your back plate in, go put it in. Now. Everyone. Alright? Loading up in five. Let's go."

Only about five or six guys scurried off to their tents to grab their back plate—but that was five or six too many. A few minutes later we loaded up the Humvees and headed out on the operation. It all went smoothly. We hit the target, grabbed the bad guys, gathered the intelligence we needed, and then headed back to base. During the debrief, I addressed the issue of the back plates, not by yelling or screaming or even threatening accountability by constant inspections of everyone's gear. I knew accountability wasn't the answer—we just didn't have time to hold everyone accountable before each and every operation. Instead, I explained *why* it was important for them to wear their plates.

"I know some of you haven't been wearing your back plate. Right?" I looked around the room. A few guys nodded.

"Bad idea," I continued. "Bad idea. Why wouldn't you wear your back plate?" I questioned one of the guys.

"Trying to be lighter," he said. "The lighter we are, the faster we can move."

"I get that," I answered. "But can you move faster than a bullet?" That got a little chuckle from the group.

"Yeah, but I'm not trying to outrun a bullet," one young, confident SEAL said. "In fact, I'm not running away. So the enemy isn't going to see my back." This also got a reaction from the group with some head nods and grins. I even heard "Hell, yeah" from a couple of guys at the back of the room. It was a bold statement. A confident statement. A courageous statement. But it crossed the line from bold, confident, and courageous into cockiness and arrogance.

I understood how the confident young SEAL had arrived at that conclusion and how anyone in the platoon might have arrived at the same thing. We had been winning against the enemy—and winning easily. We had been shot at only a couple of times and nothing very significant. We were dominating and felt untouchable.

"Okay. I'm glad you aren't going to run away from the enemy. I don't think anyone in this room will," I told the group, and I truly believed this. Our platoon was solid.

"But let me ask you this," I continued. "Do you always know where the enemy will be? Do you always think he is going to be in front of you? Don't you think we could get ambushed or flanked from behind and you might get shot from that direction when you hadn't anticipated it?"

The room got quiet. Of course that could happen—at any time.

"Listen. I'm glad we are kicking the enemy's ass," I said, "and we are going to keep kicking his ass. But we cannot get arrogant or complacent. The enemy might never get the drop on us. But at the same time, he might get the drop on you on the next mission. And while being light is good and allows us to be quick, being quick isn't going to stop a bullet from entering your back and killing you. And it isn't just about you; it isn't just you, individually, at risk. If one of you gets shot, that means others have to carry you. Think about how much that will slow us down in a serious gunfight, when we want to be light and fast.

"But it is about much more than that," I said. "If one of us gets killed, it is a win for the enemy. And on top of that—and more important—it is a loss for America, for the Navy, for the Teams, and for your family. And we need to do everything we can to prevent that loss. That includes wearing all the ballistic protection we can. Understood?"

The room was quiet. I had made my point.

As the deployment continued, we still didn't have time to inspect everyone's gear. But we made it a point to make sure everyone understood the bare minimum they needed to carry. They also understood what items were not optional and, more important, *why* they were not optional. Once my troops understood *why* a piece of lifesaving equipment was needed and how it impacted not only them but the mission as well, they made sure not only to have the proper gear with them but also that the gear was ready for use.

This didn't happen because I "held them accountable." It happened because they now understood *why* the particular piece of gear was important for them, for the mission, and for the team. Now they were holding *themselves accountable*. Furthermore, when the troops understand why, they are empowered—and with that empowerment, they begin to police themselves and each other, which provides redundancy and unification of effort.

This is not to say that I never inspected gear. That is the dichotomy: while a leader wants team members to police themselves because they understand *why,* the leader still has to hold people accountable through some level of inspection to ensure that the *why* is not only understood but being acted upon. So my platoon chief, LPO, or I would still regularly inspect gear when able—but that was not our primary tool for accountability. We didn't need to hold the troops' hands to make sure they were accountable. They *held themselves accountable,* which proved far more effective.

Once the platoon realized the importance of executing in accordance with the standard and how violating the required gear list impacted the overall mission, we didn't have to rely solely on gear inspections. Each team member applied peer pressure to keep others in check. And that peer pressure from within the team was far more powerful than any pressure I could apply from above them in the chain of command.

The balance between the troops understanding the *why* mixed with intrusive accountability provides the best possible outcome for a team. As a testament, through the rest of the deployment, I never caught another man without body armor again.

Principle

Accountability is an important tool that leaders must utilize. However, it should not be the primary tool. It must be balanced with other leadership tools, such as making sure people understand the *why,* empowering subordinates, and trusting they will do the right thing *without* direct oversight because they fully understand the importance of doing so.

Unfortunately, leaders often get the idea that accountability can solve everything—and in a sense they are right. If a leader wants to ensure a subordinate follows through with a task, the leader can inspect repeatedly to confirm that the task gets done. With enough oversight, task completion can achieve 100 percent success. This is why leaders often want to use accountability to fix problems: it is the most obvious and simple method. The leader tells a subordinate to carry out a task; the leader watches the subordinate do the task; the leader inspects the task once it is complete. There is almost no room for error.

Unfortunately, there is also almost no room for the leader to do anything else besides monitor the progress of that specific subordinate in that specific task. If there are multiple subordinates with multiple tasks, a leader very quickly becomes physically incapable of inspecting them all. On top of that, while focused down the chain of command and inward toward the team, the leader will have no ability to look up and out—up toward senior leadership to build relationships and influence strategic decisions and out toward the strategic mission to anticipate future operations and understand developments. Finally, when the leader is not present to provide immediate oversight, the subordinate may or may not continue to properly execute a particular task.

Instead of using accountability as the primary tool of leadership, leaders should implement it as just one of many leadership tools. Instead of holding people accountable, the leader has to *lead.*

The leader must make sure the team understands *why*. Make sure its members have ownership of their tasks and the ability to make adjustments as needed. Make sure they know how their task supports the overall strategic success of the mission. Make sure they know how important their specific task is to the team and what the consequences are for failure.

Now, this does not mean that accountability should never be used. In *Extreme Ownership,* chapter 2, "No Bad Teams, Only Bad Leaders," we wrote that "when it comes to standards, as a leader, *it's not what you preach, it's what you tolerate.*" It is imperative that leaders hold the line and uphold the standards where it matters most. That is another dichotomy nested in accountability: there are absolutely cases when accountability should and must be used. If a subordinate is not performing to standard, despite understanding why, despite knowing the impact on the mission, and despite being given ownership, then a leader must hold the line. That method is accountability. The leader must drill down and micromanage tasks in order to get the subordinate on track. But the leader cannot stay there. The leader must eventually give subordinates leeway to perform based on their own intrinsic drive—not because they are being held accountable, and not based on the micromanagement of the leader, but because they have a better understanding of why.

And that is where balance must be found: use accountability as a tool when needed, but don't rely on it as the sole means of enforcement. A reliance on heavy accountability consumes the time and focus of the leader and inhibits the trust, growth, and development of subordinates.

Instead, balance accountability with educating the team and empowering its members to maintain standards even without direct oversight from the top. This is the hallmark of the highest-performing teams that dominate.

Application to Business

"They just won't do what we tell them to do!" the national operations manager told me. "They just don't seem to care!"

The company had started using a new software program about three months earlier to track their product as it was installed and utilized by the customers, which consisted of medium- to large-size businesses. It was a well-thought-out system, built on an existing platform that allowed technicians in the field to input what equipment had been installed, the tests that were completed, issues overcome, and shortfalls of the system. It also interacted with the company's customer relationship management system, providing salespeople with information about the customers if they needed to approach them about renewal or upgrades.

"What exactly is it that the field technicians won't do?" I asked.

"They won't use the system. They won't enter the information. They show up on-site with the customer to take care of an install or a troubleshooting scenario, they do their work, then boom—that's it. They enter the bare minimum into the system, but no details."

"What are the details they should be entering?" I asked.

"The details are critical—not for them, but for the follow-on," the ops manager said. "If something else goes wrong and another technician has to go out and troubleshoot, it saves a lot of time and effort if they know what the previous technician did. On top of that, the details really help our salespeople. When they call to offer new services or a renewal of existing services, if they don't know what the customer has been through, they get blindsided. It makes it seem as if no one at the company cares about the customer at all. Try selling to someone that already thinks your company doesn't care about them."

"I can see where that would be problematic," I acknowledged. "So what have you done to get them to do what they are supposed to do?"

"We put a whole bunch of accountability checks into place," he said. "We started with the technicians themselves. We told them they needed to fill in the details. That barely had any impact. Next, we went to the team leaders. We told them we wanted entries in every field of the software—and that we would give bonuses based on the number of fields filled out."

"And how did that work?" I asked.

"It cost us money but didn't get us anywhere," the ops manager replied. "The technicians did as they were told: they filled out every field. But they did so with worthless one- and two-word answers."

"Ouch," I said.

"Yeah. Ouch," the ops manager agreed. "Next up were the regional operations managers. We figured if we held them accountable they would make it happen. So we told them if the technicians in their regions didn't start filling out all the fields—with legitimate details—we were going to drop their volume bonuses by ten percent. We saw a little uptick after that for about two weeks. Then, things went backward—back to where the technicians weren't filling out anything at all, not even a word in most of the fields."

"Not good," I commented.

"No. Not good at all," the ops manager said. "Especially because we reached pretty deep into our budget to have this new software designed, built, and implemented."

"Alright," I declared. "Let me go and talk to some of the team leaders, regional managers, and frontline technicians and see what I can figure out."

Over the next few days, I set meetings and went around talking to everyone involved down the chain of command. I started with the regional managers. It didn't take long to figure out what was going on with them. They had tried to hold the team leaders and technicians accountable for filling in every field—especially when their volume bonus was threatened with a 10-percent cut. But it didn't take them long to figure out that if their technicians spent the additional time filling in all the fields, they couldn't cover as many installations or customer service calls. By not covering as many installations, they made less money, and that cost them more than the 10 percent penalty for noncompliance with the software. Once they realized this, the regional managers backed off holding the front line accountable.

The team leaders had another story. They were busy. They handled the schedules for their teams, and it was a huge job: appointments, cancellations, customers not present, jobs taking too long and interfering with other jobs, and, of course, dealing with absent technicians and getting their jobs covered. On top of that, as the technical experts, they spent a fair amount of time on the phone with technicians troubleshooting more complex problems. Finally, they were also the first point of impact for customer complaints. Any issue with the product or the technician came directly to the team leader first—and those calls had to be handled delicately and tactfully. With all of this on their plates, they didn't have time for much else. And they certainly didn't have time to load individual technicians' screens after every call to ensure that the data was being entered. So even though they understood that it needed to happen, they simply didn't have the time to execute it.

Finally, I got into the field and talked to some of the technicians. They had some significant problems. First of all, entering information into the system took longer than the senior leadership knew. In the field, different customers in different areas had varying levels of cell phone reception. In areas with poor signals, loading each page could take a minute or two—and there were eight pages to load, so this was a huge waste of time. Furthermore, each page started with the need to reenter the customer's name, address, and account number. Copy and paste wasn't a solution because you couldn't copy more than one field at a time, requiring you to flip back and forth between screens, which took forever. Last, instead of having some multiple-choice options for the most common answers, every answer had to be typed in, which wasted even more time. On top of all that, and most important, no one on the front lines really understood how the data was going to help *them*.

When I reported back to the national operations manager with all this information, he was shocked.

"Okay," he said in a depressed voice. "Accountability didn't work. Now what?"

"Now you *lead*," I told him.

He took a moment to let that sink in.

Finally, he broke. "Well then, I am at a loss. How am I supposed to lead here?"

It was a great sign. He was humble enough to admit he needed some help—and what's more, humble enough to ask for it.

"Okay, it isn't that bad," I replied. "Luckily, you have a bunch of good people out there who want to do the right thing. First, you have got to solicit input on how to make the software better. There are some things that would really simplify it. Multiple-choice answers for one. Making the customer information flow from one screen to the next would be helpful—these guys are typing the same information on every page. And there should be fewer pages. Simplify. I know you rarely have to print these things out, so why do they need to be compatible with a paper format? Put more questions on each screen so the techs aren't loading screen after screen—that wastes all kinds of time in the field. Those are just some initial suggestions after talking to only four or five of your techs. I'm sure a broader inquiry would yield even more ideas to streamline the software based on direct feedback from the guys who use it."

"That makes sense," the ops manager replied. "I thought we had gotten enough feedback."

"Maybe you did in the beginning," I said. "But once a complex thing like this hits the field, you need to continually get feedback to make it better. That's just the way it is."

"Got it. Anything else?" the ops manager asked.

"Absolutely," I said. "The biggest thing I figured out in talking to the frontline troops about this is that they have no idea why they are doing this—and, most important, how it affects *them*."

"How it affects them?" he repeated.

"Yes. Right now, they don't get it," I said.

"But they know this data will help us hold on to customers

and allow us to upsell them on better, more expensive products," the ops manager said. "Obviously, that is going to make the company more profitable. What else is there to get?"

"Okay. Think about what you just said," I stated. "If the company makes more money, if the company is more profitable, do you think that a frontline technician cares?"

"I hope he cares! It is his paycheck!" the ops manager yelled.

"Hope isn't a course of action," I said. "And, from his perspective, he has been getting a paycheck consistently for as long as he's been employed here—regardless of how profitable the company is or isn't. It simply doesn't impact him."

"He should still care about it," the ops manager insisted.

"Of course he should," I agreed. "And in a perfect world, every employee would care deeply about the profitability of the company he or she works for. But these folks have other things to care about. Husbands and wives. Kids. Soccer games. Bills and cars and mortgages and the game on Friday night and the broken water heater and the kid heading off to college. They have a ton to care about—and like it or not, the profitability of the company is not high on their list."

"So then what do we do?" the ops manager asked. "If they don't care, why should they give any extra effort?"

"They have to understand *why*—but that *why* has to have a thread that ties back to them, to what is in it for *them*," I told him.

"And how do I do that?" he asked. "How can I make them care about the company's profits?"

"You have to think it through," I said. "It's like this. If you can capture this data that you want, you will be able to better arm both technicians in the field and your salespeople, right?"

"Absolutely. That's the whole point," the ops manager agreed.

"And once the technicians and salespeople are armed, they can do a better job, right?" I continued.

"Definitely," he answered.

"Okay," I said. "Now follow me: Armed with this data, the technicians will be able to provide better and faster customer service, and the salespeople will be able to sell more product to more customers. When we provide better service and sell more products, our business grows. When our business grows, we make more money—"

"That's what I said! But how does that help?" the ops manager interrupted.

"Listen," I told him. "When the company makes more money, we can invest more money in advertising and infrastructure. Once we put more money into advertising and infrastructure, we will gain even more customers and be able to support them even better. The better we perform as a company, the more customers we acquire. The more customers we acquire, the more work there is for technicians, which means overtime and overtime pay. And once the company maxes that out, we will need more technicians. The more technicians we need, the more we have to pay them to be here. So this means down the line, we will increase pay for technicians, especially experienced ones. And lastly, the more technicians and clients we have, the more team leaders and regional supervisors we will need. This opens up a pathway to advancement for every technician at this company. So profitability of the company not only puts money into the pockets of the owners—which the frontline technicians probably don't care too much about—but more important, it impacts the technicians directly: it opens up opportunity for more pay, higher salaries, and a pathway for career advancement. That's the thread that ties all of this together and aligns everyone at the company—the corporate leadership team right down to the field technicians. That's leadership."

The operations manager nodded. The light had come on. It was clear.

Over the next two days, I helped him put together a simple, clear presentation that explained the thread of *why*. We also talked about the fact that he would still have to occasionally inspect people's work to ensure that things were being done—there still had to be some level of overt accountability. But most of the accountability would come intrinsically, from the individual leaders and the field technicians themselves, who were now empowered by understanding the *why*. They would help keep each other accountable, when they fully understood the impact and the direct benefit to them.

A few days later, the national operations manager briefed the plan during an all-hands morning call. He also put one of the tech-savvy regional managers in charge of compiling feedback about the software system so it could be improved. Most important, he drove home how every member of the company would benefit from collecting data to the best of their ability—which would help every employee improve their lives.

The troops now understood that, and they went to work.